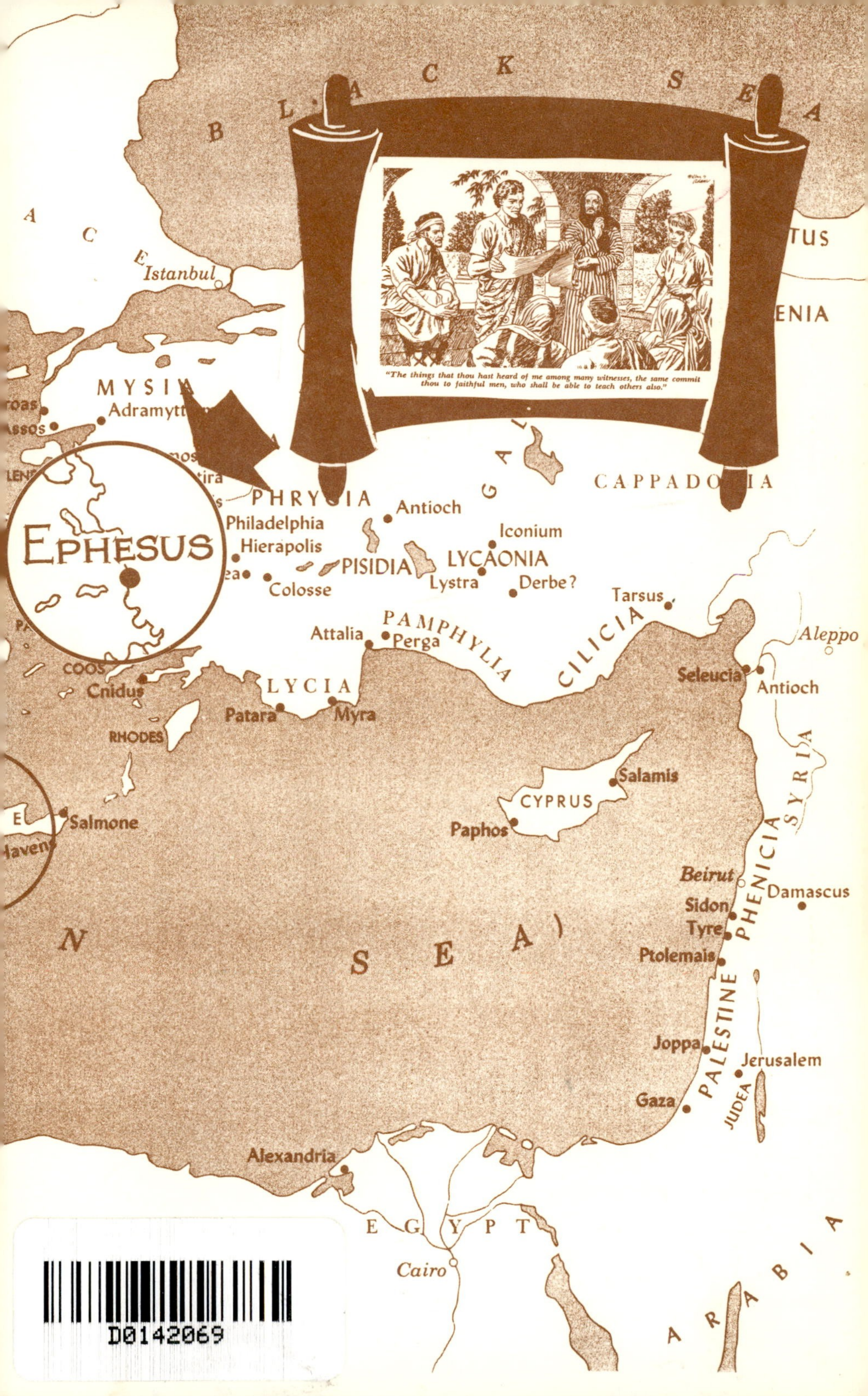
B L A C K S E A
"The things that thou hast heard of me among many witnesses, the same commit thou to faithful men, who shall be able to teach others also."
Istanbul
MYSIA
Adramytt
EPHESUS
PHRYGIA
Philadelphia
Hierapolis
Colosse
PISIDIA
Antioch
GAL
Iconium
LYCAONIA
Lystra
Derbe?
CAPPADO IA
TUS
ENIA
Tarsus
CILICIA
PAMPHYLIA
Attalia
Perga
LYCIA
Patara
Myra
COOS
Cnidus
RHODES
Salmone
Seleucia
Antioch
Aleppo
SYRIA
Salamis
CYPRUS
Paphos
Beirut
Sidon
Tyre
Ptolemais
PHENICIA
Damascus
N
S E A
PALESTINE
Joppa
Jerusalem
JUDEA
Gaza
Alexandria
E G Y P T
Cairo
A R A B I A
D0142069

PAUL'S LETTERS TO TIMOTHY AND TITUS

BIBLE STUDY TEXTBOOK

PAUL'S LETTERS TO TIMOTHY AND TITUS

A NEW

- *Commentary*
- *Workbook*
- *Teaching Manual*

Don De Welt

Professor at Ozark Bible College

Paraphrase by James MacKnight

College Press, Joplin, Missouri

First Printing—May 1961
Second Printing—February 1966
Third Printing—July 1972
Fourth Printing—November 1975
Fifth Printing—December 1979

ISBN 0-89900-043-6

DEDICATION

To the one who first brought me the message of life.—Archie Word

ACKNOWLEDGEMENTS:

Permissions to quote from the following books have been obtained from the copyright owners —

From *Augustana Book Concern*:
The Interpretation Of St. Paul's Epistles To The Colossians, To The Thessalonians, To Timothy, To Titus And To Philemon by R. C. H. Lenski

From *Wm. B. Eerdmans Publishing Company*:
The Pastoral Epistles by Donald Guthrie
The Pastoral Epistles by E. K. Simpson
New Testament Epistles by John H. Bratt

From *Zondervan Publishing House*:
Commentary On The Pastoral Epistles by Patrick Fairbairn

From *Dr. Wilbur Smith*:
Outline Of I Timothy

From *Baker Book House*:
New Testament Commentary by William Hendricksen
The Epistles To Timothy by Russell Bradley Jones
New Testament Epistles by Victor E. Hoven

From *Moody Press*:
Titus And Philemon by D. Edmond Hiebert
First Timothy by D. Edmond Hiebert
The Pastoral Epistles by Homer A. Kent, Jr.

From *Gospel Advocate Company*:
New Testament Epistles by David Lipscomb
An Introduction To The Epistles Of Paul by Leslie G. Thomas

From *Christian Standard*:
Studies In The Epistles And Revelation by W. B. Taylor
Bible Teacher And Leader — article by Lewis C. Foster

Contents and Analytical Outline

PAUL'S SECOND LETTER TO TIMOTHY
INTRODUCTION 1:1-5

PART ONE
EXHORTATIONS 1:6-2:26

PART TWO
WARNINGS 3:1-4:5

PART THREE
TESTIMONY 4:6-18

CONCLUSION 4:19-22

PREFACE

For those who do not have a copy of a *Bible Study Textbook* it might be helpful to say a word as to their purpose:

Here is a series of books unique in format and content. We have but one intention in these publications: To prompt the personal study of the Word of God.

We shall discuss every verse, but our discussion will be entirely subservient to our higher purpose. The constant question shall be "do you understand the meaning of the divine writer?" We shall lend whatever aid necessary to help you discover his meaning. It is not at all enough to simply say "here is what is meant," and then in so many words state it. No personal discovery by the student has been made by a teacher's plain statement of fact.

We want a creative study of the Bible. We desire to produce the situation and the tools by which you build your beautiful temple of Bible knowledge. Here are teaching aids that truly teach — *The Bible Study Textbooks*.

Don De Welt

PROLOGUE

My heart was made happy when brother De Welt requested that I give this prologue concerning his comments on *First and Second Timothy and Titus.* He is my "Timothy" and being such, I know him and his background, and what we can expect from him in this field.

Brother De Welt is a talented man in his presentation as well as being a deep student of the Word of God. His many books now in print give evidence of his labors and their wide acceptance. He is a man of deep convictions based on study. I expect this latest effort to surpass his former works, because this is his strongest field, *evangelism.*

He has had much experience in evangelism, and has had years of proving by test his ideas as he has trained young men to "do the work of an evangelist." This book should be very practical.

I appreciate brother De Welt because of his character. He is one of God's scarce personalities who appreciate the efforts of others. He is quick to express gratitude for the part others have played in his life and he deserves heaven's blessings upon his own labors.

I pray God will bless the efforts put forth in this work especially planned for Evangelists.

Sincerely,

A. Word.

GENERAL INTRODUCTION

There are several very important questions to be answered before we can proceed with an exegetical study of the letter of Paul to Timothy.

1. *Did Paul actually write this letter?* Of course we know I Timothy 1:1 says he did, but there are those who hold a different opinion. Why would anyone deny the plain statement of the text as to the authorship? Such a conclusion is based upon a presupposition. It is presupposed by some that the books of the New Testament were not written in the first century nor by the persons whose names they bear. What shall we say to these things? It would be an easy matter to simply deny the accusation, but this would also be a presupposition. It is not the purpose of this text to give an exhaustive study of the subject. Others have done a splendid service in answering this charge. We refer you to them for the details necessary. Read: *New Testament Commentary — Exposition of The Pastoral Epistles* by Wm. Hendriksen pp. 4-33; *The Pastoral Epistles* by Homer A. Kent, Jr. pp. 24-71; *An Interpretation Of St. Paul's Epistles To the Colossians, to the Thessalonians, to Timothy, to Titus and to Philemon*, by R. C. H. Lenski pp. 473-484. *The Pastoral Epistles* by Donald Guthrie pp. 11-53.

2. *Where was Paul when he wrote these letters?* Was Paul in jail at Rome awaiting his execution? Was Paul released after his first imprisonment? These questions might not appear pertinent to our study, but they most assuredly are. Here is another question of vital importance: *Does the book of Acts contain a continuous, complete record of the life of Paul?* At this juncture someone is sure to ask, "what difference does it make?" Well, it just so happens that there are events mentioned in I and II Timothy and Titus that *can not* be harmonized with the account of Paul's life in the book of Acts. There are two possibilities: (1) We do not have a record of all the events in Acts. (2) These events took place *after* the Acts account, and just before Paul's death. The second position is the one most commonly accepted. A careful reading of the book of Acts will convince one that it would be almost impossible to open up areas for the inclusion of the following events:

a. *A trip to Crete.* On this trip Paul was accompanied by Titus. Paul left Titus on the isle to carry on the work Paul had started. Read Titus 1:5. The only mention of Crete in Luke's second treatise has to do with the shipwreck. Read Acts 27:27-28:11. Where was Titus? Where is indication that a group of churches was established on the island at this time?

b. *Paul's trip into Macedonia from Ephesus.* At this time Timothy was left at Ephesus to minister to the church. Read I Timothy 1:2. If you have read the Acts account you know of Paul's two visits to Ephesus. The first visit is eliminated as he is going the wrong direction. Read Acts 18:19-22. Paul was going to Palestine, not Macedonia. The second visit is recorded in Acts 19:1—20:1. In Acts 19:22 we are told that Timothy and Erastus had been sent ahead into Macedonia. When Paul left Ephesus for Macedonia as near as we know Timothy was *not* at Ephesus but already in Macedonia.

c. *A visit to Timothy at Ephesus from whatever place Paul wrote.* Read I Timothy 3:14. At what time in the Acts account did Paul visit Timothy at Ephesus? It could not have been in either of the recorded visits. In the first visit the church had not been established, and Paul arrived before Timothy. In the second visit Timothy was with him.

d. *Paul was in Nicopolis.* Read Titus 3:12. Where is this place? It is not easy to answer this question. It is quite possibly on the eastern coast of Achaia—or is it on the coast of Macedonia? The important point is: Paul was there. But when was he there? Why? No mention of this is made in the Acts account. No break is made in the Acts record (unless we make one) for such a visit.

e. *Paul was at Miletus.* Read II Timothy 4:20. Paul's visit to Miletus on his way to Jerusalem (Acts 20: 15-38) does not fit the tenor of II Timothy 4:20. Acts does not mention Trophimus.

f. *Paul left a cloak and parchments at Troas.* Read II Timothy 4:13. Paul was twice at Troas as recorded in Acts 20:6, 7 and II Cor. 2:12-14; in neither visit can we fit the present instructions; most especially would we reject the reference in II Corinthians 2:12-14. The urgency of the visit mentioned in II Corinthians 2:12-14 precludes the circumstances of II

Timothy 4:13. Is it at all likely, that upon the way to Jerusalem with a party of seven representatives from the churches, that Paul would have paid a leisurely visit to the house of Carpus? Perhaps so, but no mention is made of it.

g. *II Timothy* 4:20 *seems to suggest that Paul was at Corinth.* In this verse Paul is apparently discussing an itinerary of which we know nothing in the Acts record. This visit to Corinth could have been only on the part of Erastus, without Paul, but the context seems to suggest otherwise.

h. *Please read II Timothy* 1:16, 17, 2:9 *and* 4:6. *Now read Acts* 28:30, 31 . . . *Note the difference in the description of the imprisonments.* We conclude that there were two imprisonments. The first one, described in Acts 28:30, 31, from which he was released. During this period of liberty Paul wrote the letters of I Timothy and Titus. Quite possibly I Timothy was written first from somewhere in Macedonia. To say which of these letters was written first is an impossibility, but the facts fit together better when we assume I Timothy of first composition.

In answer to our original question we can say: *Paul wrote I Timothy in the year* 62 *or* 63 *A.D. after release from Roman imprisonment, while he was somewhere in Macedonia. Very shortly after in the same year Paul wrote to Titus. Upon his second arrest while in the Roman prison in* 64-68 *A.D., probably in* 67 *A.D., he wrote the last of his letters—II Timothy.*

For the benefit of those who read these words and do not know the background of Paul's epistles we present a brief outline of their composition. Before he was imprisoned Paul wrote:

1. On his second journey he wrote from Corinth the epistles of I & II Thessalonians.
2. On his third journey he wrote I Corinthians from Ephesus; II Corinthians from Macedonia, possibly Philippi; Galatians and Romans from Corinth.
3. While in prison in Rome for two full years he wrote the following letters: Ephesians, Philippians, Colossians, and Philemon.
4. After his release he wrote I Timothy and Titus. After his second arrest he wrote II Timothy. Anyone is free to disagree with the time and place of the writings of these letters. All we say is that we have decided after two decades of study, that this is the most reasonable arrangement.

3. *To who were these letters addressed? To Timothy and Titus to be sure but what do we know of these men? First as to Timothy*:

a. Paul first saw this young man in the city of Lystra on his first missionary journey. (Acts 16:1,2) Acts 20:4 seems to indicate Lystra as his home in contrast to Gaius of Derbe. In the strictest sense of the term this young man was a "half-breed", for whereas his mother Eunice and grandmother Lois were Jewesses, his father was a Greek. (Acts 16:1; II Timothy 1:5). The text would seem to indicate that his father was not a believer, even in the Jewish Faith. Timothy had not been circumcised thus indicating the lack of interest on the part of the father. There was no lack of interest on the part of his mother or grandmother, for they were devout students of the Old Testament scriptures and taught Timothy from them. Although it is not so stated it is probably true that Timothy, his mother and grandmother were all converted on Paul's first journey. Two or three things could have prepared Timothy for his acceptance of Jesus as the Messiah:

(1) A knowledge of the Old Testament scriptures. When Paul pointed out "of whom the prophets spoke" he was as ready to be baptized as was the eunuch of Acts 8.

(2) The consistent though difficult life of his mother and grandmother offered a grand example to him. Did they accept their Messiah first, or was it their son who did? Timothy saw in the day by day living of Eunice and Lois that the scriptures could be translated into life; this he wanted and this he did.

(3) He was a witness of the devotion and sufferings of the Apostle Paul. This alone without his previous knowledge and home life could have been inadequate. It undoubtedly was inadequate for many others who lived in Lystra. Timothy saw the unswerving devotion, the undying zeal, and the unselfish love of Paul among those who hated him and stoned him. Was it the tears that streamed down the face of Timothy as he stood over the broken body of Paul that Paul remembered? (Cf. II Tim. 1:4). What did Timothy feel when Paul arose from the place of stoning to return to speak to the very ones who sought his life? (Acts 14:20). If Timothy felt a spiritual kinship to Paul it was surely a mutual matter for Paul refers to him as: "my child," "Genuine child in faith," "beloved

child." We conclude that Timothy was one of Paul's converts to Christ upon Paul's first evangelistic tour.

b. Paul took him to help upon the second visit to Lystra. (Acts 16:1-3). Because of labor for Christ on Timothy's own initiative, Paul chose him to work with him. We wonder what "program of evangelism" was being followed by Timothy in the wild barbarian towns of Derbe, Iconium, and Lystra? Probably the one originated by our Lord when he said "Let your light shine before men."

   Timothy's reputation for faithfulness was well established when Paul returned to Lystra. Timothy was not working for a "promotion" to the office of evangelist. He worked for Christ because he loved lost souls and his Lord. Kent suggests Timothy might have taken John Mark's place who left Paul on the first journey.

   Before Timothy left his mother and home to travel with Paul, he must "become all things to all men, that by all means he might win some." (I Corinthians 9:20). Paul requested that Timothy be circumcised. Paul did this that any unnecessary delay and argument with Jews might be avoided. If Timothy was to enter the synagogues with Paul and share in the services, this rite was essential.

   Perhaps it was when Paul chose Timothy, that the hands of the elders of Lystra, Derbe and Iconium, along with the hands of Paul, were laid upon the head of Timothy, thus ordaining him for the work he was about to do. (I Timothy 4:14; II Timothy 1:6). There were evidently two "gifts" given here: the "gift" of the office of evangelist through the hands of the presbytery or eldership, and the "gift" of supernatural powers by the hands of Paul.

c. Timothy traveled with Paul and Silas upon their second evangelistic tour. (Acts 16:2-4; 17:14, 15; 18:5; I Thessalonians 1:1; 3:2-6; II Thessalonians 1:1). While upon this journey he was sent back to Thessalonica to help the recently established church in that city.

d. Timothy was with Paul again on his third missionary journey. (Acts 19:22; 20:4; II Corinthians 1:1-19). It would seem Timothy was given the special task of carrying not only the message of the gospel, but the messages of the Apostle Paul; both written and oral. He was sent by Paul to Corinth to bear the Apostle's special instructions (I Corinthians 4:17; 16:10). Timothy was to return to Corinth in company of Paul at a later time on the same journey (Romans 16:21). We can believe the last statement, if we believe the epistle to the Romans was written from Corinth.

e. When Paul was imprisoned at Rome, Timothy was one of the few who visited him there. (Philippians 1:1; Colossians 1:1; Philemon 1). While Paul was in prison, he sent Timothy on yet another errand. (Philippians 2:19-23).

f. Hebrews 13:23 speaks of an imprisonment for Timothy of which we have no other record.

g. The particular concern of our study is: where was Timothy when he received Paul's letter or letters? I Timothy 1:3; II Timothy 1:16-18; 4:19 seem to leave little doubt that he was in the city of Ephesus, at work with the church in this great city. We refer you to another *Bible Study Textbook* for further information about this church and city. (Read from THE GLORIOUS CHURCH pp. 12-16)

h. Timothy did not have an easy field in which to labor. A most important question has to do with the position or office held by Timothy, and whether it has any example for us. There seems to be a rather unanimous opinion among commentators, that Timothy was an apostolic representative, or one who acted for the apostle Paul in Paul's absence. We quote from Homer A. Kent who holds this view with a number of others:

"The functions which Timothy fulfilled in the early church should not be confused with the present-day pastor. Rather, in those formative days of the church, he seems to have been one of several who helped to carry out the transition from the times of the apostles to the post Apostolic era of the church. In the beginning of the church, the authority of the apostles brought into being the church, and served to guide and instruct it. Although it seems clear that from the beginning local churches were congregationally controlled, still the influence of the apostles was strong. Timothy, therefore, was an apostolic representative. He exercised the guidance and counseling ministry that Paul would have performed had he been present. Titus occupied a similar position (Titus 1:5). Thus it is probably not correct to visualize Timothy as the pastor of the local Christian church at Ephesus. Rather, he was Paul's official delegate to assist the Ephesian church with its officials in conducting affairs in the proper manner." (*The Pastoral Epistles* pp. 19, 20)

What shall we say to these things? Is there an office of evangelist today? We advance four reasons for believing we do have a present day office of evangelist:

(1) *The nature of the work assigned to the evangelist makes the office a perpetual one.* Their job was to convert sinners, to feed the flock of God, to teach the ignorant. While time endures, this will be necessary. Therefore the office must be perpetual.

(2) *Evangelists from the beginning received their commission from churches, and not directly from Christ, as did the apostles and prophets.* This can be shown in the case of Timothy, in which the hands of the eldership or presbytery were laid upon him. (Acts 14:1-3, I Tim. 4:14). The imposition of the hands of the eldership (probably of Lystra and Iconium) was for the purpose of setting him aside for the work upon which he was embarking. Paul laid his hands upon Timothy (II Tim. 1:6) to impart to him those miraculous gifts, which in that age were necessary in order to enable him to fulfill the commission which he had received from the church of Lystra and Iconium. Since we still have local churches after the order of those of that day, we have the prerogative of setting aside evangelists.

(3) *Paul told Timothy to choose certain faithful men and commit to them what Paul had committed to Timothy.* (II Tim. 2:2). This hardly needs comment; it is only necessary to ask, what was the work of Timothy, and then realize that he was to commit that work to others and then they *in turn were urged to commit the work to others.* If this admonition was followed by Timothy and those who succeeded him, we have the permanence of the office assured!

(4) *The office has actually been continued from the beginning to the present day.* That "evangelist" was the name by which these servants of the church were usually designated in primitive times, seems evident from the testimony of several of the Christian fathers. Eusebius, for instance, the learned Bishop of Caesarea, A.D. 315-340, thus speaks of evangelists who lived and labored during the reign of Trajan A.D. 98-117.

4. *What do we know of Titus?* We quote from *Bible Teacher and Leader—article by Lewis C. Foster*: "The parents and home community of Titus are not known. It is made clear, however, that he was a Gentile; and he was at Antioch of Syria either fourteen or seventeen years after Paul became a Christian. (See Galatians 1:18; 2:1). From this time on he was a close companion of Paul, entrusted with important tasks and held in high esteem by the apostle. It is strange that his name does not appear in the book of Acts. Since Luke omits his own name also, it has been suggested that Titus was a relative of the author, or in some way was so close to him that Luke deliberately refrained from mentioning him by name. At any rate, we can conclude that Titus was included in the company that went to Jerusalem from Antioch when the question of keeping the old law was disturbing the church. Acts makes it clear that "certain other of them" went up with Paul and Barnabas to Jerusalem (Acts 15:2), and then we read explicitly in Galatians 2:1 that they took Titus with them. After this occasion, Titus does not figure in the New Testament records until Paul is at Ephesus, on his third missionary journey, and is writing to the church at Corinth. Here it becomes evident that Titus, along with an unnamed brother, had been sent by Paul to Corinth to represent Paul and the gospel, perhaps to deliver Paul's first letter to them, and to defend the right. Later Paul, failing to find him in Troas, became so anxious to know of the state of affairs in Corinth that he advanced to meet the returning Titus in Macedonia. Here Paul's heart was made glad when he learned from Titus that the Corinthians had accepted his rebukes and corrections in a proper way. Out of comfort and relief Paul wrote his second epistle to them. In all there are seven references to Titus in 2 Corinthians (2:13; 7:6, 13, 14; 8:6, 16, 23; 12:18). From this we also learn that Titus had special responsibilities in making the collection for the poor in Jerusalem. Following this we know nothing of the movements of Titus until Paul addressed a letter to him in Crete. It becomes evident that after Paul's release from his first Roman imprisonment, he did missionary work on the island of Crete and left Titus there to lead in the continuing work, even as he left Timothy at Ephesus. In this epistle Titus is asked to join Paul at Nicopolis as soon as he is contacted by Artemas or Tychicus (Titus 3:12); but whether these plans

were carried out we do not know. In his last epistle Paul states that Titus has gone to Dalmatia (2 Timothy 4:10). It seems unfair to suppose that this was against Paul's wishes, as was the desertion by Demas (2 Timothy 4:10). Rather, Crescens had gone to Galatia and Titus to Dalmatia as Paul had directed them. Since no previous word had been given of work done in Dalmatia, this may have been a missionary enterprise into a new field. Dalmatia was northwest of Macedonia, and may have been Titus' next destination after a stay at Nicopolis. Some suggest that Titus was older than Timothy (compare I Timothy 4:12 and Titus 2:15) and was chosen for situations that demanded the stronger and more understanding character. The apostle calls Titus "mine own son" (Titus 1:4). He also accepts him as his "brother" (2 Corinthians 2:13) and his "partner and fellowhelper" (2 Corinthians 8:23). Although Titus is not called an "overseer" in the sense of an elder or bishop, nevertheless he was a capable shepherd for the Christian flock as a representative for the apostle Paul in the service of the Lord. It is impossible to measure the power of his influence in the church, but we can be sure it was great."

What was the purpose or purposes of these letters? Obviously the purpose was to prepare Timothy to do an effective work for Christ in Ephesus. The church had been established in this great city for some years before. Paul himself had labored in Ephesus for a longer period of time than at any other place. (Acts 20:31). Titus was sent or "left" on the isle of Crete for the same purpose. The letters are not only personal but official.

The epistle of II Timothy has less of the general instructions for the church than those of I Timothy and Titus. The student will note the sense of authority in the words of I Timothy. Timothy was expected by Paul to deliver the instructions he gave him to all the churches in Ephesus; and perchance also to the seven churches of Asia. Titus was likewise to use the letter of Paul as an authoritative document in his work among the churches in Crete.

The question has been raised as to our relationship to these letters. Are we to conclude that Timothy and Titus were special personal representatives of Paul, and therefore such instructions as found in these letters were given only and exclusively to them? No one wants to hold this position with all its implications, for there is too much in these letters applicable to present day church administration; particularly is this true of the eldership. (See I Timothy 3:1-11). Why hold the position at all if we are not willing to accept its implications? We are all willing to conclude that these two men had powers we do not now possess, but *what work were they to do apart from the exercise of supernatural powers that we cannot fulfill today?*

On what shall we base our conclusion that Timothy and Titus were to act in Paul's place in Paul's absence? Can we not carry out in our community what Paul told Timothy to do in the community of Ephesus? We yet have the heavenly oracles, and the same need. The letters were written as an encouragement to the men who received them; as a means of setting the churches in order. But these letters were also written as a grand means of establishing the kingdom of God in the world today!

5. *How shall we outline this book?*

Here are four examples by men who have done it:

WILBUR SMITH

First Timothy Outlined

Everyone agrees that the outlining of the pastoral epistles is quite difficult, since they were not written with the idea of carrying through a logical argument, as were the letters to the Ephesians and the Romans. I have spent some time attempting to outline the First Epistle of Timothy, and have taught the pastoral epistles here at the Fuller Theological Seminary in an elective course. At last I think I have worked out, together with my students, what might be considered as satisfactory an outline as can be constructed. Some of my readers might like to have such an outline possibly to insert in the margin of this portion of the New Testament.

Salutation, 1:1, 2

I. Paul's First General Charge to Timothy, 1:3-20
   1. A charge regarding the need for constant watchfulness lest false doctrines appear, 3-11
   2. A word of encouragement by Paul's review of his own experience, 12-16

3. A doxology, 17
4. An exhortation to be faithful to his original call to the ministry, 18-20

II. Certain Aspects of Life in the Christian Church, 2:1—3:16
1. The practice of prayer, 2:1-8
2. The place of women in the church, 2:9-15
3. Qualifications for church officers, 3:1-13
   a. for bishops, 1-7
   b. for deacons, 8-13
4. A personal exhortation to Timothy, 14, 15
5. A doxology, 16

III. A Prophecy Concerning Apostasy in the Last Days 4:1-5

IV. The Characteristics that Should be Displayed by a Good Minister of Christ, 4:6-16
1. In general, 6-11
2. In particular, 12-16

V. Ideals of Conduct for Certain Groups in the Church, 5:1-6:2
1. Respect for the aged, 5:1,2
2. The conduct of women, 5:3-16
3. The work of the elders, 5:17-22
4. A general exhortation, 5:23-25
5. The relation of master and servants, 6:1,2

VI. Final Exhortation and Warnings, 6:3-21
1. Some perils to be avoided, 3-10
2. A final charge to Timothy, 11-14
3. A doxology, 15, 16
4. A warning to the rich, 17-19
5. A concluding word of warning to Timothy, 20, 21

HOMER A. KENT

Outline of I Timothy Chapter One

Introductory Matters (1:1-2)

I. CHARGE CONCERNING SOUND DOCTRINE (1:3-20)
   A. The Danger to Sound Doctrine In Ephesus (vv. 3-11)
      1. Teachers who taught another doctrine.
      2. Teachers who failed to use God's Law properly.
   B. The Outstanding Illustration Of The Results of Sound Doctrine (vv. 12-17)
      1. Paul's former life of Lawkeeping was a life of unbelief.
      2. Paul's present life in the ministry was the result of mercy and grace.

   3. Paul's conversion was planned as a pattern to future believers.

C. The Responsibility Of The Minister Toward Sound Doctrine (vv. 18-20)
   1. The responsibility expressed by formal charge.
   2. The responsibility illustrated by two examples.

Outline of I Timothy Chapter Two

II. CHARGE CONCERNING PUBLIC WORSHIP (2:1-15)
- A. Prayer in Public Worship (vv. 1-7)
   1. The kinds of prayer.
   2. The objects of prayer.
   3. The reason for prayer.
   4. The basis for prayer.
- B. Men and Women In Public Worship (vv. 8-15)
   1. Conduct of the men.
   2. Conduct of the women.

Outline of I Timothy Chapter Three

III. CHARGE CONCERNING CHURCH OFFICERS (3:1-16)
- A. Office of the Overseer (vv. 1-7)
   1. Nature of the office.
   2. Qualifications for the office.
      a. General qualification.
      b. Moral qualification.
      c. Mental qualifications.
      d. Personality qualifications.
      e. Domestic qualification.
      f. Christian experience.
      g. Reputation.
- B. Office of the Deacon (vv. 8-13)
   1. Nature of the office.
   2. Qualifications for the office.
      a. Personal character.
      b. Spiritual life.
      c. Christian experience.
      d. Morality.
      e. Domestic relations.
   3. Qualifications for women servants.
   4. The encouragement for deacons.
- C. The Importance Of This Charge To the Church (vv. 14-16)

Outline of I Timothy Chapter Four

IV. CHARGE CONCERNING FALSE TEACHERS (4:1-16)
- A. The appearance of False Teachers (vv. 1-5)
  1. The time of these teachers.
  2. The description of these teachers.
  3. The teaching of these teachers.
  4. The refutation of these teachers.
- B. The Duty of the Minister Toward False Teachers (vv. 6-10)
  1. Constructive teaching.
  2. Godly living.
  3. Faithful laboring.
- C. The Encouragement of the Minister Toward a Constructive Ministry (vv. 11-16)
  1. In public life.
  2. In personal life.

Outline of I Timothy Chapter Five

V. CHARGE CONCERNING VARIOUS MEMBERS OF THE CONGREGATION (5:1-6:2)
- A. The Pastoral Care of Old and Young Members (vv. 1, 2)
  1. The persons involved.
  2. The nature of the pastoral care.
  3. The manner of pastoral care.
- B. The Pastoral Care of Widows (vv. 3-16)
  1. The kind of widows.
  2. The treatment of widows.
- C. The Pastoral Care of Elders (vv. 17-25)
  1. The honoring of elders.
  2. The discipline of elders.
  3. The selection of elders.
- D. The Pastoral Care of Slaves (6:1, 2)
  1. A slave should serve his unsaved master respectfully.
  2. A slave should give his Christian master even more service, and not look down upon him.

Outline of I Timothy Chapter Six

VI. CHARGE CONCERNING THE MINISTER HIMSELF (6:3-21a)
- A. The Minister is Charged to Avoid Improper Motives (vv. 3-10)
  1. The evidence of wrong motives.

2. The nature of wrong motives.
3. The prevention of wrong motives.
4. The results of a wrong motive.

B. The Minister is Charged to Maintain a Proper Walk (vv. 11-16).
1. The nature of a proper walk.
2. The performance of a proper walk.
3. The incentive for a proper walk.

C. The Minister is Charged to Perform a Faithful Ministry (vv. 17-21a)
1. This is accomplished by directing men toward spiritual goals.
2. This is accomplished by guarding the deposit of the faith.

D. Conclusion (6:21b)

D. EDMOND HIEBERT

AN OUTLINE OF I TIMOTHY

THE SALUTATION, 1:1,2
1. The Writer, v. 1
2. The Reader, v. 2a
3. The Greeting, v. 2b.

I. THE CHARGE TO TIMOTHY CONCERNING FALSE TEACHERS, 1:3-20
1. The Charge to Timothy to Preserve the Purity of the Gospel, vv. 3-11
    a. The nature of the charge, vv. 3,4
        1) The impartation of the charge, v. 3a
        2) The contents of the charge, vv. 3b, 4
    b. The aim of the charge, v. 5
    c. The reason for the charge, vv. 6-11
        1) The failure of the false teachers, vv. 6, 7
        2) The true knowledge concerning the law, vv. 8-11
            a) The nature of the law, v. 8
            b) The purpose of the law, vv. 9, 10
            c) The harmony of this view with the Gospel, v. 11
2. The Apostle's Thanksgiving for His Relation to the Gospel, vv. 12-17
    a. The thanksgiving for his appointment to God's service, v. 12
    b. The description of the one appointed, v. 13a
    c. The explanation of the appointment, vv. 13b-16

1) The outpouring of God's grace on him, vv. 13b, 14
2) The purpose of God's grace through him, vv. 15, 16
d. The doxology of praise, v. 17
3. The Renewal of the Charge to Timothy, vv. 18-20
a. The duty of Timothy, vv. 18, 19a
b. The shipwreck of certain men, vv. 19b, 20

II. THE INSTRUCTIONS CONCERNING CHURCH ORDER, 2:1-3:16.
1. The Regulations Concerning Public Worship, 2:1-3:16.
a. The duty of public prayer, vv. 1-7
1) The nature of public prayer, v. 1a
2) The scope of public prayer, vv. 1b-2a
3) The result of such praying, v. 2b
4) The reasons for such prayer, vv. 3-7
a) Its intrinsic nature, v. 3
b) Its accord with God's will, v. 4
c) Its accord with Christian doctrine, vv. 5, 6
d) Its accord with Paul's ministry, v. 7
b. The manner of public prayer, vv. 8-10
1) The praying of the men, v. 8
2) The adorning of the women, vv. 9, 10
c. The position of the women in public worship, vv. 11-15
1) The command concerning the woman, v. 11
2) The restriction upon the woman, v. 12
3) The vindication of the restriction, vv. 13-15
a) The vindication from the order of creation, v. 13
b) The vindication from the story of the fall, vv. 14, 15
2. The Qualifications of Church Officers, 3:1-13
a. The qualifications for a bishop, vv. 1-7
1) The desirability of the office, v. 1
2) The qualifications for the office, vv. 2-7
a) The first seven qualifications, v. 2
b) The second seven qualifications, vv. 3-6
c) The qualifications as to community standing, v. 7
b. The qualifications for deacons. vv. 8-12
1) The personal qualifications of the deacons, vv. 8, 9
2) The testing of deacons, v. 10
3) The qualifications of the women (deaconesses), v. 11
4) The domestic qualifications of deacons, v. 12
c. The reward of faithful service, v. 13

3. The Personal Word to Timothy in View of Christian Truth. 3:14-16
   a. The purpose in writing to Timothy, vv. 14, 15a
   b. The nature of the church, v. 15b
   c. The substance of Christian truth, v. 16

III. THE ADVICE TO TIMOTHY IN VIEW OF THE CHARGE. 4:1-6:2

1. His Personal Work in View of the Apostasy, 4:1-16.
   a. The objective warning against false teaching, vv. 1-5
      1) The prediction of the apostasy, v. 1a
      2) The characterization of the apostates, vv. 1b, 2
      3) The teaching of the apostates, vv. 3-5
         a) The nature of the teaching, v. 3a
         b) The refutation of the teaching, vv. 3b-5
   b. The subjective fortification against error, vv. 6-16
      1) The fortification through a faithful ministry, vv. 6-11
         a) The characteristics of a good minister, v. 6
         b) The activity of a good minister, vv. 7-9
            (1) Neg. — The refusal of myths, v. 7a
            (2) Pos. — The exercising of himself unto godliness, vv. 7b-9
         c) The motivation of the good minister, v. 10
         d) The duty of the good minister, v. 11
      2) The fortification through becoming conduct as a minister, vv. 12-16
         a) The indication of his personal duties, vv. 12-14
            (1) To make his youth respected because of his example, v. 12
            (2) To attend to the public services, v. 13
            (3) To exercise his gift, v. 14
         b) The exhortations diligently to fulfill these duties, vv. 15, 16

2. His Official Work with Various Groups, 5:1-6:2
   a. The attitude in dealing with individual members, 5:1,2
   b. The duty in regard to widows, 5:3-16
      1) The duty of supporting widows, vv. 3-8
         a) The command to honor genuine widows, v. 3
         b) The definitive classification of widows, vv. 4-6
            (1) The widow having children, v. 4
            (2) The widow who is a genuine widow, v. 5

(3) The widow living in pleasure, v. 6

c) The instructions concerning parental support. vv. 7, 8

2) The instructions concerning the enrollment of widows, vv. 9-15

a) The qualifications of those enrolled, vv. 9, 10

b) The rejection of the young widows, vv. 11-13

(1) The command to reject the young widows, v. 11a

(2) The reasons for the rejection, vv. 11b-13

c) The apostolic directive for young widows, vv. 14, 15

3) The duty of a believing woman, v. 16

c. The duty toward elders, 5:17-25

1) The duty of honoring good elders, vv. 17, 18

a) The statement of the duty, v. 17

b) The substantiation of the duty, v. 18

2) The instructions concerning the trial of an elder, vv. 19-21

a) The caution in receiving an accusation against an elder, v. 19

b) The judgment upon the sinning, v. 20

c) The impartiality in the judgment, v. 21

3) The advice concerning the ordination of elders, v. 22

4) The suggestion concerning Timothy's use of a little wine, v. 23

5) The enunciation of principles for testing candidates, vv. 24, 25

d. The instructions concerning the slaves, 6:1, 2

1) The duty of slaves toward unbelieving masters, v. 1

2) The duty of the slave of a believer, v. 2a

3) The duty of Timothy to teach these things, v. 2b

IV. THE CONCLUDING INSTRUCTIONS AND EXHORTATIONS TO TIMOTHY, 6:3-21a

1. The Description of the False Teacher, vv. 3-5

a. The identification of the false teacher, v. 3

b. The verdict on the false teacher, vv. 4,5

2. The Relation of Godliness and Wealth, vv. 6-10

a. The gain of true godliness, vv. 6-8

1) The gain of godliness with contentment, v. 6

2) The nature of godly contentment, vv. 7, 8

b. The danger to those seeking wealth, vv. 9, 10
  1) The nature of the danger, v. 9
  2) The reason for the danger, v. 10a
  3) The verification of the danger, v. 10b

3. The Exhortation to an Active Life in View of Christ's Return, vv. 11-16
  a. The characterization of the one addressed, v. 11a
  b. The statement of the specific duties, vv. 11b, 12
  c. The restatement of the charge, vv. 13-16
    1) The solemnity of the charge, v. 13
    2) The contents of the charge, v. 14a
    3) The termination of the charge, vv. 14b-16
      a) The statement of the termination. v. 14b
      b) The explanation of the termination, vv. 14b-16

4. The Charge Concerning the Rich, vv. 17-19
  a. The persons to be charged, v. 17a
  b. The contents of the charge, vv. 17b, 18
    1) Neg. — The dangers they are to avoid, v. 17 b
    2) Pos. — The duties they are to fulfill, v. 18
  c. The encouragement in carrying out the charge, v. 19

5. The Final Appeal to Timothy, vv. 20, 21a
  a. The positive appeal to guard the deposit, v. 20a
  b. The safeguard in rejecting the spurious, vv. 20b-21a

THE BENEDICTION, 6:21b

DONALD GUTHRIE

I TIMOTHY: ANALYSIS

I. THE APOSTLE AND TIMOTHY, i. 1-20
  (a) Salutation, i. 1, 2
  (b) The contrast between the gospel and its counterfeits, i. 3-11
  (c) The apostle's personal experience of the gospel, i. 12-17
  (d) The apostle's charge to Timothy, i. 18-20

II. WORSHIP AND ORDER IN THE CHURCH, ii. 1 - iv. 16
  (a) The importance and scope of public prayer, ii. 1-8
  (b) The status and demeanour of Christian women, ii. 9-15
  (c) The qualifications of Church officials, iii. 1-13
  (d) The character of the Church, iii. 14-16
  (e) Threats to the safety of the Church, iv. 1-16
    (i) The approaching apostasy, iv. 1-5
    (ii) Methods of dealing with false teaching, iv. 6-16

III. DISCIPLINE AND RESPONSIBILITY, v. 1 - vi. 2
- (a) Various age groups, v. 1, 2
- (b) Widows, v. 3-16
  - (i) Widows in need, v. 3-8
  - (ii) Widows as Christian Workers, v. 9, 10
  - (iii) Younger widows, v. 11-16
- (c) Elders, v. 17-20
- (d) Timothy's own behaviour, v. 21-25
- (e) Servants and Masters, vi. 1, 2

IV. MISCELLANEOUS INJUNCTIONS, v. 3-21
- (a) More about false teachers, vi. 3-5
- (b) The perils of wealth, vi. 6-10
- (c) A charge to a man of God, vi. 11-16
- (d) Advice to wealthy men, vi. 17-19
- (e) Final admonition to Timothy, vi. 20-21

6. *How will you outline the letter?* Please make up your own outline. Do this by reading the epistle no less than five times. Check the four outlines as you read the letter. If you can not agree with the partitioning of the commentators you are under no obligation to accept such. You *are* obligated before God to attempt a careful analysis for your own understanding; and that you might be able to teach others.

AN EXEGETICAL STUDY OF 1 TIMOTHY

We prefer a dividing of the text in the following order:

Introduction 1:1, 2

I. Sound Doctrine 1:3-20
- 1. Danger to sound doctrine. 3-11
- 3. Example of sound doctrine. 12-17
- 3. The preacher and sound doctrine. 18-20

II. Public Worship 2:1-15
- 1. Prayer. 1-7
- 2. Men and women in worship. 8-15

III. Church Officers. 3:1-16
- 1. The elder. 1-7
- 2. The deacon. 8-13
- 3. Importance of instructions. 14-16

IV. False Teachers 4:1-16
- 1. Their coming. 1-5
- 2. The preacher and the false teachers. 6-10
- 3. The true service of God. 11-16

V. Care of Members of the Church. 5:1-6:2
   1. Care of young and old. 1, 2
   2. Care of widows. 3-16
   3. Care of elders. 17-25
   4. Care of slaves. 6:1, 2

VI. The Minister Himself. 6:3-21a
   1. Motives. 3-10
   2. Proper walk. 11-16
   3. Faithful ministry. 17-21a

Conclusion 6:21b

We shall follow this outline throughout the rest of our study.

INTRODUCTION 1:1,2

Text 1:1,2

1 Paul, an apostle of Christ Jesus according to the commandment of God our Saviour, and Christ Jesus our hope: 2 unto Timothy, my true child in faith: Grace, mercy, peace from God the Father and Christ Jesus our Lord.

Thought Questions 1:1,2

1. When, and where, and why did God "command" Paul to be an apostle?
2. In what sense can God be referred to as our "Saviour"?
3. Christ is "our hope" in a particular sense; explain.
4. Is there any significance in the arrangement of the name "Christ Jesus" instead of Jesus Christ?
5. Why call Timothy a "true child"? Did Paul mean there were some who were not?
6. Show the inter-relation of the words: grace, mercy, peace. Could we arrange these words in a different order? Should we do so? Why?

Paraphrase 1:1,2

1 I Paul, an apostle of Jesus Christ, write this epistle by the commandment of God, the contriver of our salvation, and of the Lord Jesus Christ, on whose death, and not on the sacrifices of the law, our hope of eternal life is founded.
2 To Timothy, who is my genuine son in the faith, being like-minded, with myself: May gracious assistances, merciful deliverances, such as I have obtained, and inward peace from God our Father, and Christ Jesus our Lord, be multiplied to thee.

Comment 1:1,2

Vs. 1. Although this is a personal letter it carries Apostolic authority. It is to be read to others and referred to, again and again for divine confirmation of these things taught by Timothy. The reference to Paul's apostleship was not for Timothy's benefit, but for those of Ephesus among whom Timothy was working. Is Paul stating here that God commanded him to be an apostle, or that God commanded him to write the letter? We much prefer the thought of his apostleship. It seems artificial to supply the thought that God commanded him to write. We can recall immediately when and where God called or commanded him to be an apostle. The word "apostle" means "one sent". There were some persons designated as apostles, who were sent from the churches. (Cf. Phil. 2:25, II Cor. 8:23, Acts 14:14) There were only twelve and Paul as apostles of Christ Jesus, or sent from Christ Jesus.

Why say Christ Jesus and not Jesus Christ? Remember that each name has a meaning. The writer is not using the order with no thought. The office of the Christ, i.e. "the anointed one" is more prominent here. In its context we can see why. Paul is "one sent" by the "anointed one" and this is in accord with the command from such.

God is here called "our Saviour". The expression is found only in the Pastorals. Why? Could it be that Timothy and those of Ephesus needed to be reminded of the ultimate source of our salvation? Christ could never have provided our salvation if God had not sent Him. Paul said elsewhere — "in hope were we saved" (Romans 8:24). It is God who saved us, but it is Christ Jesus who provides the hope in such salvation. Thus Paul is commanded by the "fountain of our salvation" and "the embodiment of our hope" to be an apostle.

Vs. 2. Are we to understand that Paul is addressing Timothy as his son in the faith or is he referring to the genuiness of Timothy's Christian character? There is a division of opinion on this point. Since Timothy was a convert of Paul, and since he did refer to such relationship in other places, such would not be unusual here. The issue to decide, is whether Paul wants to relate Timothy to himself, or to what Paul has just written. Paul spoke of his own relationship to God and Christ; what is the relationship of Timothy? Is Timothy a genuine child of "*the faith*"—or a genuine child of Paul's in the faith? Which is it? Are not both true?

The divine blessing pronounced by Paul on Timothy is a most interesting one. In other epistles "grace and peace" are in the greetings, but nowhere do we find "mercy" except in the Pastorals. Why would Timothy need mercy—perhaps more than others? Mercy has to do with God's acceptance in spite of our failures. Was Timothy in some special need of such treatment? Perhaps he was. Some see an inter-relationship between these words. Grace first, to forgive our past sins, mercy to overlook our present failures, this results in peace in our hearts.

How did Paul imagine such blessings would be bestowed? In obedience to the divine laws of God we shall have the divine benefits attached thereto.

Fact Questions 1:1,2

1. Explain the use of the word "apostle" both generally and specifically.
2. What is the application of the word "command" as here used?
3. Specify just how God becomes our "Saviour".
4. Jesus is "our hope" in what areas?
5. In what sense was Timothy a "genuine child"?
6. Show the inter-relationship of: "grace, mercy and peace."

1. SOUND DOCTRINE 1:3-20

1. DANGER TO SOUND DOCTRINE 3-11
    a. False Teachers. 3-7

Text 1:3-7

3 As I exhorted thee to tarry at Ephesus, When I was going into Macedonia, that thou mightest charge certain men not to teach a different doctrine, 4 neither to give heed to fables and endless genealogies, which minister questionings, rather than a dispensation of God which is in faith; so do I now. 5 But the end of the charge is love out of a pure heart and a good conscience and faith unfeigned: 6 from which things some having swerved have turned aside unto vain talking; 7 desiring to be teachers of the law, though they understand neither what they say, nor whereof they confidently affirm.

Thought Questions 1:3-7

7. What seems to be the specific purpose of this letter to Timothy?
8. How would Timothy know if the doctrine of certain men was false or true?

9. Just imagine such teachers in our churches today; how could we carry out Paul's instructions?
10. Why were such persons so interested in fables and genealogies? Where did they find them?
11. Paul did not want "questionings"; he *did* want "a dispensation of God"; Explain the difference.
12. What is meant by saying "*the end* of the charge"? Is Paul suggesting that some of the teachers in Ephesus did not have a pure heart?
13. How could anyone teach that which he did not know? Explain.
14. What were these men confidently affirming?

Paraphrase 1:3-7

3 As I entreated thee to continue in Ephesus, when I was going into Macedonia, I now, by commandment of God, require thee so to do; that thou mayest charge the Judaizers not to teach differently from the inspired apostles of Christ.

4 Nor to inculcate fabulous traditions, invented to prove that men cannot be saved unless they obey the law of Moses; and uncertain genealogies, by which every Jew endeavors to trace his descent from Abraham, and which by their uncertainty occasion disputes, rather than the great edification which is through a right faith only.

5 Now the scope of the charge to be given by thee to these teachers is, that instead of *inculcating* fables and genealogies, they inculcate love to God and man proceeding from a pure heart, and directed by a good conscience, and nourished by unfeigned faith in the gospel doctrine.

6 From which things some teachers having swerved, have in their discourses turned aside to foolish talking; talking which serves no purpose but to discover their own folly, and to nourish folly in their disciples.

7 As thou mayest know by this, that they set themselves up as teachers of the law of Moses, though they understand neither what they themselves say concerning it, nor the nature of the law they establish.

Comment 1:3-7

Vs. 3. It is just as important to conserve the results as it is to obtain them. Paul was as concerned about the faith of the Christians in Ephesus after they became converts as he was before they accepted. The "grevious wolves", and the perverse teachers from among the elders at Ephesus, had evidently arisen. (Acts 20:29,30). The purpose for Timothy's stay in Ephesus was a doctrinal problem. He was to do a job of teaching. Paul felt it to be a very urgent matter. There was and is a norm of truth. Any deviation from this norm is serious and must be corrected. The correction is going to be authoritative. Timothy is to give orders as a superior officer in the army of God. Those in the army of God are to give heed. Any teaching, different from, or added to the one already delivered by the apostles, is to be rejected and corrected.

Vs. 4 The particular (although evidently not the only) difficulty in the area of teaching, had to do with a certain type of pedigree tracing. Evidently it meant a great deal to be able to show that Abraham (or some other illustrious Jewish leader) was your great-great-great grandfather. In the attempt to trace such descent, certain stories would be discovered about your relatives, which were in truth but fables. Endless questions could be asked and discussed. For an example of this practice, the Jewish *Book of Jubilees* would be a good source. This did not help anyone—least of all did it promote the cause of Christ in Ephesus. It must be corrected!

Vs. 5. Paul wants Timothy to know that he is not simply to authoritatively contradict such false teachers, but to, in the correction, produce pure hearts, good consciences, and unhypocritical faith. Could it be that such false teachers were teaching as they did because they had none of these virtues? It would seem then that their fine-spun name tracing was a smoke-screen for a sinful heart. How much false doctrine has moral implications, only God can know.

Vs. 6. Paul specifically states in this verse that some of the teachers (elders?) had missed the mark. How easy it is to be caught up in some side issue and miss the purpose of God. Much class discussion today is as vain and empty as that described here by Paul. It needs correction for the same reason.

Vs. 7. How could anyone confidently affirm that of which he was ignorant? It is not to be understood that these teachers were entirely ignorant of the law of Moses; indeed they professed to be "specialists" in the Law. They majored in minors and missed the whole purpose of the very subject they were professing to teach. Worse yet, they taught a different purpose than that intended by God. If these teachers understood the true meaning of these fables, they would never have taught them. It is sad and serious to be spiritually blind, but how tragic to observe the blind leading the blind to the ditch!

Fact Questions 1:3-7

7. Why did Paul leave Timothy in Ephesus?
8. If there was no New Testament in the day when Paul wrote to Timothy, what would Timothy use as a standard of truth?
9. Why the great interest of some in genealogies?
10. Why did the discussion about genealogies become unprofitable?
11. What is the meaning of the phrase: "the end of the charge"?
12. What was "the mark" or "the target" missed by these teachers?

b. Misuse of the Law. 8-11

Text 1:8-11

8 But we know the law is good, if a man use it lawfully, 9 as knowing this, that law is not made for a righteous man, but for the lawless and unruly, for the ungodly and sinners, for the unholy and profane, for murderers of fathers and murderers of mothers, for manslayers, 10 for fornicators, for abusers of themselves with men, for menstealers, for liars, for false swearers, and if there be any other thing contrary to the sound doctrine; 11 according to the gospel of the glory of the blessed God, which was committed to my trust.

Thought Questions 1:8-11

15. In what sense can we say the law is "good"?
16. How could the law be used "unlawfully"?
17. How does the list of sins here given relate to the persons with whom Timothy was dealing?
18. Why give such an extended list? Is there some particular significance in the grouping?
19. Why have law at all if men are going to be unrighteous?
20. What is the distinction between a "manslayer" and a "murderer of fathers"?
21. What would be a modern name for "Menstealers"?; for "abusers of themselves with men"?
22. Explain verse 11 in context.

Paraphrase 1:8-11

8 I acknowledge indeed that the law of Moses is an excellent

institution, if one use it agreeably to the end for which it was given.
9 Now we know this, that the law is not made for justifying a righteous man, but for condemning and punishing the lawless and disorderly, namely, atheists and idolaters; persons polluted with vice and who are excluded from things sacred, murderers of fathers and murderers of mothers, those who slay others unjustly;
10 Fornicators and sodomites, man-stealers, liars, those who perjure themselves; and if any other practice be opposite to the doctrine which preserves the soul in health, the law was made to restrain and punish it.
11 This view of the law I give according to the glorious gospel of the infinitely and independently blessed God, with the preaching of which I am entrusted.

Comment 1:8-11

Vs. 8. Paul does not wish to create the impression that he has rejected the law of Moses. Some prejudiced Jews might so conclude by what he has just said. The law does indeed have a good purpose. It is not to serve as a source of name hunting. There is a play on words in this verse: "use the law lawfully". These Jewish leaders were so proud of being law teachers, and at the same time in their practice they were actually "unlawful."

Vss. 9 & 10. The true use of the law is now to be shown. Christians do not need the law. They serve a higher law: the law of love, and as a result are not affected by the prohibitions of the law of Moses. If these false teachers were teaching the law to the Christians in Ephesus, what Paul has written would indeed contradict their work. Why this long list of persons affected by the law? Maybe the law teachers were so completely ignorant of the law that they needed this elementary information. It could have been some of these teachers were practicing some of the sins here mentioned. In this case they would be condemned by the very subject they were teaching.

Commentators see a similarity in Paul's prohibitions here, to those of the Ten Commandments. Note this table of comparison as given by Homer Kent:

The first table of the Decalogue is covered in general terms:

I Timothy 1:9, 10	Exodus 20:1-17
Lawless and disobedient	1. Thou shalt have no other gods before me.
Ungodly and sinners	2. Thou shalt not make unto thee any graven image.

Unholy and profane	3. Thou shalt not take the name of the Lord thy God in vain.
	4. Remember the sabbath day to keep it holy.

By these three pairs of words the second table is covered more completely:

Father-smiters and mother-smiters	5. Honor thy father and thy mother.
Murderers	6. Thou shalt not kill.
Fornicators, Sodomites	7. Thou shalt not commit adultery.
Kidnappers	8. Thou shalt not steal.
Liars, perjurers	9. Thou shalt not bear false witness.
Any other thing.	10. Thou shalt not covet. (*Ibid.* pp. 87, 88)

Vs. 11. The above information as to the proper use of the law is in perfect agreement to, and a part of, the Good News entrusted to Paul. The Gospel (or the Faith) would teach that sinners are to be brought under the judgment of God by the law. When they are thus shown to be guilty and condemned before God's righteous law, they will hear with eagerness the Good News that "Christ died to save sinners". Such Good Tidings are described as being "of the glory of the blessed God", or of the "glorious gospel". The word "glory" could be understood as "character"; thus the Good News shows forth the character of God. Indeed it does: God is shown as one of infinite love and wisdom, "that he himself might be just, and the justifier of him that hath faith in Jesus." (Rom. 3:26)

Fact Questions 1:8-11

13. Paul has not rejected the law; others have. Show how they have.
14. Is the law misused in our teaching today? How? In what sense is the Christian free from the law?
15. Why does Paul make reference to the Ten Commandments?
16. Paul says the Gospel has something to say about the law—what is it?
17. In what way does the Gospel manifest the character of God?

2. EXAMPLE OF SOUND DOCTRINE. 12-17

Text 1:12-17

12 I thank him that enabled me, even Christ Jesus our Lord, for

that he counted me faithful, appointing me to his service; 13
though I was before a blasphemer and a persecutor, and injurious:
Howbeit I obtained mercy, because I did it ignorantly in unbelief;
14 and the grace of our Lord abounded exceedingly with faith
and love which is in Christ Jesus. 15 Faithful is the saying, and
worthy of all acceptation, that Christ Jesus came into the world
to save sinners; of whom I am chief: 16 howbeit for this cause
I obtained mercy, that in me as chief might Jesus Christ show
forth all His longsuffering for an ensample of them that should
thereafter believe on him unto eternal life. 17 Now unto the
King eternal, immortal, invisible, the only God be honor and glory
for ever and ever. Amen.

Thought Questions 1:12-17

23. Please be able to relate this section with the whole chapter. How do verses 12-17 relate to what has proceeded and what follows?
24. In what way did Christ enable Paul to enter His service?
25. In what sense did Christ count Paul "faithful"? Refer to verse 12.
26. Define each of the three words in verse 13.
27. Is Paul saying in 13b that he was saved in his ignorance? If not, what is he saying?
28. Just how is the word "grace" to be understood as in verse 14?
29. Show the relationship between the three words: grace, faith, and love, as in verse 14.
30. Why refer to the statement in verse 15 as "a faithful saying"?
31. Give the meaning of the word "chief" as here used by Paul.
32. Paul gives two reasons for his obtaining mercy, one in verse 13, and one in verse 16; explain the one in verse 16.
33. Paul's conversion should be a great encouragement to all—why?
34. Define three characteristics of God as found in verse 17.

Paraphrase 1:12-17

12 Now I thank Christ Jesus our Lord; who strengthened me for
preaching it (the glorious gospel), by bestowing on me the gifts
of inspiration and miracles, because he knew that I would be
faithful to my trust, when he appointed me to the apostleship;
13 Who was formerly a defamer of him and of his doctrine, and
a persecutor of his disciples, and an injurious person in my behaviour towards them. But I received pardon because I acted
from ignorance, being in a state of unbelief, and fancying that I
was doing God service.

14 And in thus pardoning me, and making me his apostle, the goodness of our Lord hath super-abounded toward me, accompanied with the faith and love which is required by Christ Jesus, but in which I was greatly deficient formerly.
15 This saying is true, and worthy of cordial and universal reception, that Christ Jesus came into the world to save sinners, of whom, on account of my rage against Christ and his disciples, I reckon myself the chief; I mean of those who have sinned through ignorance.
16 However, though my sin was great, for this cause I received pardon, that in me, the chief of those who sin through ignorance, Jesus Christ might show forth the greatest clemency in forgiving offenders, for an example of mercy to encourage them who should in future ages repent and believe on him, in order to obtain everlasting life.
17 Now, ravished with the goodness of God, in making me an example of pardon for the encouragement of future penitents, I say, to the Ruler of the ages, who is immortal and invisible to the wise God above, be honour and glory, for ever and ever. Amen.

Comment 1:12-17

As Donald Guthrie has stated, "This section appears to be a digression" . . . . but it is not. Paul has said that the "end of the charge was love out of a pure heart, and a good conscience and faith unfeigned". These qualities Paul obtained from the "Good News" or the Sound Doctrine. Timothy can now present to these law teachers an example of the results of the right use of the Law and the Gospel. Paul is saying, "If Christ can change me, and He did, then He can change anyone; preach it!" Cease dabbling in law speculation.

Vs. 12. The gratitude of the Apostle is genuine. The enabling power of Christ and God are a favorite theme of Paul's letters.
He is to say: "I am what I am because of the grace of God"—(I Cor. 15:10), "My grace is sufficient for thee." (2 Cor. 12:9), "I can do all things through Christ who strengtheneth me". (Phil. 4:13)

As to just where and when and how Christ enabled Paul, we need but refer to the place "nigh unto Damascus". There are three records of this event: (Acts 9, 22, 26). Perhaps the order of names in this verse is significant: Christ, which means "the anointed of God", "Jesus", which means Saviour, "Our Lord", which means Sovereign. This is the one who is well able to enable. How could Paul be counted "faithful" *before* he was converted? We understand this word to mean "trustworthy" as here used. Christ knew the character of Paul from the time of his birth (Gal. 1:15). It was because of this dependable quality that he called him. Because of his sin Paul felt unworthy to be called or counted trustworthy. How wonderously precious must Christ have been to Paul that he could thank Him for calling him into a life of privation, imprisonment and death. And yet he was glad to share in this service.

Vs. 13. Here is an elaboration of the reason for the thankfulness. Paul says of himself that he was: "a blasphemer i.e. one who speaks against"—and this he did openly and often; "a persecutor" —he not only spoke against Jesus himself but in his persecution he "strove to make others blaspheme" (Acts 26:11). To summarize his evil work he says he was "injurious" or a violent, insolent man. He was the most loathsome of men. Still speaking of his appointment to the service of Christ, Paul uses the word "mercy". He says he obtained mercy because he did all that he did against Christ in ignorance and unbelief. He was unlike his countrymen who had access to the knowledge of Jesus as their Messiah. He was unlike some who refused to believe in spite of the evidence. Is not Paul's word applicable to all who obtain mercy? It is only when we are informed and believe, that we are granted mercy.

Vs. 14. What is called "mercy" in vs. 13 is called "grace" in vs. 14. Of course the emphasis in vs. 14 is upon the "unmerited favor" shown to Saul of Tarsus. In vs. 13 the thought of meeting the need of Saul is in the forefront with the use of the word "mercy". "Where sin abounded, (as in the life of Paul), so grace did abound more exceedingly" (Romans 5:20). The love and confidence Christ had for Paul overflowed, and received in kind. Paul responded with faith and love for the one who so loved and trusted him. In it all was a deep awareness of his own unworthiness.

Vs. 15. It might be well to say just here that the expression: "Faithful is the saying", seems to be the preface to a statement used in Paul's day which Paul here adapts to his purpose. There are five such "Faithful sayings" in the Pastorals. They are found in: I Tim. 3:1; I Tim. 4:8, 9; II Tim. 2:11-13; Titus 3:4-8a; and here in I Tim. 1:15. We might refer to these five sayings as "slogans" or "axioms". They were current and very popular in Paul's day. Such sayings summed up "The Faith". The saying in vs. 15 expresses the very heart of the gospel (Cf. I Cor. 15:1-4). Paul calls Timothy to recall this reliable saying and relate the apostle to it. Christ came to save sinners. He saved me, and I indeed was the chief of sinners, so deeply in need of saving. There is much to be said to present day application of this grand statement. We are sorely tempted to become homiletical instead of exegetical.

Vs. 16. Here we are introduced to another reason for the mercy shown to Paul. Vs. 13 attributes God's grant of mercy to ignorance and unbelief on the part of Paul. Vs. 16 attributes the purpose of mercy to the presenting of an example to the world of God's longsuffering. Paul is saying that what happened to him is a sketch of what could happen to anyone. The power of Christ is seen in Paul. No one is too sinful, or too stubborn, or too ignorant to receive mercy. Paul was to demonstrate this in his own preaching. He came to know it was true as he saw "barbarians" converted to Christ and by Christ. Paul's experience gives the bold outline of God's Power and Mercy. The personal details will be different as each person fills them in to complete the picture of his own life experience with Christ. Paul's Damascus encounter will ever remain the outline sketch of God's infinite mercy.

Vs. 17. A spontaneous expression of joy and adoration is so typically Pauline. The past three verses are cumulative in their feeling; a climax is reached at the end of verse sixteen, hence the doxology of verse 17 is a natural response.

God is the king of "ages"—all ages. In the context we might say that He is also the Saviour of all men of all ages. All the qualities of God here described should be associated with the thought of His providing salvation in Christ. Notice: He is king, therefore able to save. He is ruler over all men of all ages and hence can save all of them; He is not subject to corruption; He shares His nature with man and thus gives him an eternal salvation; He is invisible to mortal eye; He is of Spirit-quality thus superceding this temporal sphere. God is the only one who could and does save; to Him we ascribe all honor and adoration without end. Amen.

Fact Questions 1:12-17

18. How does this section develop the purpose of the charge?
19. Discuss the subjective and objective aspects of Christ's enabling power with Paul.
20. How are we to understand the word "faithful" as used in verse 12?
21. Give the meaning of the three words used to describe Paul in verse 13.
22. Explain the relationship of ignorance and mercy.
23. In what sense did grace "super-abound"?
24. In what way was Paul "chief" of sinners?
25. State five ways in which Paul is an example to all who would be saved?

3. THE PREACHER AND SOUND DOCTRINE 18-20

Text 1:18-20

18 This charge I commit unto thee, my child Timothy, according to the prophecies which led the way to thee, that by them thou mayest war the good warfare; 19 holding faith and a good conscience; which some having thrust from them made shipwreck concerning the faith: 20 of whom is Hymenaeus and Alexander; whom I delivered unto Satan that they might be taught not to blaspheme.

Thought Questions 1:18-20

35. State in one sentence the charge that Paul gave to Timothy.
36. What were the "prophecies" mentioned in vs. 18? Cf. I Tim. 4:14; II Tim. 1:6.
37. Whatever these prophecies were, Timothy was going to use them to help him in the battle of the faith. Explain.
38. Show the great importance of sustaining the proper relationship of faith with conscience.
39. Show how the figure of a shipwreck is appropriate.
40. Two men are to be taught a lesson; how and why?

Paraphrase 1:18-20

18 This charge to the Judaizers, not to teach differently, I commit to thee, son Timothy, to deliver to them; and I do it amiably to the revelations which were before made to me concerning thee, and which I now mention, that through the recollection of these revelations and the honour which was done thee by them, thou mayest strenuously carry on the good warfare against the enemies of truth in Ephesus.

19 In carrying on this warfare, hold fast the true faith, and at the same time a good conscience, using no improper methods in spreading the gospel; which faith and good conscience some teachers having put away from worldly motives, with respect to the faith have made shipwreck; they have corrupted the gospel, and destroyed their own souls.

20 Of whom are the two Judaizing teachers Hymenaeus and Alexander, whom, for their obstinately persisting willfully to corrupt the gospel, I have delivered to Satan to be by him tormented with bodily pains that they might be taught by a chastisement miraculously inflicted on them not to revile either Christ, or his doctrine concerning the salvation of the Gentiles. Let the faithful in Ephesus avoid these wicked teachers.

Comment 1:18-20

Vs. 18. Please notice the reference here to the charge mentioned earlier in Verse 3. What Paul has said between Verse 3 and Verse 18 would prepare Timothy to deliver the charge and accomplish the purpose for which it was given. Paul is here saying that his willingness to entrust Timothy with the high responsibility of such a charge can be found in "the prophecies that led the way" to Timothy. There are many and varied comments about the meaning of the phrase before us. We have preferred a comparison of I Tim. 4:14 with this text to offer an explanation. We might also compare II Tim. 1:6 in this connection. The gift of prophecy was exercised when the hands of the elders were laid upon Timothy. It could have been that Paul exercised such a gift when he laid his hands upon Timothy. In either case we would say that someone looking ahead by the power of this prophetic gift saw the wonderful possibilities in this young man.

Naturally the prophetic promises were mentioned to Timothy in such a way as to impress themselves upon his heart. By recalling them he could use such encouragement to help him in "warring the good warfare". Perhaps Timothy was to remember such inspired words concerning himself and take heart that, if those who were guided by the Holy Spirit believed in his ability, who was he to hesitate?

Vs. 19. It is not to be imagined that Timothy did not have faith or a good conscience. It is rather to introduce the reason for the defection of some, that Paul exhorts Timothy to hold faith and a good conscience. "What God hath joined together let not man put asunder"—When faith and conscience are separated there is always shipwreck ahead. Are we to understand that these men wrecked the ship of The Faith or wrecked their own personal ship of faith? We must conclude it is a subjective matter. To discuss whether these men were lost or not in this experience surely seems to be beside the point. Such men were in deadly danger; they were in the grasp, and under the power of Satan; to remain in such a condition would result in only one end.

Vs. 20. Several were involved in the problem outlined by Paul, but only two are mentioned by name. It would seem that only when nothing more could be done are "certain ones" designated. It is futile to try to identify the Alexander mentioned here with the several over Alexanders mentioned in the New Testament. The Hymenaeus here mentioned can be identified with the one in II Timothy 2:17, 18; 4:14. How could Satan become a teacher against blasphemy? This is not easy to answer. Perhaps the answer is in the character of those being disciplined.

Fact Questions 1:18-20

26. Explain the use of the term "charge" as found in Vs. 18.
27. Show the possible connection between I Tim. 4:14 and Vs. 18.
28. Why are faith and conscience inseparable?
29. What was wrecked in the shipwreck?
30. Why name the two men of Vs. 20?
31. How would Satan be able to teach them not to blaspheme?

EXEGETICAL EXAMINATION ON I TIMOTHY CHAPTER ONE

1. Give from memory an outline of this chapter.
2. Explain the "commandment" of God as in Verse 1.
3. Tell why you believe what you do about Timothy's relationship to Paul as his child.
4. Explain "endless genealogies"—why endless?
5. Define: "dispensation of God which is in faith".
6. What is: "the end of the charge"?
7. In what sense is, "the law good"?
8. Why list all the sinners of Verses 8-11?
9. Give the meaning of the phrase: "contrary to the sound doctrine".
10. Give the meaning of the word, "faithful", as in Verse 12.
11. Why would God grant mercy to someone who acted in ignorance and unbelief any more readily than He would to one who did not? Or is this the meaning of the phrase?

12. In what way did Paul become an example to all those who would come after him?
13. Explain "the prophecies" as in Verse 18. How would Timothy use them?
14. What was it that caused the shipwreck of some?
15. How would the action taken upon Hymenaeus and Alexander teach them?

II. PUBLIC WORSHIP 2:1-15

1. PRAYER 1-7

Text 2:1-7

1 I exhort therefore, first of all, that supplications, prayers, intercessions, thanksgivings, be made for all men; 2 for kings and all that are in high place; that we may lead a tranquil life in all godliness and gravity. 3 This is good and acceptable in the sight of God our Saviour; 4 who would have all men to be saved, and come to the knowledge of the truth. 5 For there is one God, one mediator also between God and men, himself man, Christ Jesus, 6 who gave himself a ransom for all: the testimony to be borne in its own times; 7 whereunto I was appointed a preacher and an apostle (I speak the truth, I lie not) a teacher of the Gentiles in faith and truth.

Thought Questions 2:1-7

41. The word "therefore" in 2:1 connects verses 2:1-7 with those proceeding; show the connection.
42. How is the word "first" to be understood? Is Paul giving instructions for the "pastoral prayer"?
43. Define each of the four words relating to prayer and show their inter-relation.
44. Why mention: "kings, and all that are in high place"?
45. Are we to understand from Paul's admonition that our praying is going to affect the decisions of State? How? Why?
46. Define the difference in the use of the word "quiet" and the use of the word "tranquil". God, our Saviour, is most pleased when we pray after the order here prescribed; why?
47. If God wants all men saved why doesn't He save them?
48. There are four arguments for universal prayer. These arguments are found in verses 5-7. See if you can define them.
49. Why mention the humanity of Christ Jesus as in Vs. 5?
50. What is the meaning of the expression "ransom for all"?
51. What is "the testimony", of Verse 6?
52. Unto what was Paul appointed?

Paraphrase 2:1-7

1 Now I exhort, first of all, that in the public assemblies, deprecations of evils, and supplications for such good things as are necessary, and intercessions for their conversion, and thanksgiving for mercies, be offered in behalf of all men, for heathens as well as for Christians, and for enemies as well as for friends;
2 But especially for kings, and all who have authority in the state, by whatever name they may be called, that, finding us good subjects, we may be suffered to lead an undisturbed and peaceable life, while we worship the only true God, and honestly perform every civil and social duty.
3 For this, that we pray for all men, and especially for rulers, although they be heathens, is good for ourselves, and acceptable in the sight of God our Saviour.
4 Who commandeth all men to be saved from heathenism ignorance and Jewish prejudices, and to come to the knowledge of the truth, that is, of the gospel, through the preaching of the word.
5 For there is one God, the maker, benefactor, and governor of all, and one Mediator between God and men; consequently, all are equally the objects of God's care: This Mediator is the man Christ Jesus.
6 Who voluntarily (John x. 18.) gave himself a ransom not for the Jews only, but for all. Of which doctrine the publication and proof is now made in its proper season; so that, since Christ gave himself for all, it is certainly the will of God that we should pray for all.
7 For the bearing of which testimony concerning the benevolence of God towards all men, and concerning Christ's giving himself a ransom for all, I was appointed an herald, or messenger of peace, and an apostle divinely inspired, (I call Christ to witness that I speak the truth and lie not), a teacher of the Gentiles in faith and truth; that is, in the true faith of the gospel.

Comment 2:1-7

Vs. 1. The use of he word "exhort" indicates something far stronger than just a suggestion. Paul wants these instructions carried out to the letter, as well as in the spirit in which they were given. Notice the word, "therefore"; Paul is saying: upon the basis of what has been said in chapter one, primary in importance is the proper attitude in public worship, particularly in prayer. When Timothy, or any one of the church leaders prayed in public, here are the instructions as to attitude and requests.

The four words here used each have a different meaning and application; however, there is much overlapping in application or use. Supplications are those expressions in prayer that relate to the deepest needs of the heart; such needs are far more personal than those expressed by "prayers". General requests are covered in the second word. Please do not fail to associate such praying with the object: "all men." "Intercessions" is not as specific here as we usually think of it. Here the thought is much more one of pleading on behalf of others, than acting in the official capacity as a mediator. How very negligent we are in the area of "thanksgiving" in prayer. Just what is it about "all men" that would be a cause for thanksgiving? To ask such a question is an indication of our need for such an exhortation.

Are we to pray for sinners? This verse should forever settle that question. If we would exercise these four elements in prayer for "all men" we would indeed be praying for sinners; and doing it just like God intended.

Vs. 2. "All men" is generic; "kings, and all that are in high place" are some of the specific men for whom we should pray.

Why pray for these men? Because it will effect certain changes in them and their administration that would not otherwise prevail. God *is* still ruling in the affairs of men. It is still God who raises up and casts down the rulers of this nation and word. God does not operate on man's schedule—but He acts in answer to the prayers prayed like Daniel of old did (Cf. Dan. 6:10). Not only so, but the very attitude necessary to pray after this manner, would help the one praying to be able to lead a quiet and tranquil life in all godliness and gravity. Such will be true in any society at any time. "Tranquil" refers to the outward calm. "Quiet" refers to the inward condition of the one praying.

When God answers our prayers we should show our gratitude by living a life pleasing to God.

Vs. 3. The expression "good" is to be thought of in the same sense as the use of the word "good" when God looked upon His creation and said "it is good"; i.e., a pleasure to the All-Mighty. Because God is a Saviour for all men, it is most acceptable to Him that we pray for the salvation of all men.

Vs. 4. The thought begun in Vs. 3 is completed in Verse 4. Such praying is admirable in God's sight because He wants all men to be saved, or come to an acknowledgment of the truth.

God has made provision for the salvation of all men. He loves all men. He has commissioned that the good news be preached to all men; therefore it is with satisfaction that He hears prayers ascending on behalf of all men. We like the distinction made by Homer Kent in the use of the verbs:

> "Furthermore, God wishes all men to be saved. The verb "thelo" is employed which denotes a desire springing out of the emotions or inclinations, rather than out of deliberation "boulomia". Hence this is a reference to God's moral will which applies to all men. However, this moral will of God may fail, and often does. Men sin, although God does not want them to. Consequently, if men are lost, it is because they opposed God's will which gave His Son to save them. This does not teach universalism, for God does not violate man's opportunity to choose. The passive voice of the infinite "sothenai" (to be saved) may be suggestive. God wishes all men to be saved, that is, to experience salvation through the appointed channel of personal faith in Christ. If the text had used the active voice, "Wishes to save all men," one would wonder why God does not then do so." (*Ibid.*, p. 103)

Vs. 5. We like the thought that in Vss. 5-7 we have four arguments in favor of praying for all men: (1) The unity of God—"There is one God;" (2) The unity of the Mediator,—"and one mediator;" (3) The availability of the ransom,—"who gave himself a ransom *for all*; (4) The commission to the Gentiles—Vs. 7. (For this we are indebted to Homer Kent). If there is only one God (and we know there is), if there is only one Mediator (and we are sure of this), and they were provided for all men—how could we be exclusive in our concern and prayers?

Vs. 6. Christ is not only the one Mediator but also the one payment for man's soul. God has given His Son as an exchange for all men.

The act of His giving Himself as a ransom price on behalf of man, relates directly to His worthiness to be the universal Mediator. We like the thought that there must have been one who was both God and man in order to be a Mediator. Only this one could meet the great "kidnapper's ransom price"; it was the God-Man Christ Jesus!

The expression: "the testimony to be borne in its own times" is not easy of understanding; the question is: "*what* is to be the content of the testimony"?

We prefer the thought this phrase compares very favorably with Gal. 4:4 and has reference to the "fulness of time when God sent forth His Son". He was to be the one mediator; the one ransom. It is now time to give this testimony or good news.

Vs. 7. The fourth and last reason for universal prayer on behalf of all men is found in the commission our Lord gave to Paul. If Christ sent Paul to preach to the Gentiles, (as he did Peter to the Jews), then surely we should pray for these objects of God's concern and subjects of Paul's work.

The descriptive words: "preacher", "apostle", "teacher", "in faith and truth", indicate his task. He was "one sent" to "herald forth"; in so doing to "teach" all. This was to be done in faith, with the truth.

Fact Questions 2:1-7

26. In what sense is the expression "First of all" used?
27. Please define the terms: "supplications, prayers, intercessions, and thanksgivings" as here used.
28. In what particulars are we to pray for all men?
29. What is the difference, if any, from a tranquil life, and a quiet life?
30. Show the distinction in the use of the terms: "godliness and gravity".
31. What is "good and acceptable with God"?
32. In what sense does God will that all men be saved?
33. Are being saved, and coming to the knowledge of the truth, two different experiences?
34. How does the thought of the oneness of God relate to the context?
35. Show the contextual connection of the One Mediator.
36. What is "the testimony to be bourne in its own times"?
37. Unto what was Paul appointed a preacher and an apostle, a teacher of the Gentiles in faith and truth?

2. MEN AND WOMEN IN WORSHIP 8-15

Text 2:8-15

8 I desire therefore that the men pray in every place, lifting up holy hands, without wrath and disputing. 9 In like manner, that women adorn themselves in modest apparel, with shamefastness and sobriety; not with braided hair, and gold or pearls or costly

raiment; 10 but (which becometh women professing godliness) through good works. 11 Let a woman learn in quietness with all subjection. 12 But I permit not a woman to teach, nor to have dominion over a man, but to be in quietness. 13 For Adam was first formed, then Eve; 14 and Adam was not beguiled, but the woman being beguiled hath fallen into transgression: 15 but she shall be saved through her child-bearing, if they continue in faith with love and sanctification with sobriety.

Thought Questions 2:8-15

53. Is Paul excluding the women from public prayer by his use of the term "men" in Vs. 8?
54. What is meant by the expression: "every place"?
55. What are "holy hands"? Is this describing a posture in prayer?
56. Why say "without wrath and disputing"? How could men pray at all if such conditions prevailed?
57. To what does the phrase, "women in *like manner*" refer?
58. Why would Christian women adorn themselves in anything else than modest apparel?
59. Does "shamefastness' relate to the use of cosmetics? Explain.
60. Is it wrong to wear jewelry of any kind? Explain.
61. A woman professing good works should adorn herself with what raiment?
62. Why introduce the thought of women learning? Please indicate how it relates to the context.

Paraphrase 2:8-15

8 I command, therefore, that the men pray for all, (ver. 1), in every place appointed for public worship, lifting up holy hands; hands purified from sinful actions; and that they pray without wrath and disputings about the seasons and places of prayer.

9 In like manner also I command that the women, before appearing in the assemblies for worship, adorn themselves in decent apparel, with modesty and sobriety, which are their chief ornaments, not with plaited hair only, or gold, or jewels, or embroidered raiment; in order to create evil desires in the men, or a vain admiration of their beauty;

10 but, instead of these vain ornaments, let them (as becometh women professing the Christian religion) adorn themselves with works of charity, which are the greatest ornaments of the female character, and to which the tender-heartedness of the sex strongly disposeth them.

11 Let every woman receive instruction in religious matters from the men in silence, with entire submission, on account of their imperfect education and inferior understanding.

12 For I do not allow a woman to teach in the public assemblies, nor in any manner to usurp authority over a man; but I enjoin them, in all public meetings, to be silent.

13 The natural inferiority of the woman, God shewed at the creation; for Adam was first formed, then Eve, to be a help meet for him.

14 Besides, that women are naturally inferior to men in understanding, is plain from this—Adam was not deceived by the devil but the woman being deceived by him, fell into transgression.

15 However, though Eve was first in transgression, and brought death on herself, her husband, and her posterity, the female sex shall be saved equally with the male, through child-bearing; through bringing forth the Saviour; if they live in faith, and love, and chastity, with that sobriety which I have been recommending.

Comment 2:8-15

Vs. 8. The actual lifting of the hands toward God in an expression of supplication and petition was a very common occurence in the Old Testament; also in the synagogues and in the early church; hence we refer the expression to the physical act. When hands are thus held up before God, let them be the expression of a pure heart; a good conscience; and an unhypocritical faith; then will the hands be holy or clean.

Let prayers for the rulers be without a desire for vengeance upon them. Let no hatred or animosity enter the heart, as mention is made of the names of those who rule. This would not be an easy matter when Nero was on the throne.

Under the world conditions of the first century, it would not be easy to believe prayers would effect any real change, or produce any good, hence the use of the word "disputing", or "doubting". Paul wants the Christians in Ephesus and all places, to pray in simple faith in God's ability and love.

Vs. 9. The three words, "in like manner," have occasioned no small discussion among commentators. We take them to refer to the sphere of the women's activities as compared with that of the men. As the men were to follow carefully the instructions given to them regarding leading in prayer, the women "likewise" are to follow carefully the instructions about to be given to them.

Both the men and the women here mentioned are appearing in public. How they act and look and feel, is very important. We have noticed how men are to behave themselves; the discussion turns now to the women. Woman does not have a place of congregational leadership; hence her appearance is discussed rather than her position or work.

Paul is saying: when women dress for church please remember the following divine instructions: "Be orderly and modest in arranging your appearance; particularly with your clothes and hair." The word "adorn" had the meaning of orderliness; the word "modest" does not only refer to the cut of the dress but to the attitude of the one wearing it.

Every woman knows what is considered modest in the society in which she lives. Extremes are thus avoided by placing the responsibility of the one who wears the clothes.

The word "shamefastness" is an obsolete word which simply means "modesty"; the word "modesty" in the first half of this verse refers to the appearance of the clothes; here the word refers to the attitude of the heart of the woman.

"Sobriety" refers to that inner self control that would hinder any Christian woman from appearing in public in any garb that would reflect on her Christian character.

To be specific Paul refers to a custom which evidently was very common in some assemblies of his day. "Not with braided hair, and gold or pearls or costly raiment." We like the comment of Lenski upon this point:

> "Isa. 3:18-24 names some of the extravagant female ornaments. Paul says: 'not braids and gold or pearls or expensive clothes.' I Pet. 3:3 writes: 'not the outward adorning of plaiting of hair and of wearing of things of gold or putting on apparel.' This is the vanity of personal display in order to attract general attention, in particular to fill other women with envy, to outshine rivals. These are 'braids' or 'plaits' of hair, the putting it up in showy, unusual fashion so as to become conspicuous, and not just common and customary braids.
>
> Paul does not say where the gold or pearls are worn, whether in the braided hair, or in chains about the neck, or in pins, etc. on the dress. Display of jewelry is referred to. Aside from religion, good taste forbids such display. The two 'or' are not disjunctive so that, when gold is worn, pearls would not be;

but conjunctive, which is a common use of 'or' that draws attention to each item separately, to the gold for one thing, to the pearls for another, and also to the expensive clothes. The fact that flashy jewelry would be displayed with costly 'clothing' is apparent. Such a woman wants to make a stunning impression. Her mind is on herself; she is unfit for worship.

This verse does not refer to merely sex attraction. How many women who are past the age are given to the silly vanity of dress? Paul is not insisting on drab dress. Even this may be worn in vanity; the very drabness may be made a display. Each according to her station in life: the queen not the same as her noble mistress. Each with due propriety as modesty and propriety will indicate to her both when attending divine services and when appearing in public elsewhere." (Lenski, Pp. 559-560).

Vs. 10. The adornment of women professing godliness when they prepare to worship in public is "good works". How could good works be worn? The development of character through good works is the adornment of the heart. Such a heart condition will react on the selection of clothes.

Vs. 11. Verses 11-15 are a unit. In verses 11, 12 we have a charge to women. In verses 13-15 we have two reasons for the charge. We refer the admonition here given to the public service: women are not to lead out in such meetings; they are rather to be the silent learners. We, of course, think of the companion verses to this in I Corinthians 14:34,35. Possibly the conditions in Ephesus would have called forth such prohibitions.

Vs. 12. The expression "I permit not" is not to be passed off lightly as local or temporary, as we have heard it done in too many places. Paul speaks with divine authority to us as well as to the church at Ephesus. Are we to assume there are actually two prohibitions here? We are to read in a subsequent letter that Paul permits and encourages women to teach (Cf. Titus 2:3-5) so we must confine it to certain conditions and times. We would say then, that in gathering of the whole public assembly, the woman is not to teach. The expression "to have dominion over a man" could well be translated "lord it over" a man. In the public meetings where men are present, women are not to teach, nor in any way "lord it over" them, but in contrast they are to be "in quietness".

Vs. 13. "Adam was first formed, then Eve"; at first reading, this might appear as a rather superfluous reason for giving man precedence over the woman; but look again. How was man created? "out of the dust of the ground"!; and how was woman created? Out of man; man was a separate being before woman was created. I Corinthians 11:9 is a commentary on this thought. Man holds a direct relationship of responsibility to God; the woman through the man to God, i.e. in the husband and wife relationship. Only when this arrangement was altered did the first pair lose Paradise.

Vs. 14. The social position of the woman is as well established in the order of temptation and sin as in the order of creation. The woman was altogether deceived by the serpent and came into transgression. This would indicate a definite lack on her part. To quote another, "She wants, by the very constitution of nature, the qualities necessary for such a task—(i.e. ruling in the church) in particular, the equability of temper, the practical shrewdness and discernment, the firm, independent, regulative judgment, which are required to carry the leaders of important interests above first impressions and outside appearances, to resist solicitations, and amid subtle entanglements and fierce conflicts to cleave unswervingly to the right." (*Fairbairn*, p. 129). This, Eve did not do. Why she did not do it, the inspired writer is to say, has to do with her essential nature. Adam, on the other hand, was not deceived by the serpent. Adam was indeed a sinner, and responsible for his own action as well as his relationship to his wife. If Adam is the head of the woman, why does he not act like it? Both Adam and Eve were out of place. However, the only point being made here is that in the nature of the two, one is made to lead and the other to follow.

Vs. 15. This verse contains one of the most difficult of expressions in the whole letter. What shall we say of the promise of salvation to woman through "child bearing"? Does this refer to "the Messiah" or "The Child"? Is Paul offering salvation to women through the pains of bearing children? Are the "they" of the latter part of the verse the same as "woman" of the first part? Let each student answer these questions before he proceeds to formulate an opinion. *Gutherie* outlines the three leading views on this verse:

1. *Refers to the Messiah*—woman has been given the capacity to save herself and all others because it was through woman that the Saviour was born.
2. *The word "saved" is to be taken in the natural or physical realm* and refers only to the promise of the safe deliverance of children if the proper conditions are observed.
3. *Woman is to save herself* in the process of seeing to it that her children are saved.

Fact Questions 2:8-15

38. Give the meaning of the expression "every place."
39. Is Paul suggesting that men actually, physically, lift up their hands in prayer? Explain.
40. Give the meaning of "holy hands."
41. How would wrath and disputing relate to prayer?
42. Explain the phrase: "women in like manner"?
43. How shall we determine what apparel is modest?
44. Meaning of the words: "shamefastness and sobriety."
45. Is Paul against all braided hair?
46. Women are to adorn themselves with something—what is it?
47. When and where is a woman to learn in quietness?
48. Does the act of teaching give a woman dominion over a man?
49. Explain the two reasons for the subjection of women, as given by Paul.
50. How does the thought of verse 15 fit this particular context?

EXEGETICAL EXAMINATION OVER CHAPTER TWO OF I TIMOTHY

1. Give an outline of this chapter. It would be very helpful to you, if you were able to divide it with more detail than just the two main divisions.
2. Define the meaning and application of the four terms describing prayer as in Vs. 1.
3. What is "good and acceptable in the sight of God"—Explain why "acceptable" to God.
4. Give the four arguments for universal prayer.
5. What is "the testimony to be borne in its own times"?
6. Explain how "wrath and disputing" relate to prayer as in Vs. 8.
7. Explain what you believe about the little phrase "women in like manner", as in Vs. 9.

8. Explain "shamefastness and sobriety".
9. Paul did, and did not, permit women to teach—explain when, where, and why.
10. Explain the two reasons for the subjection of woman to man.
11. Explain Vs. 15.

III. CHURCH OFFICERS 3:1-16

A. Office of the Overseer (3:1-7)

1. THE ELDER. 1-7

Text 3:1-7

1 Faithful is the saying, if a man seeketh the office of a bishop, he desireth a good work. 2 The bishop therefore must be without reproach, the husband of one wife, temperate, sober-minded, orderly, given to hospitality, apt to teach; 3 no brawler, no striker; but gentle, not contentious, no lover of money; 4 one that ruleth well his own house, having his children in subjection with all gravity; 5 (but if a man knoweth not how to rule his own house, how shall he take care of the church of God?) 6 not a novice, lest being puffed up he fall into the condemnation of the devil. 7 Moreover he must have good testimony from them that are without; lest he fall into reproach and the snare of the devil.

Thought Questions 3:1-7

63. Why use the prefatory words: "Faithful is the saying"?
64. Why would this be such a desirable work? Is this a work, or an office?
65. Is the bishop the same man as the elder? Prove your answer.
66. No man can be completely "without reproach"; how shall we understand this phrase?
67. Does the text say an elder *must* be a married man? Explain.
68. Explain in your own words the meaning of the term "temperate."
69. In what particulars must a bishop be "sober-minded"?
70. Are we discussing ideals, or actual essential qualifications?
71. In what sense must a bishop be "orderly"?
72. How would it be known that a man was "given to hospitality"?
73. Some elders are "apt not to teach"; explain the phrase "apt to teach".
74. How would one serving as an elder, ever be involved in an accusation of being "quarrelsome over wine"?
75. How are we to define and apply the term "striker" as here used?
76. Show the contrast between "a striker" and one who is "gentle".

77. Almost every leader in the church has been accused of being "contentious" at one time or another; how shall we decide who is and who is not?
78. What are the symptoms of one who is sick with "love for money"?
79. In what sense is a man to rule his own house? Cf. 5:14.
80. Does Paul mean by the qualifications that a man *must* be married and have a family to be an elder?
81. Who determines whether children are "in subjection"?
82. What is "the condemnation of the Devil"? Why would a novice be particularly susceptible?
83. How does, "the reproach of the Devil" differ from, the "condemnation of the Devil"?

Paraphrase 3:1-7

1 When about to elect bishops, thou shouldst remember that this saying is true, if one earnestly seeketh the office of a bishop, he desireth a work, which, though very laborious, is both honourable and beneficial, as it promotes the glory of God and the good of mankind.

2 Therefore a bishop ought to be free from blame; the husband of one wife, at a time; attentive to this duty and to his people; prudent in his conduct; of comely behaviour; hospitable to strangers; fit to teach, by having good knowledge of the things he is to teach, a clear manner of expressing his thoughts, and an earnest desire to instruct the ignorant.

3 He must not be addicted to wine, nor of such a hasty temper as to be a striker of those who provoke him, or one who gains money by sinful, or even dishonourable occupations, but equitable in judging of the offences which any of his flock may commit; not a noisy, abusive, quarrelsome talker, nor covetous in his dealings.

4 He must be one who possesseth such wisdom and firmness as to govern properly his own family. In particular, he must have his children in subjection to him; as becometh the gravity of his character, and his reputation for prudence.

5 For if one be not capable of governing so small a society as his own family, but suffers his children to be disobedient and vicious, how shall he govern in a proper manner that greater and more important society, the church of God?

6 A bishop must not be one newly converted, lest being puffed up with pride on account of his promotion, he fall into the punishment inflicted on the devil.
7 Moreover, before his conversion, he must have behaved in such a manner as even to have a good testimony from the heathens; that he may not be liable to reproach for the sins he committed before his conversion, and fall into the snare of the devil, who by these reproaches may tempt him to renounce the gospel.

Comment 3:1-7

Vs. 1. There is some little disagreement as to whether we should relate the expression. "Faithful is the saying . . . ." with "but she shall be saved through her child bearing"—or "if a man seeketh the office of a bishop he desireth a good work." We prefer to associate the expression with 3:1 rather than 2:15, although we offer nothing but opinion for the preference. There are three other times when the expression "Faithful is the saying" is used: I Tim. 1:15; II Tim. 2:11; Titus 3:8. They offer no help, for the expression: "faithful saying" both follows and precedes in these examples. Whatever else we can say, it is certain that the office of overseer is one to be greatly desired.

It should not be necessary to say that there is but one office for "elder" and "overseer". Here are two names for the same office—Cf. Acts 20:17, 28 and Titus 1:5 for interchangeable use of the terms.

Paul writes of a strong desire for this office and work. This desire should be in the candidate, it should arise as he contemplates the work he is to do. The glory of service and work for the Lord should ever be before possible candidates for the office of elder. In most places neither the office nor the work are well enough known to create any desire for the overseership. When elders are doing their God-given work among the congregation, men will want to be like them. We read of elders visiting the sick, (James 1:27; 5:12, 14) feeding the flock on the word and protecting the flock from enemies—(Acts 20:29-31). When such work is being done or pointed out as being necessary, men will be attracted to the office. Let us mark carefully *both* words: it is *worthy*, and it is *work*.

Vs. 2. We offer no special outline of arrangement for the qualifications (although we have read a good number of arbitrary groupings). Let us simply proceed in the order Paul gives:

"*without reproach*"—We ought to say that it is our firm persuasion that Paul expected the congregations in Ephesus to be able to clearly see and approve every one of these qualifications in the lives of every one of their elders. Indeed with only two exceptions ("apt to teach" and "not a novice") *all* the qualifications are to be found in all Christians.

"Without reproach" means "not to be taken hold upon"—if one is to be taken hold of there must be a handle, i.e. some obvious flaw in his character upon which men seize to bring upon him blame and reproach. The candidate for this office should be without a handle.

"*the husband of one wife*"—There is so much controversy and contention on some points of Scripture that one hesitates to advance any opinion. It has been my careful conclusion that Paul is discussing the moral quality of the candidate for the eldership. He is saying such a man must be the husband of only ONE wife—not more than one. The elder must be a "one woman" type man, both in thought and practice. A most thorough-going study of this subject can be found in *Scriptural Elders and Deacons* by H. E. Phillips, pp. 97ff, published by Phillips Publications, Gainesville, Florida. This is the most complete review of the subject I have found—although I do not concur in his conclusion.

"*temperate*"—The word here translated "temperate" is translated "sober" later in the qualifications. Originally the word meant a complete abstinence from wine. Here it is used metaphorically of our attitude of life. It is translated "vigilant" in the King James Version. Perhaps the English meaning associated with the words "sober" and "vigilant", carries a complete definition of this qualification.

II Timothy 4:5 compares very well with I Timothy 3:2. The thought of being "temperate" refers to an attitude of mind which is reflected in the life. This attitude is not of "just taking a little", but of sober, careful judgment in all matters.

"*sober-minded*"—balanced judgment; not carried away by every "wind of doctrine". Men are needed in the church today who hold such deep-seated convictions that no amount of difficulty will move them from their faith and work.

"*orderly*"—this has more than reference to appearance, although we believe it relates to that. An unordered, slovenly appearance is usually indicative of an unordered, slovenly mind.

The elder should be a true gentleman in the best use of the word.

"*hospitable*"—Lenski has wisely observed that "hospitable" and "apt to teach" belong together as something the elder is to impart to others. Rom. 12:13; Heb. 13:2; I Pet. 2:9 should be read concerning hospitality. The social and political circumstances of Paul's day, to say nothing of the economic status of the Christians, would make hospitality especially welcome. The genuine desire to make our house the home of needy, Christian strangers, rich or poor, is so very sadly lacking and sorely needed in the church today.

"*apt to teach*"—This does not refer to a willingness to teach, but to the ability to do so. As to whether a man has such ability can best be decided by those with whom he labors and whom he tries to teach. Each and every elder should have such ability. Read I Tim. 5:17 as to the teaching responsibility.

Vs. 3. "*no brawler or quarrelsome over wine*"—This is to say no "winebibber"; we would refer to him today as a "wino". What conditions prevailed in the church that such a prohibition needed to be included?

"*No striker; but gentle*"—These two qualifications should be considered together. A striker is one who is ready with the fists at the slightest provocation. Some have learned to use their tongues instead of their fists but they are still a "striker". In contrast is the one who is "gentle toward all." Here is the thought of yielding but not compromising.

"*Not contentious*"—Not one who likes to fight, but one who does not like to fight—not the fighting kind.

"*No lover of money*"—Of course this refers to loving what money can do. It is this quality of heart that makes a man covetous. The idolatry of money-worship is ever near us.

Vs. 4. "*one that ruleth well his own household*"—The thought of overseeing in the household or family situation in the same manner as in the church situation is the point here. Go home with the prospective elder and observe the conduct of his wife and children. Do they respect him? Is he regarded as competent by those who know him best? The obedience of the children should be held as a serious responsibility by the Christian father.

Vs. 5. If a man fails at home he will surely fail in public. The care of the church is of a much more complicated nature than that of the home, and yet it compares favorably in several particulars The inescapable conclusion is: to be deficient in one is to be deficient in both.

Vs. 6. *Just who is a novice?* When is a man to be considered a "new convert"? This is surely a relative matter. The appointment of elders on the first missionary journey in the churches of Derbe, Lystra, Iconium and Antioch (Cf. Acts 14:23), is a point in question. How long had such men been Christians? We could assume that some of them were elders in the synagogue before they became Christians, but that would only be an assumption. The power of pride must here be considered. How large a part does ego have in a man's character? Some men are far more vain than others. How long will it be before the power of Christ in the heart will overcome the power of pride? Such questions must be answered before we can refer to such a man as a novice, or not a novice.

"*the condemnation of the devil*"—Is this referring to the particular punishment God will give the devil? Or does this mean the condemnation brought on by the devil? The third possibility refers to the judgment or punishment meted out by the devil on those who fell under his power. We prefer the first of these —i.e., the particular judgment God has reserved for Satan. This was brought about through the pride of Satan: he thought of himself much more highly than he ought to have thought; he assumed an office to which God had not appointed him; and in which he was not prepared to serve; for this cause God removed him from heaven. The new convert who is "wrapped in his own pride", as if wrapped in fog, cannot be a proper candidate for the office of elder, and is about to repeat Satan's sin, and if so would receive Satan's condemnation. How much better to anticipate and prevent, than not to anticipate and regret.

Vs. 7. Prior to his conversion, and subsequent to it, the candidate for the eldership must have conducted himself in such a manner, that those non-Christian friends and neighbors who knew him best, would be able to tell how uprightly and unblameably he conducted himself. We are not referring to his Christian friends or neighbors, but rather to those on the "outside". Can those who work with him or near him say of him that he does his work well and treats his fellow workmen in a fair and unselfish manner? The reproach and snare of the devil is not at all the same as "the condemnation of the devil".

If a man were appointed to the office of elder, and yet he was the butt of ridicule and jokes by those "on the outside" because of his inconsistent conduct, then indeed he has fallen into the devil's trap, and justly deserves to be reproached or accused by Satan. The devil sets the trap and then reproaches those who fall into it. This snare or trap is prepared each time we profess one thing and live another. What a pit in which to fall!

Fact Questions 3:1-7

51. What is the "faithful saying", and why so called?
52. Is an elder and a bishop the same man? Prove your answer.
53. How does one obtain a strong desire for the office?
54. Give the meaning of the expression, "without reproach"?
55. Could any single man be an elder? Explain.
56. Meaning of the expression, "temperate"?
57. If a man was "temperate" wouldn't he already be "sober-minded"?
58. Aren't some "unorderly" men doing more for God than some "orderly" ones? How does this relate to the qualifications?
59. Is there some way in which we can tell when a man is "given to hospitality"? If so, how?
60. Who shall decide if a man is "apt to teach"? How?
61. Explain how a "brawler" could even be considered for the eldership—to say nothing of being qualified for the office.
62. What type of gentleness must be manifest in the character of the elder?
63. When is a man contentious and not just constructively critical?
64. Is it possible to "love money", and still not have much of it? What is the deeper difficulty?
65. Who would venture to say when any man "ruled well his own household"? How could this knowledge be obtained? What about invading the privacy of the home?
66. What are the symptoms of "being puffed up"?
67. Satan has set a very deadly snare—it is discussed in the 7th verse. Explain how to avoid it.

BALLOT

ELDER

NAME______________________________

THE QUALIFICATIONS OF AN ELDER

(Check on line where candidate qualifies)

Positive qualifications

1.______*He must desire the office and seek it.* I Tim. 3:1. This would suggest that a man should consider the office one of privilege, and he should constantly be preparing his life so as to be a fit candidate for it.

2.____*The bishop must be without reproach or blameless.* I Tim. 3:2a; Titus 1:6a; 7a. He would hold this position before man and not God, for no one is blameless or without reproach before God. As the persons of the congregation, where he is contemplating the office of elder, view his life, they should be able to find nothing blameworthy about it.

3.____*The husband of one wife.* I Tim. 3:2a; Titus 1:6b.

4.____*The elder must be temperate.* I Tim. 3:2c; Titus 1:8f. Three thoughts are expressed in the Greek: "Having power over one's self, abstaining from wine, curbing one's desires or impulses."

5.____*Sober-minded.* I Tim.. 3:2c; Titus 1:8c. The thought in the Greek is, "of sound mind, sane in one's senses." (Cf. Eph. 5:4).

6.____*Orderly.* I Tim. 3:2c. "Of good behavior, modest."

7.____"*Given to hospitality.*" I Tim. 3:2f; Titus 1:8a. (Cf. I Tim. 5:10).

8.____*He must be a sound, capable, and willing teacher of the Word.* I Tim. 3:2g; Titus 1:9.

9.____*Not given to wine* (K.J.V.); *no brawler* (R.V.) I Tim. 3:3a; Titus 1:7d. A brawler is one who quarrels noisily, creates an uproar or starts a row.

10.____*He must not be a striker.* I Tim. 3:3b; Titus 1:7c. The word in the Greek means, "smiter, pugnacious, quarrelsome."

11.____*Gentle.* I Tim. 3:3c. "Equitable, fair, mild." The bishop must be willing to be taught; willing to admit error and to change his mind; not weak but approachable.

12.____*He must rule his own house.* I Tim. 3:4-5; Titus 1:6c.

13.____*He must have a good testimony from without.* I Tim. 3:7. He must be one who practices what he preaches.

14.____*A lover of good.* Titus 1:8b.

15.____*He must be holy.* Titus 1:8e. (Cf. Heb. 12:14)

16.____*He must be just.* Titus 1:8d. "Righteous, observing divine and human laws, upright, passing just judgment on others." (Cf. John 7:24).

Negative qualifications

1._____*Not contentious.* I Tim. 3:3d. "Given to angry debate, quarrelsome." One who loves strife and wrangles over non-essentials, could not qualify as a bishop.
2._____*No lover of money.* I Tim. 3:3c; Titus 1:7f; I Peter 5:2.
3._____*Not a novice.* I Tim. 3:6. "A new convert, a beginner" would be considered a novice.
4._____*Not self-willed.* Titus 1:7b. "Self-pleasing, arrogant."
5._____*Not soon angry.* Titus 1:7c. "Easily provoked, irritable."
6._____*His wife must not be a slanderer, but grave, temperate, and faithful in all things.* I Tim. 3:11.

2. THE DEACONS 8-13

Text 3:8-13

8 Deacons in like manner must be grave, not double-tongued, not given to much wine, not greedy of filthy lucre; 9 holding the mystery of the faith in a pure conscience. 10 And let these also first be proved; then let them serve as deacons, if they be blameless. 11 Women in like manner must be grave, not slanderers, temperate, faithful in all things. 12 Let deacons be husbands of one wife, ruling their children and their own houses well. 13 For they that have served well as deacons gain to themselves a good standing, and great boldness in the faith which is in Christ Jesus.

Thought Questions 3:8-13

84. Deacons should be like the elders; in what particular?
85. Is there a better word for "grave"?
86. In what way would deacons be tempted to be "double-tongued"? Explain.
87. Is there any possibility that "a little wine" would be permissable? Explain.
88. Is "filthy lucre" confined solely to money? Why so called?
89. How does Paul use the word "mystery" as related to "the faith"?
90. If the deacons serve only in the material area, how is it that they are to hold the "mystery of the faith"?
91. What would stain the conscience of the deacon? Why so important to have a good conscience?
92. Does verse ten suggest a period of probation for the deacons? Explain.
93. Who could ever be "without blame"? Discuss this in connection with deacons.

94. Does verse eleven make provision for female deacons? Discuss. Cf. Rom. 16:1,2.
95. In what respect is the qualification "not slanderers" particularly appropriate?
96. Why the general qualification "faithful in all things"?
97. Is it here suggested that deacons must be married? Why?
98. If a deacon "must" be married then it follows that he "must" have more than one child, and that such children must be old enough to be "ruled"—is this so? Discuss.
99. What is "the good standing" obtained by deacons? Is this a step toward becoming an elder?
100. How could service in our present office of deacon, produce any boldness in the faith? How did it do it in the days of Paul?

Paraphrase 3:8-13

8 The deacons, in like manner, must be of a grave character, not double-tongued, speaking one thing to this person, and another to that, on the same subject; not giving themselves to much wine; not persons who earn money by base methods.

9 He must hold fast the doctrines of the gospel with a pure conscience; He must not, from fear or self-interest, either conceal or disguise these doctrines.

10 However, let these also be tried first, by publishing their names to the church, that if anyone hath aught to lay to their charge, he may show it; and after such a publication of their names, let them exercise the deacons office, if no person accuses them.

11 The women, in like manner, who are employed in teaching the young, must be stayed in their deportment; not slanderers and tale-bearers, but vigilant and faithful in all the duties belonging to their office.

12 Let the deacons be husbands of one wife only at a time, having showed their temperance by avoiding polygamy and causeless divorce. They must likewise rule with prudence and firmness their children, and every one in their families.

13 For they who have performed the office of a deacon with ability and assiduity, secure to themselves an honourable rank in the church, and great courage in teaching the Christian faith. For even the wicked must respect persons who show so much benevolence and activity, in relieving the poor, the afflicted and the persecuted.

Comment 3:8-13

Vs. 8. We should have little hesitancy in acepting the office of deacon; let us not stumble over the general use of the word; surely we will agree that many persons are called "servants" (the same word here used to refer to deacons), but this does not mean that all such persons are "deacons" in the sense here used. Philippians 1:1 should settle the matter: "Paul and Timothy, servants (bond servants) of Christ Jesus, to all the *saints* in Christ Jesus that are at Philippi, with the *bishops* and *deacons*." All Christians are not deacons anymore than all older men are elders.

The "Like manner" of verse eight refers to the necessity of being qualified for the office. Once again let us say that such qualifications are not given as ideals alone, but as definite qualities of character to be found in the men who serve.

Lack of dignity (not pompousness) is seen on every side. This is true because the service of deacon is not held in a serious or "grave" light. It is only when we are serious about the task that such seriousness will be reflected in our life. But whose responsibility is it to present a clear picture of the privileges and opportunities of the office of deacon? We need far more good evangelists like Timothy.

Why would a deacon be most especially tempted to be "double-tongued"? Would it be because of his oft visiting on behalf of Christ? How sorely tempted we are at times to say one thing to one person and something else to another, and on the very same subject. This must not be. We must fear the displeasure of God far more than that of man. Let the deacon consistently tell the truth at all times, with all people.

A reference has already been made to excessive use of wine. This must have been a problem in the church. It is a problem in our present society to an extent that we do not like to admit. There is no provision here for use of wine in any form. The text simply states that a candidate for the office of deacon must not be a drunkard. (Please see our special study on Bible and Wine in the last pages of this book.)

"Greedy of filthy lucre" goes much deeper than "love of money"—"lucre" means "base gain" of any kind. The thought of using the office for such gain is always present. The advantage of the Lord and not of self, is the uppermost thought of the truly qualified deacon.

Vs. 9. To compare the present day qualifications for deacons with the expression "holding the mystery of the faith in a pure conscience" is a glaring example of how far short we are of having men who meet such qualifications. Today the thought that a deacon should be a genuine student of the Bible seldom enters the mind. "The mystery of the faith" does not refer to some secret truths, but rather to that which was once concealed but is now revealed. The deacon is to have a grasp of the gospel in such a manner that he will be able to share it with others. This requires study and preparation on his part. Such a wonderful treasure must be kept in a clean vessel—"a pure conscience". The deacon must not suffer from the accusations of his own conscience, because of the inconsistencies in his daily conduct with "the faith" he understands and professes.

Vs. 10. How shall we carry out the injunction of Vs. 10? Shall we place certain men "on probation" as deacons and then if they prove themselves capable, appoint them to the office? This is strongly urged by some commentaries. However, the thought in the word "prove" does not suggest such a formal testing.

The lives of the candidates for the office should be carefully observed over a period of time by the congregation. Those qualities of character necessary to carry out the worthy work of the deacon will be observed by the Christians. This has to do with a testing of character and work in the ordinary course of the church life. What a responsiblity this places upon the minister to make the congregation aware of what a deacon should be and do. After a careful informal examination such men who are to serve as deacons should be found "blameless".

Vs. 11. A good deal of discussion is always in order just here as to whether we have a provision made for the office of "deaconess." A reference is also always made to Rom. 16:1, 2. We must say Paul is not referring to women in general, for this would hardly be in place in the midst of a discussion of church officers. It must then refer either to female deacons or to the wives of the male deacons. The latter conclusion is our preference. We say this because of the absence to any other reference to deaconess. The term deacon is a masculine one. All the deacons mentioned are men(unless we are to understand Phebe was a deaconess in an official sense). The words of Guthrie are very much to the point just here: "The reference is too general to postulate with certainty a distinct order of deaconesses, but some feminine ministration was necessary in visitation and in attending to women candidates for baptism. For such work certain moral qualities would be essential whether for deacon's wives or for deaconesses in their own right."

The expression "faithful in all things" is a very general one, but it has none-the-less strong implications: such women should live a life of complete consistency. The other qualifications have been discussed in connection with the elders and deacons.

Vs. 12. What we have said of the elders as to this qualification can be here applied to deacons.

Vs. 13. Perhaps the present day application of the text should not be our first thought in our comment upon it, but one cannot help but relate the service and standing of deacons here described with some men now serving as deacons. What type of service would be necessary to obtain a good standing in the sight of God and man? to say nothing of "great boldness in the faith"? Surely the responsibilities would entail far more than we usually relate to the deacons work. The New Testament deacon will be so conspicuous in his work among the flock that they will notice it. They will mark him in their own mind as a true servant of Christ. He will so teach and evangelize in his personal attentions to the saints as to gain by experience "great boldness in the faith." These are but a few obvious applications of the text.

Fact Questions 3:8-13

68. We should not hesitate to accept the office of deacon as a part of the present day church organization;—why?
69. How does the responsibility of the evangelist relate to the office of deacon?
70. Why would a deacon be especially tempted to be "double-tongued"?
71. Is any use of wine permissable? Explain.
72. What is "filthy lucre"? Explain.
73. How shall a deacon acquire the ability to "hold the mystery of the faith"?
74. Are deacons to be placed "on probation"? Explain.
75. Is provision made for female deacons? You are under no obligation to accept our opinion.
76. True deacons will develop a "good standing" before men and God, and "great boldness in the faith". Explain how this is done.

BALLOT

DEACON

NAME______________________________

THE QUALIFICATIONS OF A DEACON

(Check on line where candidate qualifies)

1._____*Grave.* Serious about his important work.

2._____*Blameless.* After a careful informal examination, such men who are to serve as deacons should be found "blameless".

3._____*Holding the mystery of the faith in a pure conscience.* The deacon must not suffer from the accusations of his own conscience because of his inconsistencies in his daily conduct with "the faith" he understands and professes.

4._____*Proved.* The lives of the candidates for the office should be carefully observed over a period of time by the congregation.

5._____*Not double-tongued.* How sorely tempted we are at times to say one thing to one person and something else to another, and on the very same subject. This must not be. Let the deacon consistently tell the truth at all times with all people.

6._____*Not given to much wine.* There is no provision here for use of wine in any form. The text simply states that a candidate for the office of deacon must not be a drunkard.

7._____*Not greedy of filthy lucre.* This goes much deeper than love of money. "Lucre" means base gain of any kind. Do not use the office for self promotion.

8._____*Husband of one wife.* The deacon must be a "one woman type" man.

9._____*Ruling his children and his own house well.* Ideal family relationships help to qualify a man for service in the household of the faith.

3. IMPORTANCE OF INSTRUCTIONS 14-16

Text 3:14-16

14 These things write I unto thee, hoping to come unto thee shortly; 15 but if I tarry long, that thou mayest know how men ought to behave themselves in the house of God, which is the church of the living God, the pillar and ground of the truth. 16 And without controversy great is the mystery of godliness; He who was manifested in the flesh, Justified in the spirit, Seen of angels, Preached among the nations, Believed on in the world, Received up in glory.

Thought Questions 3:14-16

101. Why didn't Paul instruct Timothy before leaving him at Ephesus?
102. What "things" are referred to in Vs. 14?
103. In what way is the church "the house of God"?
104. In what sense is the church the "pillar and ground of the truth"? What truth?
105. Explain the use of the term "mystery" as used by Paul.
106. When was Christ "manifest in the flesh"?
107. Give the meaning of the expression, "justified in the spirit."
108. Give occasions when Christ was "seen of angels".
109. Why mention that He was, "preached among the nations"?
110. Is the term "world" different from "nations" as used here?
111. Was Christ received up "into glory" or "in glory" according to Vs. 16?

Paraphrase 3:14-16

14 These things I write thee, although I hope to come to thee soon, to give thee more complete instruction concerning thy behavior.

15 Or if by any accident I am obligated to tarry long, I have written these things, that thou mayest know how thou oughtest to behave thyself in the house of God, which is neither the temple at Jerusalem, nor the temple of Diana at Ephesus, but the church of the living God, consisting of all believers, and which is the pillar and support of the truth.

16 Thou oughtest to behave properly in the church; for confessedly most important is the doctrine of the gospel which is kept therein; namely, that to save sinners by his death, the Son of God was manifested in the flesh; was justified through the Spirit, who raised him from the dead; was, after his resurrection,

seen of the apostles his messengers; was preached to the Gentiles as their Saviour; was believed on in many parts of the world; was taken up into heaven in a glorious manner.

Comment 3:14-16

Vs. 14. Wherever Paul was when he wrote this letter he anticipated a visit to Timothy. We like to believe he had been in prison at Rome, then was released, and went into Macedonia from whence he wrote this letter. This letter seems to take on an official tone here. The words here written, i.e. from 1:1-3:16 are to be used in the place of the personal presence of the apostle.

Vs. 15. In my absence, be it short or long, these instructions are to be read and followed. The student should note that the American Standard Version refers to the behavior of "men", and King James Version to "Timothy". The absence of the pronoun in the original makes either one of them correct. In either case the meaning turns out the same. Timothy's behavior was to be a pattern for others. The household of God is alluded to in 3:5, and is here specified. It should not be necessary to say the expression "house of God" has no reference to a church building. In the New Testament "the house of God".. consistently refers to the people. We are "a habitation of God in the Spirit." In contrast to the dumb, dead idols worshipped in Ephesus and Asia, this is the "called out" of the "*living* God."

The difficulty in understanding the church as "the pillar and ground of truth" can be explained as: *pillar*, supporting the truth by defending it against its enemies; and the *ground of the truth*, in the sense of preserving it through the centuries.

Vs. 16. Shall we connect this verse up with "the truth" of verse 15 b, i.e. "pillar and ground of "*the truth*"? If so then verse 16 will be an enlargement of "the truth". Or, shall we associate this with the work of the deacons and elders? If we do this, then what we shall say here in Vs. 16 is the motivation for the work of these officers. We prefer the latter emphasis. Some have thought this verse to contain the words of an early Christian hymn. The words of the hymn by common consent were accepted as expressing in few words the heart of the Christian faith. Here is more or less "a statement of faith". The words "mystery of godliness" can be understood as meaning—"revealed mystery of living like God wants us to". We explained "mystery" in Vs. 9. It is used in the same sense here.

"*Manifest in the flesh*": Note please, the different phases of Christ's life and work emphasized in these expressions: First the incarnation: "Manifested" carries the thought of *unveiling*, He who existed in the form of God chose to empty himself and be clothed with flesh. He was both concealed and revealed. God was seen in human flesh. "Emmanuel" was His name, "God with us". It was the flesh He chose as a medium of manifestation. It was in the flesh He unveiled deity. We like to think of Bethlehem as associated with this expression; but we could not appreciate Bethlehem without a knowledge of the rest of the truth in this verse.

"*Justified in the Spirit*": We take the word "spirit" to refer to the inward man, and not to the Holy Spirit. As to His flesh He was veiled and *unveiled*. It was a humble garment that scarcely concealed the glorious person. As to His spirit: He made claims of divinity that need vindication. He was not "a liar". This vindication was provided by His miracles; but most of all He was "declared to be the Son of God with power by the resurrection from the dead" (Rom. 1:4). Thus all that the inward man claimed was upheld or justified.

"*Seen of angels*": We can not resist the desire to share with you the words of Simpson on this phrase: "If Sheol was strangely moved at the arrival thither of the once resplendent son of the morning, little wonder that heaven was stirred by the descent to our sphere in voluntary self-abnegation of the only-begotten of the Father. With what tremulous interest must these legions of His have followed the steps of His humiliation from the throne of awful majesty to the cross of agonizing shame! And how, as the infernal plot against Him thickened, must they have witnessed with amazement the non-intervention of Omnipotence on His behalf! Far more than twelve legions of angels must have waited breathlessly for that signal to flash across the upper skies which should snatch heaven's Darling from the 'power of the dog'. Surely the resurrection daybreak dawned on them as well as on the dazed disciples 'like some sweet summer morning after a night of pain' and the triumph of His reascension, escorted by their bright squadrons homeward, had been to them its meridian glow. But imagination must fold her fluttering wing, lest we incur the Colossians' rebuke (2:18) for prying into angelology! Enough to know that these unseen spectators from another world have drunk in the vision of the 'Word made flesh' and can be summoned to bear record to its supreme reality." (Ibid.)

"*Preached among the nations or Gentiles*": If we attempt to follow the life of our Lord in these expressions, we will now say we are discussing the results of His mission on earth. He was born in Bethlehem or "manifested in the flesh". He was active in a miraculous, model ministry, sacrificial death, and glorious resurrection, thus "justified in the spirit". All through His earthly advent He was "seen by angels"; The answer is: So He could be "preached among the nations". How important then that we preach the gospel to all the nations. The Christians of Timothy's day fulfilled our Lord's purpose. We now are as provincial as the Jews of Paul's time. The Jews were accused of believing the Messiah was sent but for one people, and we deserve the same condemnation! We do not say it, but we do practice it!

"*Believed on in the world*": We take the former phrase to refer to the cause, and this phrase to the result. We have read the learned discussions of these phrases, as divided up into couplets and formed into interrelating arrangements; we have felt that such discussions were rather arbitrary in their conclusions.

The exaltation of our Lord is surely seen in the response of men from every nation.

"*Received up in glory*." Please note that this does *not* say He was received up "*into*" glory. This has reference to His home, not His home-coming. From the Mount of ascension Jesus returned to share "the glory He had with the Father before the world was made".

Fact Questions

77. Where was Paul when he wrote this letter?
78. What indication of "an official tone" is here observed?
79. What instructions are to be read and followed?
80. Who is to know how to "behave himself" in the house of God?
81. In what sense is the church "the pillar and ground of the truth"?
82. How shall we relate Vs. 16 with Vs. 15? Show also its connection with Vs. 14.
83. How shall we fit together the six phrases of Vs. 16; or should we attempt to see any order in this verse?
84. Explain in your own words the meaning and relation of each of the six expressions.

EXEGETICAL EXAMINATION OVER I TIMOTHY CHAPTER THREE

1. In what way and for what reason is verse one "a faithful saying"?

2. Discuss the meaning of the phrase: "husband of one wife," with special reference to the thought of the necessity of being married.
3. Discuss the three following qualifications: "temperate, sober-minded, orderly".
4. Discuss: "not contentious, no lover of money".
5. What is "the condemnation of the devil" in vs. 6?
6. What is "the reproach of the devil"?
7. Discuss: "not given to much wine," and "not greedy of filthy lucre".
8. What intimations of the deacons work can be seen in the qualifications?
9. Discuss "let them first be proved."
10. Are we to understand women can fill the office of deacon? Discuss: "women in like manner."
11. How would a deacon gain "great boldness in the faith"?
12. Give the meaning of the expression: "that men may know how to behave themselves in the house of God"?
13. In what way is the church "the pillar and ground of the truth"?
14. Discuss: "Manifested in the flesh, justified in the spirit, seen of angels".
15. Discuss: "Preached among the nations, believed on in the world, received up in glory".

IV. FALSE TEACHERS 4:1-16

1. THEIR COMING 1:5

Text 4:1-5

1 But the Spirit saith expressly, that in later times some shall fall away from the faith, giving heed to seducing spirits and doctrines of demons, 2 through the hypocrisy of men that speak lies, branded in their own conscience as with a hot iron; 3 forbidding to marry, and commanding to abstain from meats, which God created to be received with thanksgiving by them that believe and know the truth. 4 For every creature of God is good, and nothing is to be rejected, if it be received with thanksgiving: 5 for it is sanctified through the word of God and prayer.

Thought Questions 4:1-5

112. To whom did the Spirit address the words of 4:1?
113. Define the limits of "later times".
114. Are we to understand that some evil forces are at work in a direct manner with the spirit of man?

115. How would it be possible for demons to be teachers?
116. Satan works through men; why will some men speak lies in preference to the truth?
117. Who applies the hot iron to the conscience?
118. To what purpose do some command that a man live a life of celibacy?
119. What do meats have to do with holiness?
120. In what sense is "every creature good"?
121. We are to reject nothing God has created but be thankful for all. Explain why.
122. Just how are marriage and meats "sanctified through the word of God and prayer"?

Paraphrase 4:1-5

1 But, although the church, by preserving the mystery of godliness in the world, be the support of the truth, the Spirit expressly saith to me, that in after-times many in the Christian church will apostatize from the faith of the fundamental doctrines of the gospel, giving heed to teachers who falsely pretend to be inspired, and to doctrines concerning the power of angels and departed saints, and the worship due to them, whereby the worship due to Christ, as Governor and Mediator, will be wholly neglected.
2 This belief of the doctrine concerning demons, and the other errors I am about to mention, will be propagated under the hypocritical pretence of humility, and superior holiness, by lying teachers, who are seared in their conscience, and who will invent innumerable falsehoods, to recommend their erroneous doctrines and corrupt practices to the ignorant multitude.
3 These lying teachers will forbid the clergy, and such of both sexes as wish to live piously, to marry; and command the people to abstain from certain meats, which God hath created to be used with thanksgiving by the faithful, who thoroughly know the truth concerning that matter;
4 That every creature of God, fit for man's food, is good, and may be used, being received with thanksgiving to God the giver; and no kind is to be cast away, either from peevishness, or from the fancy that it is unlawful.
5 For, under the gospel, all meats are made lawful to us by the command of God, allowing us to eat of every kind in moderation; also by prayer to God, that he would bless us in the use of it.

Comment 4:1-5

Vs. 1. The use of word "but" seems to indicate some contrast; this is indeed what is intended. "Great is the mystery of godliness", but great also is "the mystery of lawlessness". This prediction or announcement is a very emphatic one. We believe the communication was to Paul by the power of the Holy Spirit; it is here transmitted to Timothy, and through Timothy to the church. "The later times" has reference to no one particular period but rather to the total time from Pentecost to the Second Coming; we say this on the basis of a study of this expression and the expression "the last days". During this period "some shall fall away from the faith"; could the "some" of this text be those described in Acts 20:29,30? We must conclude that the body of belief was so well defined that defection from it could be immediately known. If some were "in the faith" and then fell away from it, what will be their end? If apostates do not return, shall they yet be saved in their error? We only pose these questions because we feel a false emphasis has been given by some.

Are we to understand that those who fall away from the truth do so because they are influenced by supernatural evil powers? We believe it is even so. Satan has his power, and his preachers, and in this sense he is a counterpart, as well as a counterfeit of the true. The "seducing spirits" are from beneath, and are in contact with the "lying teachers". The teaching of such men proceeds from and through "demons". The tragedy is not that we have such hypocrites, for they have always been with us, but that multitudes will give heed to their Satan inspired doctrines.

Vs. 2. The pronouncements of such evil men are always given as if they proceeded from God. Only by attributing their teaching to a divine source could they beguile the heart of the innocent and lead astray the very elect. These men know they are liars but they have conveniently and intentionally forgotten the truth. The great influence of Satan here described should be a warning to all. The condition of a man's conscience is a mark of his spiritual progress or failure. These teachers of lies were able to do so because their conscience had been and was "cauterized". Just how such a condition arises is not at all easy to say. We are sure it does not happen all at once. Such persons are "past feeling". Cf. Eph. 4:19.

Vs. 3. Timothy will immediately be able to recognize such teachers by the context of their teaching. We must try to remember the historical setting of these words. Such false teachers were to arise in Timothy's day, and shortly thereafter, who would teach that God did not create matter because matter is evil.

According to such errors an evil deity created matter. The command by such persons to abstain from meats and marriage is based upon the supposed evil of matter. Various applications of this concept have been used by Satan down through the years. Sin will never be overcome by treating the instrument through which it works. Perhaps diets of the extreme nature, so popular in our day, and the constant reference to the widespread immorality, is treating the result rather than the cause. There is nothing wrong with food (meats) or with marriage; the difficulty is in gluttony—"whose god is their belly", and "lust" —"who mind the things of the flesh". To those who know and believe this, meats and marriage are received with deepest gratitude.

Vs. 4. This is an enlargement of what has already been said. When God finished the different phases of creation, He said of the objects He had created, "it is good". Since God is Himself the very essence of goodness, nothing He would create or make could be otherwise than good. Note the force of the word "rejected": it is no light thing to cast aside that which God has blessed. The definite inference in the little expression: "if it be received with thanksgiving", seems to be that some reject God's gift because they fail to see their good purpose. If we look at life through God's eyes we will see His loving provisions for man, and will thus receive them with gratitude.

Vs. 5. The word "sanctified" simply means "set apart" but carries with it the connotation of being set apart for a holy purpose. Where and when did this happen? Please read Genesis 9:3, 4 for some help in this connection. God's definite statement of purpose in animal and plant creation as given in this passage, answers the question.

How does prayer "set apart" the food we eat? To ask is to infer the answer. We all should pray over our food before we eat it, and thus thank the giver of every good and perfect gift. To insist as some commentators do that we must include some of the word of God in our prayer, i.e., to quote Bible references in our prayers, seems to be insisting on too much. Out of the depths of a grateful heart, we can thank our Father "for our daily bread".

Fact Questions 4:1-5

85. How shall we relate this section to the one preceding? Show the contrast.
86. The paraphrase seems to relate this section almost exclusively to a prophecy of the sins of the Roman Catholic church. Do

you agree with the application? Explain.

87. Upon what do we base our conclusion that "the later times" refers to the special period from Pentecost to the Second Coming?
88. Show how Acts 20:29, 30 relates to this section.
89. What is "the faith" from which some "fall away"?
90. If some fall away from the faith, does this mean they were never in the faith? Explain.
91. Satan is at work today. Can Satan speak to you and me? If so, how? Is Satan speaking to man today? How?
92. What is the mark of a man's spiritual progress or failure? Discuss.
93. Explain the greatest tragedy in the evil work of Satan.
94. Explain the immediate as well as future application of Vs. 3.
95. What modern day application can we see in Vs. 3?
96. How does the nature of God relate to the goodness of His creation?
97. What is the force of the word "rejected"?
98. Discuss Gen. 9:3, 4 in connection with Vs. 5.
99. Explain how meats and marriage are "set apart" by prayer.

2. THE PREACHER AND THE FALSE TEACHERS. 6-10

Text 4:6-10

6 If thou put the brethren in mind of these things, thou shalt be a good minister of Christ Jesus, nourished in the words of the faith, and of the good doctrine which thou hast followed until now: 7 but refuse profane and old wives' fables. And exercise thyself unto godliness: 8 for bodily exercise is profitable for little; but godliness is profitable for all things, having promise of the life which now is, and of that which is to come. 9 Faithful is the saying, and worthy of all acceptation. 10 For to this end we labor and strive, because we have our hope set on the living God, who is the Saviour of all men, specially of them that believe.

Thought Questions 4:6-10

122. What is the meaning of the expression "put the brethren in mind"?
123. What "things" are meant in Vs. 6?
124. Do you believe the term "minister" in Vs. 6 is used in an official sense? Explain.
125. How are we to understand the connection between "reminding the brethren" of certain things, and being "nourished in the words of the faith"?

126. Was Timothy neglecting the faith and the good teaching? Why mention the faith and teaching?
127. Just what is involved in "old wives' fables"?
128. Be practical in answering this question: "How can I exercise myself unto godliness?"
129. Specify the profitableness of bodily exercise.
130. Is Paul saying: we should control our bodies; but more important is the control of the spirit?
131. How would Paul's admonitions relate to those who are over-weight, and otherwise self-indulgent?
132. Godliness, or the Christian way of life, offers the very best for the life which now is. Show how this is true economically, socially, politically.
133. Is there a life "that is to come"? If so, how will godliness affect it?
134. Why is it that so many of us feel that after death there is an existence, but not a whole life to be lived?
135. Just what is "the faithful saying"?
136. To what end or goal did Paul and his fellow-workers labor and strive?
137. If we sometimes feel the Christian life is not worth the effort, what is wrong? Specify.
138. In what sense is God the Saviour of all men?
139. How shall we understand that in a special sense He is the Saviour of them that believe?

Paraphrase 4:6-10

6 By laying these things, concerning the lawfulness of all sorts of meats, and concerning the corrupt doctrines and practices which are to arise in the church, before the brethren in Ephesus under thy care, thou wilt be a faithful minister of Jesus Christ, nourished by the precepts of the true faith and of the sound doctrine, to the knowledge of which thou hast attained by my instructions.

7 But the foolish stories and old wives' fables which the Judaizers tell to establish their false doctrines, reject, as tending to impiety; and employ thyself in those exercises of the understanding and of the affections, in which godliness consists.

8 For the bodily mortification which the Jewish fables are framed to recommend, is attended with little advantage; but the exercise of godliness, that is, the practice of piety and morality, is profitable for advancing all our interests, temporal and eternal, having the blessings of the present life and of that to come promised to it.

9 What I have said concerning the unprofitableness of bodily exercise, and the profitableness of godliness, is true, and worthy of the most hearty reception.
10 On account of this, I both endure great hardships and suffer reproach from Jews and Gentiles, that I trust to be made happy both here and hereafter, neither through bodily exercise, nor through the sacrifice of beasts, nor through the power of any idol, but by the living God, who is the preserver of all men, but especially of believers.

Comment 4:6-10

Vs. 6. We cannot help but notice Paul's evaluation of a "good servant" or "minister" and the image of one so popular in our day. Paul states in no uncertain terms, not only here but elsewhere, that a good minister is known by what he believes as well as what he does. The word "minister" as here used is not in the official sense. The same word was used of "the deacon". Timothy is to instruct the Christians of Ephesus, and particularly the elders of the various churches, in a kind but convincing manner, concerning the apostasy of the later times. If such persons are thoroughly indoctrinated, Timothy can consider his divine position and responsibility fulfilled. In carrying out this injunction of the apostle, Timothy will be feeding his own soul; how vastly important this is! It is possible to feed others and yet starve to death yourself. It is also very possible to have the humility necessary to "practice what we preach". Paul does not imagine that Timothy has neglected the good teaching; he rather points out that Timothy has been following the right diet; it is now a matter of getting others to do likewise.

Vs. 7. The word "refuse" means to ignore, to avoid, to turn a deaf ear to such stories. We are not to imagine that "old wives" are the leaders in this false teaching, it is rather that some leaders in the churches are acting and talking like old senile women. Perhaps that is another reference to the "fables and endless genealogies" of 1:4. We do not equate "old wives' fables" with "the doctrine of demons" in 4:1. This is a separate instruction from what has already been given concerning apostasy. It would take a good deal of time and energy to follow out the details of these fables; and since man has just so much time and energy, let us not dissipate it with such foolishness. In contrast, let us give ourselves to developing godliness! If we are going to become like God, then we shall do so because we have studied and practiced

His will as revealed in His Word. The word "exercise" suggests just how strenuous and energetic must be our pursuit of godliness. "Timothy is to knit his sinews for the race of godliness."

Vs. 8. The use of the word "exercise" would immediately suggest to Timothy the gymnasium. This being true, Paul used such imagery to his own advantage. Go ahead with your muscle development, but remember its limitations; it is indeed profitable (and more such exercise is very much needed today), but we must not forget that our bodies are for God as well as our spirits. Some have thought the reference to bodily exercise indicates abstinence from meats and marriage, however, this hardly fits the use of the term "exercise" with its physical-culture background. It ought to be said that if one cannot control the passions of the body, he has no place instructing others in the higher control of the spirit.

There is a remarkable connection between the fitness of the body and the health of the spirit. When our bodies are strong and healthy, how much easier is it to exercise ourselves unto godliness! Somehow when we are sick in body we are also sick in spirit. This need not be the case, but it usually is; however, the emphasis should not be on bodily fitness, for when it is at its top performance it is only an instrument of the inward man. The strength of the inward man is far more important. When we watch the diet of the inward man, when we are very careful as to the strength of the will, the health of the emotions and conscience, then life takes on a glorious aspect. We can enjoy life to the fullest here, for we know it's true point and purpose, while we eagerly anticipate the fuller and more wonderful life that is to come.

Vs. 9. Just what is "the faithful saying"? We believe we have just discussed it. The thoughts of Vs. 10 offer a conclusion to what has been said, and therefore are hardly to be considered as a faithful saying. Such a statement as Vs. 10 would be incomplete without Vs. 8. All men everywhere should hear the message of Vs. 8. Particularly is this true of young men. We cannot help but think of the general care of the body, as well as the care of muscle. The over emphasis on the care of the body is such a serious mistake: it only offers a little pay, it is not enough to satisfy all our needs. How short and temporary is the return for such care. On the other hand, how full and complete the returns, in godly development, of the care of the spirit. No wonder it is a saying recommended to all men, of all time and place.

Vs. 10. Paul is not ashamed to say that this was the end, or purpose of his strenuous efforts—i.e., of developing the inward man. When the reward is commensurate with the effort, no one begrudges the effort. We can give ourselves completely to this matter of living for Christ, because we have a living God to aid us along the way, and to reward us at the end of the way.

In what sense shall we understand the little phrase: "who is the Saviour of all men, especially of them who believe"? *First*, fit it into the context. Paul has just said of godliness, that it has "promise of the life which now is, and of that which is to come" —is not this speaking of present salvation as well as final salvation? *Second*, every time it appears, we should not equate forgiveness of sins with the word "salvation". God is the Saviour of all men in the sense that all men depend on Him for all they have in the physical world—indeed all they have in any realm of living ultimately comes from God. Without God man would be lost physically—mentally—morally. This is true of all men, whether they recognize it or not. But most especially is this true of those who believe—for they know the source of all things in the life which now is, and of that which is to come. We would do anything necessary to obtain godliness or salvation because we know how much we need it, and because we know the living God who can and will give it.

Fact Questions 4:6-10

100. How can we know "a good minister of Christ Jesus"?
101. What is the meaning of the expression "put the brethren in mind"—of these things?
102. When could Timothy feel he had fulfilled his divine responsibility?
103. In carrying out the instructions of Paul, Timothy is to be greatly benefited. Explain how.
104. Why not rebuke the ones who tell "old wives' fables"? What was to be done?
105. What is "the little profit of bodily exercise"? Are we wrong if we do not have it?
106. Is it possible to control the "inward man" without thought to the "outward man"?
107. How shall we strengthen the "inward man"?
108. Show how Vs. 10 could not contain the "faithful saying".
109. Why is an over concern for the body a serious mistake?
110. Toward what did Paul labor and strive?
111. What is it that sustains our efforts to live for God?

112. In what sense are we to understand that God is "the Saviour of all men"?

3. THE TRUE SERVICE OF GOD. 11-16

a. In Public Life 11-13

Text 4:11-13

11 These things command and teach. 12 Let no man despise thy youth; but be thou an ensample to them that believe, in word, in manner of life, in love, in faith, in purity. 13 Till I come, give heed to reading, to exhortation, to teaching.

Thought Questions 4:11-13

140. Show the difference in the instructions given in Vs. 6 and Vs. 11.
141. What is the distinction between "commanding", and "teaching"?
142. Why would anyone look down on Timothy? Who would do it?
143. How was Timothy to avoid being despised?
144. Is an "ensample" the same as an "example"? Explain.
145. Explain in your own words, just how Timothy was to be an "ensample".
146. The meaning of the word "reading" of Vs. 13, is not what we usually associate with the word. Give the meaning of the word as here used. (Cf. Acts 13:15)

Paraphrase 4:11-13

11 These things solemnly enjoin as God's express commands, and teach the believers to act suitably to them.

12 Let no one have reason to despise thy admonitions on account of thy youth; but be thou a pattern to the faithful in gravity of speech, in propriety of behaviour, in fervency of love to God and man, in meekness but firmness of spirit, in soundness of faith, in chastity.

13 Till I return, apply thyself to reading the scriptures to the people in the public assemblies. Read them likewise in private for thine own improvement: also apply thyself to exhorting those who err, and to teaching the young and ignorant.

Comment 4:11-13

Vs. 11. In contrast to "suggesting to the brethren" in Vs. 6. Timothy is here told to "command and teach". What is it that merits such importance? Are we to understand the command and teaching to relate to what follows in verse 12-16, or what has preceded in 6-11? The subject matter of 12-16 is of such a personal nature that we cannot imagine Timothy is receiving a charge concerning it. We prefer rather, to think the command has reference to the truth and error of Vss. 6-11. Timothy is to approach the brethren in the manner of a counselor, but he is at the same time to remember the necessity of getting his points across; to do this it will be necessary to instruct and inform. Open the minds of the brethren concerning these false teachers; impress upon them the imperativeness of your message; do all of this by way of instruction as a teacher.

Vs. 12. Now follows some very personal and practical instructions for Timothy as an individual. There are two misconceptions to be cleared up here: First, that Timothy was timid, this thought can not be demonstrated. The boldest of young men might need encouragement. It is just as easy to believe Timothy is being encouraged to *continue* in the right attitude and work.

Second, that Timothy was a mere stripling. He must have been in his teens when Paul chose him to help on the second journey. More than ten years have passed. Timothy could have been as old as forty when this word was written. There is abundant evidence to show that a man in Timothy's day was considered young until the age of forty.

The word "despise" means "to look down upon". The way to avoid such an attitude from some of the older men, is not by way of demanding respect, but rather by earning it. If we do not look down on ourselves and yet maintain humility, it will not be long until we can convince others that they should adopt the same attitude; not toward us so much as toward the work we are trying to do. This *earned* respect will be gained by setting up a pattern in the following five areas:

(1) *In word* or in conversation: "Out of the abundance of the heart the mouth speaketh". How carefully we should choose our words at all times. This should be a warning against the "idle talk" of so many present day preachers. Such talk not only wastes God's time but hurts God's work by a poor example.

(2) "*In manner of life*" or in general demeanor: it isn't what we do on Sunday that gives the example, it is our conduct day by day. We might not like to "live in a goldfish bowl"; if such is your attitude, choose another work. The minister asks, by his very position, for examination of his daily conduct as an example to those who believe.

(3) "*In love*": Please read I Corinthians Chapter 13 each day

for thirty days. Begin to see the members of your congregation in the applications of the expressions given in this chapter. Begin in a very practical way to use such expressions as: "hopeth all things"—"believeth all things"—"endureth all things"—"taketh not account of evil". God and man will see your good example.

(4) *"In faith"*: Is it difficult to believe God for His promises? What boldness some men of this world have in their self-confidence, and yet we cannot believe God! Why can Khruschev say "your grandchildren will all be Communists"? —because he believes in the power of Communism. Where is the man who will say to all the peoples of the world, because he believes in the power of the gospel, "all your grandchildren will be Christians"? It can be true! Who will believe it and preach it?

(5) *"In purity"*: How difficult it is to be consistent in all areas. If the minister of the Word cannot convince the community that he is above reproach in his relations to the opposite sex, he has failed in a very serious realm; he had just as well move, for he is through as a representative of Christ Jesus.

Vs. 13. The general concensus of opinion among commentators is that the public reading of the Scriptures, the public exhortation, and the public teaching from the preacher, is referred to here. The article "the" can appear before each word; so it becomes: *the* reading—*the* exhortation—*the* teaching. We are reminded of the order of service in the synagogues. In the synagogue, after reading a portion of scripture from the Old Testament, its application to life was pointed out; following this, the finer points of meaning from an exegetical viewpoint were given. It is quite possible, such was also the order in the congregations of Christians in Ephesus. Timothy was to carefully supervise each portion of the service in each congregation. Compare Luke 4:16 and Acts 13:15 for examples of the services in the Jewish assemblies.

Paul anticipated a visit to Timothy. We do not know the details of this visit. See our *introduction* for the possible time and place.

Fact Questions 4:11-13

113. What was it Timothy was to "command and teach"?
114. What are the two misconceptions to be cleared up?
115. What is "demanded respect"?
116. What is "idle talk"? Why is it used by many?
117. How shall we earn the respect of older men?
118. The preacher must "live in a goldfish bowl". Explain.

119. What was the very practical suggestion as to how we can become an example "in love"?
120. How does our present world conflict demonstrate both a lack of faith and a possession of it?
121. In what areas must the man of God be pure?
122. Was Timothy the reader of the scripture in the church service? Explain.
123. Did Paul visit Timothy at Ephesus? Explain.

b. To be an Example in Personal Life. 14-16

Text 4:14-16

14 Neglect not the gift that is in thee, which was given thee by prophecy, with the laying on of the hands of the presbytery. 15 Be diligent in these things; give thyself wholly to them; that thy progress may be manifest unto all. 16 Take heed to thyself, and to thy teaching. Continue in these things; for in doing this thou shalt save both thyself and them that hear thee.

Thought Questions 4:14-16

147. Are we to infer from Vs. 14 that Timothy was neglectful? Explain.
148. What was "the gift" given to Timothy?
149. How could you explain the expression "which was given thee by prophecy"?
150. Who were "the presbytery"?
151. What are "the things" of Vs. 15?
152. Why be concerned that some would see his spiritual progress?
153. Just what is involved in the expression "take heed to thyself"?
154. If Timothy was already saved, why the admonition of Vs. 16b?

Paraphrase 4:14-16

14 That thou mayest understand the scriptures, neglect not to exercise the spiritual gift which is in thee, which was given thee by the imposition of my hands, according to a prophetic impulse, together with the imposition of the hands of the eldership at Lystra, who thereby testified their approbation of thy ordination as an evangelist.

15 Make these things, the things mentioned in ver. 13, the objects of thy constant care: Be wholly employed in the practice of them, that thy proficiency in knowledge and goodness may be evident to all.

16 Take heed to behave suitable to thy character as an evangelist,

and to teach true doctrine; and continue to take heed to save thyself, and be the instrument of saving them who hear and obey thy instructions.

Comment 4:14-16

Vs. 14. Timothy has not neglected the supernatural endowment. The expression "neglect not" can mean: "keep on not neglecting". This is a word of encouragement not of rebuke. It is interesting to notice that whereas Timothy had supernatural gifts, yet personal faith and fidelity were not at all eliminated. We believe "the gift" here granted "by" or "in accompaniment with the hands of the presbytery" could be one of two things: (1) The gift of the office of evangelist—given by the elders of the churches of Lystra and Iconium when he was ordained. Cf. Acts 16:1-3; 13:1-3. The facts in this subject are two in number: *one*—the presbytery or elders *did* lay their hands on Timothy. The reason we offer for such imposition of hands by elders, is for a formal setting aside of men for a special work. *Two*—Timothy was an evangelist—Cf. II Tim. 4:5. When and where and how did he become such? It seems altogether reasonable to believe that at the time Paul called Timothy to help him, the elders of the churches of Lystra and Iconium concurred in his call, and set Timothy aside for the work and office of evangelist, by the laying on of their hands.

The little expression "by prophecy" will bear explanation. One or more of the elders could have had the gift of prophecy and exercised it at the time of Timothy's ordination; he would thus prophesy of the very valuable work Timothy would do in the future. This would be a great encouragement to all. Or it could have been that the Holy Spirit through the gift of prophecy told one of the elders of the marvelous potential of this young man for the office of evangelist, and he was thus prompted by the Spirit to suggest the ordination.

(2) The gift could have been one of the nine supernatural gifts of I Cor. 12:11, given to Timothy by the laying on of Paul's hands at the same time that the elders laid their hands upon Timothy. Cf. II Tim. 1:6. In this case Paul is considered one of the elders. This would not be strange since Peter referred to himself as a "fellow elder". Cf. I Peter 5:1. In this case the expression "by prophecy" would refer to Paul's prophetic insight regarding the future work of Timothy. We prefer the first explanation. We cannot be dogmatic as to just what "the gift" is.

Vs. 15. There were no half-way measures with Paul, he was completely dedicated to the Law once, when converted he was just as committed to the Gospel. This same attitude of complete dedication he urged upon Timothy. Let us hold back nothing in the service of Christ. As the song writer has expressed it "give all thy being's ransomed powers."

In sustaining such an attitude there is great good to be done. Among those who need the Lord we serve, we set an example that makes it much easier to carry the message to them. The members of the congregation are watching, and more especially, the elders of the flock. Your exemplary conduct will not go unrewarded. Respect and interest are the natural fruit of a faithful, zealous, growing ministry.

Vs. 16. The little expression "take heed" is full of meaning: look carefully, keep a close watch. Three areas will bear such scrutiny: (1) *Yourself*—i.e. your own heart; (2) *Your teaching*—are you teaching God's word or human opinions? (3) *Your consistency*—or *constancy*. If Timothy will measure up on these three counts, he will save not only himself but those who watch and hear him. What a glorious opportunity and responsibility!

EXEGETICAL EXAMINATION OVER CHAPTER FOUR OF I TIMOTHY

1. Discuss as to origin and practice, "seducing spirits and doctrines of demons".
2. Who has a "seared conscience"? Why? What effect did such persons have on the Christians?
3. Why would anyone "command others to abstain from marriage and meats"?
4. Give the two reasons for rejecting the false teachings of certain men.
5. Specify some of "the old wives' fables".
6. Explain the two-fold advantage of exercising ourselves unto godliness.
7. To what end did Paul and others labor and strive?
8. In what sense shall we understand that, "God is the Saviour of all men"?
9. Explain Vs. 14.
10. What genuine advantage is there in continuing to teach and live for Christ?

V. THE CARE OF THE VARIOUS MEMBERS OF THE CHURCH 5:1—6:2

1. CARE OF YOUNG AND OLD. 1,2

Text 5:1,2

1 Rebuke not an elder, but exhort him as father; the younger men as brethren: 2 the elder women as mothers; the younger as sisters, in all purity.

Thought Questions 5:1,2

154. Is the "elder" here an older man, or an officer in the church?
155. Just what is the meaning of the word "rebuke"?
156. Why not rebuke an elder if he needs it?
157. "Rebuke" is here contrasted with "exhort"; please explain what is involved.
158. Are we to look on the older man as a father of the church, or as our own father?
159. Is the thought of "do not rebuke" involved in our dealing with the rest of the group in verses 1, 2?
160. Wouldn't the younger men lose their respect for the evangelist if he treated them as his equal? Explain.
161. How can we develop the capacity to look upon the older women as mothers?
162. Why mention "in all purity" in reference to the younger women? Was Timothy tempted in the moral realm?

Paraphrase 5:1,2

1 When reproof is necessary, do not severly rebuke an old man; but beseech him, as thou wouldest beseech thy father in the like case; and the young men who sin, as if they were thy own brothers.

2 The old women beseech, as if they were mothers to thee, and the young, as if they were thy sisters, observing the strictest chastity in speech and behaviour towards them.

Comment 5:1,2

Vs. 1. We move from the needs of Timothy as an individual to the needs of some of the members in the churches where he served. This advice or divine direction is given to help when problems arise. When an old man needs correction, how shall it be done? Do not go after him with "hammer and tongs". Because of the age and experience of such a one, the younger man would be tempted to lose patience with him; do not do so. Some grow older and wiser and some only grow older. Regardless of the attitude of the older man, the man of God should treat him with the same respect he would give his own father. The word "exhort" which is to replace the word "rebuke" means to bring comfort and encouragement.

How shall Timothy treat the younger men who need correction

or help? In the same manner as he would treat his own brother. Treat the older men with respect—the younger men as equals. **Vs. 2.** It would be natural in the light of what has been said about men to now consider the women. Our Lord's attitude toward those with whom He worked must be ours: "behold, my mother . . . and my sisters." (Matt. 12:49). We love the older women as we would our mother—the younger ones as our sisters. Does the little phrase "in all purity" refer only to proper moral conduct in association with the younger women? It surely has this meaning, but it could refer to the unhypocritical attitude of the man of God in his association will all ages and sex.

Fact Questions 5:1,2

124. Why did Paul give Timothy the advice of 5:1,2? Was Timothy lax in his proper attitude?
125. Is Paul contradicting himself in 5:1 and 5:20, or in 5:1 and II Tim. 4:2? Explain. (The answer is in the meaning of the word "rebuke".)
126. Why would a younger man lose patience with an older man, before he would with a younger man?
127. Where can we find an example from our Lord in our attitude toward those with whom we work?
128. How shall the phrase "in all purity" be applied?

2. THE CARE OF WIDOWS 5:3-16

Text 5:3-16

3 Honor widows that are widows indeed. 4 But if any widow hath children or grandchildren, let them learn first to show piety towards their own family, and to requite their parents: for this is acceptable in the sight of God. 5 Now she that is a widow indeed, and desolate, hath her hope set on God, and continueth in supplications and prayers night and day. 6 But she that giveth herself to pleasure is dead while she liveth. 7 These things also command, that they may be without reproach. 8 But if any provideth not for his own, and specially his own household, he hath denied the faith, and is worse than an unbeliever. 9 Let none be enrolled as a widow under threescore years old having been the wife of one man, 10 well reported of for good works; if she hath brought up children, if she hath used hospitality to strangers, if she hath washed the saints' feet, if she hath relieved the afflicted, if she hath diligently followed every good work. 11 But younger widows refuse: for when they have waxed wanton against Christ, they desire to marry; 12 having condemnation, because they have

rejected their first pledge. 13 And withal they learn also to be idle, going about from house to house, and not only idle, but tattlers also and busy-bodies, speaking things which they ought not. 14 I desire therefore that the younger widows marry, bear children, rule the household, give no occasion to the adversary for reviling; 15 for already some are turned aside after Satan. 16 If any woman that believeth hath widows, let her relieve them, and let not the church be burdened; that it may relieve them that are widows indeed.

Thought Questions 5:3-16

163. Is not a widow always a widow until married again? What then is the meaning of the expression "a widow indeed"?
164. How shall we understand the use of the word "honor" in 5:3?
165. Explain the meaning of the word "piety" as used in Vs. 4.
166. Is it clear as to just who is "to show piety"? Prove your answer.
167. To our parents we owe a great debt—what is it?
168. Where has God spoken in His word concerning the responsibility of children and grandchildren toward their parents?
169. In what sense does the true widow "have her hope set on God"?
170. Is there some distinction in "supplications and prayers?"; if so, what?
171. Is the time of private prayer suggested by the expression "night and day"?
172. Why the sudden change in thought from Vs. 5 to Vs. 6?
173. What has died in the pleasure loving widow?
174. Just what is it that Timothy is "to charge" upon the congregation?
175. Who is to be "without reproach"? How does this relate to the subject of the care of widows?
176. Just what constitutes "providing for our relatives"? Would government support be included?
177. In what sense has a person "denied the faith" when he does not care for his own? In what sense is he "worse than an unbeliever"?
178. Widows were to be "enrolled" in something; what was it? Why the sixty year age limit?
179. Does the expression "the wife of one man" include the necessity of marriage, or simply refer to "a one man woman", —i.e. no polygamist? (Will you use the same logic on I

Tim. 3:2 when referring to the elder?—the same words are used).

180. Who is going to bring the report of good works as stated in Vs. 10a? Specify some possible "good works".
181. Does 10b mean that every "enrolled" widow *must* have had children—or that *if* she did they should have been brought up in the right manner?
182. These women were to be qualified long before they were widows—what is here said about them is said for the whole church, for any woman is a potential widow. Just what is involved in showing "hospitality" to strangers?
183. Please do not avoid a discussion of "foot washing" just because some have abused it. Somebody washed feet—who was it? When was it? Why was it? Was it a church ordinance?
184. Do not forget John 13:12-16.
185. Can we say that hospitals, motels, and the "community chest" do the work of the widows today?
186. Is it a sin for younger widows to marry? See Vs. 11 and Vs. 14.
187. What is "the first pledge" of the younger widows?
188. How would the advice in Vs. 14 solve the problems of Vs. 13?
189. In what sense could a church become responsible for the actions of the younger widows described in Vs. 13? What is "a tattler"; a "busy-body"?
190. In what sense are the women "to rule the house"?
191. Paul sees a grave danger in being a widow, and a serious responsibility on the part of the church. How shall we explain the danger and assume the responsibility? Cf. vs. 15.

Paraphrase 5:3-16

3 With respect to widows who are to be maintained by the church as teachers, my command is, Employ and maintain those only who are really widows, or desolate.

4 But if any widow have children or grandchildren able to maintain her, let not the church employ her as a teacher; but let these relations learn first piously to take care of their own family, and, then to make a just return of maintenance to their aged parents for their care in bringing them up. For this attention to parents in poverty is good for society, and acceptable in the sight of God. See ver. 8, 16.

5 Now, to shew thee who the widows are of whom I speak, she who is really a widow and desolate, besides being poor and friend-

less, is of a pious disposition; she trusteth in God for her support, and continueth in deprecations and prayers night and day. Such a widow will take pleasure in instructing the young.
6 But the widow who liveth in gaiety and luxury is dead while she liveth in that manner, and should not be employed as a teacher of the young.
7 Now, these things concerning the obligation lying on children to maintain their parents, charge the Ephesians to perform, that they may be blameless in that matter.
8 For if any one professing Christianity maintaineth not his own poor relations, and especially those with whom he hath lived in family, he hath renounced the faith of the gospel, and is worse than an infidel; many of whom would be ashamed of thus violating the obligations of nature and humanity.
9 Let not any widow be taken into the number of teachers of the younger under sixty years old, having neither been an harlot, nor a concubine, but the wife of one husband at a time; consequently, hath governed her passions properly in her youth.
10 Farther, she must be one who is borne witness to for good works; that she hath brought up children religiously and virtuously, that she hath formerly lodged strangers, even though heathens, that she hath washed the disciples' feet in their journeys, when they went about preaching the gospel, that she hath relieved the afflicted; in short that she hath diligently performed every charitable work.
11 But the younger widows reject as teachers, because, when they cannot endure that restraint to which they have subjected themselves for Christ's sake, they will marry, and, by encumbering themselves with a family, they will render themselves unfit for teaching:
12 Subjecting themselves to condemnation, both from God and men, because, by marrying, they have renounced their first engagement to serve Christ.
13 And at the same time also they learn to be idle, wandering about from house to house, on pretence of following the duties of their office: And not only idle, but tale-bearers also, and meddlers in other people's affairs, publishing the secrets of families, which they ought not to divulge.
14 I command, therefore, young widows to marry, if a fit opportunity offers, to bear children, to govern the house with prudence, and, by behaving in all respects properly, to give no occasion to the adversaries of our religion to reproach the gospel, on account

of the bad behaviour of those who profess it.
15 I am anxious to have these rules observed, because already some widows, whom the church hath employed as teachers, by marrying, are turned aside from the work to follow after Satan.
16 If any Christian man or Christian woman have poor widows nearly related to them, let them relieve them, if they are able, and let not the church be burdened with maintaining such as teachers, that it may relieve those who are really desolate, by employing and maintaining them as teachers of the younger women.

Comment 5:3-16

It does seem because of the length of this section, we should offer some subdivision of the passage. The following from *Edmond Hiebert* is good:

1. The duty of supporting widows, V. 3-8.
    a) The command to honor genuine widows, V. 3
    b) The definitive classification of widows, V. 4-5.
        (1) The widow having children, V. 4
        (2) The widow who is a genuine widow, V. 5
        (3) The widow living in pleasure, V. 6
2. The instructions concerning the enrollment of widows, V. 9-15
    a) The qualifications of those enrolled, V. 9, 10
    b) The rejection of young widows, V. 11-13.
        (1) The command to reject the young widows, V. 11a
        (2) The reason for the rejection, V. 11b-13.
    c) The apostolic directive for young widows, V. 14, 15
3. The duty of a believing woman, V. 16

We shall now take up a verse by verse comment, but please keep the outline before you so as to be able to analyze the entire passage.

Vs. 3. The word "honor" carries the thought of very definite assistance as well as respect. The word "widow" means "bereft" or left alone. There are two widows who do not live up to their name: those who have children or grandchildren to support them, and those who give themselves to pleasure. We cannot say that here in Vs. 3 alone, we have reference to regular financial help by the church for widows who are "widows indeed".

Vs. 4. A "widow indeed" is one who does not have help from children. In fulfillment of the fifth of the ten commandments, children are to care for their parents. Our religion is little more than a pretense if it does not enter our family relationship. Paul does not mention whether we consider our mother or grandmother worthy of support, he states that God considers her worthy; for the Christian this should settle the matter. Care for parents in their declining years is but small payment for the many years they cared for us. We were helped in every way by them when we could not help ourselves. Can we not return in kind such care? It is good to know that God sees and appreciates our efforts if no one else does.

Vs. 5. In sharp contrast, two kinds of women are described in V. 5, 6. Three qualities are given concerning the first: (1) "desolate" or utterly alone. Our hearts should go out to aged women who are too old to work, and have no children or grandchildren to help them. (2) "hath her hope set on God". If widows of Paul's day and time could hope in God, who are we to lack in faith today? We think of the widow of Zarephath (I Kings 17:8-12) who said, "as Jehovah liveth" she and her son were going to starve to death. The hope of such widows is not for food but for heaven. If God does not supply physical sustenance then He will provide something far better. We are not suggesting God does not provide food, for He does, but such hope is not some type of divine social security benefit. (3) She lays before God all of her specific needs (supplications) and does not forget the needs of others (prayers); this she does in the hours of the night, as well as when cares and concern come during the day.

Vs. 6. In the luxurious city of Ephesus there would be temptations to "give oneself to pleasure"; what would seem to be "life" was in fact "death". "To live after the flesh is to die" Rom. 8:13.

Sin of any kind is a disappointment. Such disappointment is especially keen as it relates to the sins of the flesh. God is disappointed because we have abused a high and holy relationship, not only between a loving heavenly Father and his disobedient child, but between children. Christ is disappointed because we have rejected His Lordship, the one thing above all else He deserves in our lives. The Holy Spirit is grieved and quenched in His holy work. Others who trusted us are sad and confused by our actions. Little ones might be caused to stumble and be lost. We are disappointed because we did not find what we expected—because we failed to read all the price tag. All of this spells *spiritual death*, the cost of lustful living. The "gay young widow" is anything but "gay" when she awakens to the reality we have just described.

Vs. 7. The world is watching the Christian. When we fail to care for our own, we are bringing reproach upon the name and cause of Christ. Timothy was to recognize the seriousness of such a condition. To avert it he was to give careful instruction, with the note of divine authority behind it, to all those described in Vs. 1-6: Let the older and younger men and women, all types and ages of widows, chidren and grandchildren take heed to such instruction.

Vs. 8. This verse is almost a conclusion to the one preceding it. If we do not care for our own, it will be because the command and lesson have not been heeded. The terrible seriousness of failure is emphasized: "denied the faith". The principle involved is so basic, that to fail in this is to fail in all. Please note that the body of Truth was so well defined at the time as to be called "The Faith". If we will not support our own family, we are failing where some of the world succeeds; thus we are worse than an unbeliever. No Christian man or woman is exempt from this responsibility; such care is for every mother or grandmother who might be in need. Just how such care is to be given is not specified; there is a need to be met, and meet it we must or give up our pretense of being a Christian.

Vs. 9. The church at Ephesus was well acquainted with the meaning and use of the term "enrollment", but we are not. We know the verb means to be "elected" and thus "to be enrolled" or "entered on a list." Did the congregation vote on certain widows as to whether they would be supported by the church or not? We believe the enrollment here does refer to the support of certain widows by the church. Just how such support was carried out is a matter of opinion. The two qualifications in this verse refer at the same time to age and moral conduct. As to why a widow must be older than sixty years of age, please read Paul's comment concerning the desires and actions of certain younger widows, who if enrolled would feel obligated to the church, but who would be not at all satisfied when the opportunity for marriage presented itself. Let none appear on the list for support who is not a "one man woman". The obvious meaning is that the widow should not have been the wife of more than one man. It would be ridiculous to say the necessity of marriage is included here, for such is not the point of the expression "the wife of one man". But, what of the insistence of some in forcing the necessity of marriage into the expression "the husband of one wife" (3:2)? It seems to the writer the same thought is discussed in both passages, i.e. an attitude of heart, both the prospective enrolled widow and the prospective elder must be joined to but one partner in heart and life.

Vs. 10. Certain questions must be answered in the mind of the congregation before they can offer the use of the church treasury to a widow. Look at the list: (1) Is she past sixty years old? (2) Is she a "one man woman"? (3) Who knows of the good works performed by her? What are these good works? (4) Has she been able to rear children who are a credit to the community and the church? (5) How has she treated strangers in need of hospitality? (6) What of the care of the saints?; has she washed their feet? (7) How did she care for the sick? (8) Has she been an energetic worker for good?

We do not believe a formal interrogation took place, these are but qualities one would expect to find in any faithful sister. We are not suggesting you would find them today, for you would examine many before one would appear who exemplified such virtues. As to the subject of "foot washing" we like very much the words of Lenski:

"Closely allied are the next two questions: 'whether she washed saints' feet, whether she relieved afflicted ones.' We think of John 13:15 and Luke 7:44. Travelers and guests who were received into the house had their sandals untied and their feet laved. This was the task of lowly servants, and when guests were to be honored, the host attended to it. But the matter of hospitality has already been named, and this new question cannot refer to one feature of that hospitality, to its cordiality as some think. Nor would the housewife of the Orient wash a guest's feet unless it be a woman guest's. The expression is figurative for rendering menial service, being not too proud to stoop. So also these 'saints' are not house guests but fellow Christians in the congregation who need lowly service and assistance. Thus hospitality in the woman's own home, and then helpful lowly service in the homes of destitute fellow Christians are referred to." (pp. 669, 670)

Vs. 11. In what sense shall we understand the word "refuse" as here used? It must have reference to enrollment of widows for support. There is both a general principle and specific instance to consider in this case. The general rule is: "do not enroll for full support, widows under sixty years of age." The specific instance is in reference to some younger widows: whereas they once were bereft of support and gladly received enrollment for support by the church, they now have found a prospective husband,

and that among unbelievers. The problem is that the widow has pledged herself to work for Christ and remain a widow, now she is sorely tempted to do neither one. Her desire for a husband is natural, but when it is set over against a promise to the church (and Christ) that she will remain a widow, almost inevitably the result will be that she will "exercise youthful vigor against Christ". All younger widows would not conduct themselves in such a manner, but the temptation would be present for all. Remove the circumstances by ignoring applications from younger widows for enrollment.

Vs. 12. The question as to "what is the pledge" has been cleared up, if we accept the interpretation we have just given of Vss. 10, 11. The "condemnation" is the judgment of the Lord against those who made the promise to the church and Christ that was not kept. It is more important than a breach of contract for material support. Because of the moral issue involved, she has rejected her pledge of love to Christ her Lord and Saviour. She is now about to pledge herself to a pagan husband, in doing so she rejects Christ.

Vs. 13. We are now introduced to the circumstances out of which this problem grew. *If* younger widows are enrolled to serve the church in visitation work, some of them will be tempted to become the idle tattlers and busy-bodies here described. Refuse to enroll them and you will not have the reproach against the church. It is not that some women (even church members) will not fall into such sins as here described—but at least they will not be to the mind of the unbeliever, official representatives of the body of Christ.

The "house to house" phrase could be understood in connection with the work given such widows. Idleness would develop because many would have more time and energy than work.

Vs. 14. Here are the positive instructions for younger widows: please note how perfectly the directions meet the need. What is the need?: to care for the younger women who, because of time and energy, to say nothing of more freedom, are tempted to "give themselves to pleasure". What is the answer to such a problem? "Let them marry, bear children, rule their household"; all time and energy will be taken up in the high and holy task of wife and motherhood. Such instructions are given to Christian women; no more idle visiting, no more tale bearing, no more meddling in other matters, when we give ourselves to our home and family. Paul is vitally concerned for the good name of the church in Ephesus, and in all places. To carry out the above instructions, is to stop the mouths of those who would criticize the Lord's work because of certain feminine conduct. We do not understand "the adversary" in V. 14 to refer to the devil, but rather to be used generically in reference to anyone who might oppose Christ's work.

Vs. 15. Paul's advice is urgent! Some have already fallen—some have already left the path. There is no hesitancy in saying that such are following Satan. Timothy is to urgently instruct the elders that they might instruct the church, or he is to instruct directly the assembly. Paul speaks out of sad experience ,to offer a safeguard for those who are being tempted to turn aside.

Vs. 16. There yet remains a circumstance in which some widows might find themselves. What of widows who live in the homes of wealthy church members? Perhaps their husbands, who had formerly been employed by this family, died. For whatever cause, some widows find themselves in the home of well-to-do Christians. Perhaps the widows are employed in such homes. Paul is very plain in his word to such circumstance. Let the "women", or "believer"—for so the word indicates, support such widows, that the Church might assist those who are truly "bereft" or widows. We have suggested a situation by which to explain the little phrase "hath widows", we are sure there are other ways of explaining it, e.g. "If any woman believer had widowed relatives who were in need, she should care for them . . ." (Russell Bradley Jones).

Fact Questions 5:3-16

129. How shall we understand the word "honor" as used in Verse 3?
130. How is the word "widow" used in verse 3?
131. What if our parents are not worthy of support; should we follow Paul's instructions in verse 4?
132. Give the three qualities of a "widow indeed".
133. Give an example of a widow who had her hope set on "the living God", and yet planned on starving to death.
134. Explain "prayers and supplications".
135. Show how sin is a disappointment.
136. Why the urgency as in verse 7?
137. Show just how we deny "the faith" by failing to care for our own.
138. Explain the use of the term "enrollment" as in verse 9.

139. What is the meaning of the expression "the wife of one man", or "the husband of one wife". (Cf. 3:2)
140. Give from memory four of the eight questions related to the qualifications of the enrolled widows.
141. Explain "foot washing" as related to the qualified widow.
142. In what sense shall we understand the word "refuse" as in verse 11?
143. What is "their first pledge"?
144. Why did some women become "idle tattlers and busy bodies"- Who is at fault?
145. Show how Paul's instructions in verse 14 meet the need described in verses 11-13.
146. Who is "the adversary" of verse 14?
147. Show how Paul was speaking out of sad experience, as in verse 15. Just how did Satan enter the picture?
148. Who is "the woman that believeth (who) hath widows" in verse 16?

3. CARE OF ELDERS. 17-25

Text 5:17-25

17 Let the elders that rule well be counted worthy of double honor, especially those who labor in the word and in teaching. 18 For the scripture saith, Thou shalt not muzzle the ox when he treadeth out the corn. And, the laborer is worthy of his hire. 19 Against an elder receive not an accusation, except at the mouth of two or three witnesses. 20 Them that sin reprove in the sight of all, that the rest also may be in fear. 21 I charge thee in the sight of God, and Christ Jesus, and the elect angels, that thou observe these things without prejudice, doing nothing by partiality. 22 Lay hands hastily on no man, neither be partaker of other men's sins: keep thyself pure. 23 Be no longer a drinker of water, but use a little wine for thy stomach's sake and thine often infirmities. 24 Some men's sins are evident, going before unto judgment; and some men also they follow after. 25 In like manner there are good works that are evident; and such as are otherwise cannot be hid.

Thought Questions 5:17-25

193. Are we to assume from vs. 17 that there are some elders who "rule" or that there are some elders "who do not rule *well*"?
194. Can we infer from these verses that some elders ruled and

some taught, and that such were separate responsibilties? Explain.

195. What is the "double honor"? You are called upon to *think* and advance an opinion.

196. Who is "the ox" in the figure of speech as given from Deut. 25:4?

197. Who said: "the laborer is worthy of his hire" (Cf. Luke 10:7) Paul says "the *Scripture* saith"—are we to infer that the Gospel of Luke is here called "Scripture", and placed on an equal level with the O. T. reference from Deut.?; of what importance is it if this is true?

198. Who is "the elder" of vs. 19? Is this in reference to an officer in the church or just an older man? Explain.

199. Is the mention of "two or three witnesses" hinting at a formal meeting in which accusations are made and supported?

200. In what manner are we to understand the word "sin" as in vs. 20? Just how is this to be done? Is it to be a part of our responsibility today? Who are "the rest" of vs. 20?

201. Why the strong exhortation of vs. 21? Please explain the context.

202. Why would Timothy be tempted to be partial or prejudiced? Please be practical.

203. Are we introduced to an ordination service in vs. 22? How connect laying on of hands with "other men's sins"?

204. What type of purity is suggested in vs. 22? How is this related to the context?

205. No one seems to know how vs. 23 relates to what is said in vs. 22 or vs. 24; do you? Attempt it.

206. Is Paul recommending moderate drinking of wine? If not, what is the suggestion?

207. Why didn't Paul recommend prayer and faith for Timothy's infirmities?

208. Is Paul telling Timothy to allow for a lapse of time before the selection of candidates for the eldership? Read vs. 24, 25 with this thought in mind: time will reveal character and thus indicate the disqualified and the qualified. Are we fair with the text to infer such?

209. What is the most important point of emphasis in this section as it relates to our present need for elders?

Paraphrase 5:17-25

11 Let the elders who preside prudently in your religious meetings be counted worthy of double honour; let them have a liberal maintenance from the funds of the church; especially those who, besides presiding, labour in preaching and teaching.

18 The duty of the faithful to maintain widows and elders, is enjoined both in the law and in the gospel. For the law saith to the Jews, Thou shall not muzzle the ox while treading out the corn, but allow him to eat of that which he treadeth as a recompense for his labour; and in the gospel Christ enjoins the same duty, for this reason, that the labourer is worthy of his hire.

19 Against an elder, whether he be a bishop, a president, or a deacon, receive not an accusation, unless it is offered to be proved by two or three creditable witnesses.

20 Those who, by the testimony of credible witnesses, are found in sin, rebuke before the whole church, that other elders also may be afraid to commit the like offences.

21 I charge thee, in the presence of God, and of the Lord Jesus Christ, and of the chief angels, that thou observe these rules concerning the admonition of the old and the young, and the maintaining of widows and elders, and the censuring of sinners, without being prejudiced against any person; and doing nothing from favour.

22 Appoint no one to any sacred office hastily, without inquiring into his character and qualifications: Neither, by conferring these offices on unworthy persons, partake of other men's sins. In the whole of thy conduct, keep thyself blameless.

23 Thy health being of great importance to the church, no longer drink pure water, but mix a little wine with it, on account of the disorder of thy stomach, and thy many other bodily infirmities.

24 In judging of those who desire sacred offices, consider, that of some men the sins are very manifest, leading before inquiry to condemnation. Such reject. But in others especially, their sins are so concealed that the knowledge of them follows after inquiry. For which reason no one ought to be appointed to sacred offices hastily.

25 In like manner also, the good works and good qualities of some men are very manifest: Such may be admitted to sacred offices without any particular inquiry. And those which are not manifest cannot be long hidden, if an accurate inquiry be made.

Comment 5:17-25

Vs. 17. The "honor" due widows was discussed in the last section, we have here a discussion of the "honor" due elders. All elders are to be held in high regard, but some are to be given "double honor". Just what is this "double honor"? We have read many and varied comments upon possible meanings: (1) Double pay (2) Honor plus salary (3) Twice the pay of the sixty year old widows (4) Twice the pay of the deacons (5) Honor as an older man and honor as an elder (6) Honor as a brother and honor as an elder (7) Special regard because of position and work—which would include remuneration. This last view seems most tenable. Those elders who do an outstanding job should receive special recognition from the congregation, both by word and by pay, or financial help. The particular men to receive such distinction are specified: ". . . those who wear themselves out teaching and preaching the Word". (We would look for a long while before we found such a one today). This does *not* mean that only some elders were to teach and others were not to teach, for their qualifications indicated *all* were to be able to teach, (3:2). Those who thus serve with special distinction, should be recognized by and before the congregation.

Vs. 18. This verse is an explanation of the preceding one. The word "for" would indicate its connective quality. The scriptures teach us of the responsibility of honoring such men; we are taught such from both the old and the new covenant—i.e., Deut. 25:4 and Luke 10:7. Such seems to be the thought of Paul's purpose. What did the ox receive for his work?: a part of the grain he helped to thresh; this was lawful and right. What does a laborer receive from his work?: pay. What then should a faithful man of God receive from his efforts? Can we pay the ox and the workman but not the man of God? It is important as well as imperative that elders be recognized in this light, both as to their work and their honor.

Vs. 19. Elders should be safeguarded from malicious gossip. Any overseer worthy of the name, will receive criticism in his work for Christ. Such criticism will come to the ears of the evangelist; what shall he do when he hears it? The Old Testament required two or three witnesses in the establishment of an accusation, Cf. Deut. 19:15; and so did our Lord, Cf. Mt. 18:16; and so did Paul elsewhere, Cf. II Cor. 13:1. Men or women who will not sign their name to an accusation should be rebuked for making it. We are not told just where and when and how such accusations are to be made. Are we to think of a public meeting in which accusers and accused face each other? or are we to understand this as only an informal, personal matter? This is best left up to the grace and wisdom of those involved.

Vs. 20. When an accusation is established against an elder or elders, something *must* be done. The guilty elder or elders are to be "rebuked" in the sight of all". Where and when is this to take place? The answer depends upon who is involved in the word "all"—Are we to understand this to mean the rest of the elders, or the congregation? We prefer the latter inasmuch as the congregation selected the elders, the elders oversee the local congregation, and to them they are responsible. It only seems logical that where certain elders have proved themselves unworthy, all the congregation should know about it. This rebuke "in the sight of all" presupposes that the attempts of restoration described by our Lord have been made without success. Such a rebuke or discipline is the last effort to save such men and warn the church. There should be an effect for good on the rest of the eldership as well as the community. The "rest durst not join themselves to them: howbeit the people magnified them." So said Luke of the results of the discipline of the church in Jerusalem, (Cf. Acts 5:13). A holy respect for the purity of life required by God for the officers of His church, should be the response of those who are participators and spectators in this experience.

Vs. 21. The exalted and strong words of Paul in this verse come as somewhat of a surprise. Why would it be necessary to say what he did? and how does it fit the context? Perhaps a vision of all the dear ones in the church at Ephesus, as well as those of the seven churches of Asia, came up before the eyes of his heart, as he thought of how vastly important good leadership is, and so he was prompted to say what he did. Could it be that he felt the limitation of paper and ink to communicate the depth of feelings he had about the matter of faithful shepherds, and injected this strong expression to impress upon Timothy his deep and true concern? We much prefer these thoughts to the opinion that Timothy was weak and variable in his attitude and work. If he was, why did Paul call him to the work? There were many others to whom he could have given the task.

It is more than a sobering thought that God, Christ and elect angels are all watching our actions and reading our thoughts. Remember, the all-seeing and all-knowing God is a witness to your work among men. If we are prejudiced or partial, we shall finally give an account for it. How easy it is to allow friendship and personality to turn our heads and hearts. Prejudice is preference by pre-judgment; partiality is choice because of personal advantage.

Vs. 22. Continuing the thought broken by the charge of vs. 21, Paul speaks of the ordination of elders. The laying on of hands for setting men into office was a common practice in the early church: Cf. Acts 13:1-3; II Tim. 1-6; I Tim. 4:14; Acts 6:1-6. Titus 1:5 would be a companion reference as to the responsibility of the evangelist in this work. We are not to understand that the total service is up to the evangelist; the selection according to Acts 6:3 was the responsibility of the congregation. Acts 14:23 supports this thought: the word "appointed" means "to elect with an outstretched hand". The only detailed method of selection is the reference in Acts 6:1-6. The qualifications for the office are made known by the evangelist. The congregation looks out men qualified for the office, and decides such by vote. After they have been selected they are set into the office by the laying on of the hands of the evangelist; (or the elders and evangelist). Paul's warning that this should not be done in haste is very, very important. To ordain in haste is to be "a partaker in other men's sins." Is it a sin to have a man in office who is not qualified for the work? So it would seem from this verse. To be over-influenced by personal considerations, and for such reasons to lay hands on a candidate in the sacred service of ordination, is indeed a sin of giant magnitude.

"Keep thyself pure" must be an emphasis of what has just been said: keep your motives clean and holy in your part of appointing elders.

Vs. 23. Commentators have been at an almost complete loss to show the connection of this verse to the context. The directions for the honoring, correcting and selecting of elders surely has little to do with Paul's advice to "take a little wine for your stomach's sake and thine often infirmities." Simpson suggests: "It may be that having exhorted Timothy to 'keep himself pure' Paul's mind reverts to the consecration of the Nazirite in Numbers 6 where both words for 'pure' occur (in the LXX), with its solemn abjuration of wine. Now Timothy, conversant from childhood with the Old Testament Scriptures, may have regarded this vow of abstinence as a precedent binding on himself, and so it may have been meant to remind him that wine was one of the Lord's good gifts to man, at least medicinally beneficial, and that he lay under no embargo to taboo it." (Ibid. p. 80). Lenski suggests that Paul was aware of the close relationship between the body and the mind, and wanted Timothy in the best physical condition possible so as to be able to make the wisest choices in the spiritual realm. Either of these positions seems as fair an explanation as we might advance. As to the use of the expression "a little wine" as an excuse for moderate drinking, we have nothing but contempt! The passage speaks of the use of wine for medicinal purposes and this is *all* it says about the use of wine. A complete study of the subject of "wine" as used in the Bible will be found in the *Special Study* section of this book.

Vs. 24. Once again we are back to the general subject of this section—the eldership. Do not be in a hurry to set men into this holy responsibility. If you but wait you will be able to observe their conduct and know if they are fit material for the work. In some of their lives sin will be most obvious. Such men are, as it were, led by their sins on to the judgment. It is not so with some others—you must wait awhile—but, by and by their general demeanor gives them away, and they follow where their evil desires lead them. None of this could be known if hasty judgment was made upon first impressions. This we believe is the meaning of verse 24.

Vs. 25. The opposite is also true—for which we are thankful. The good works of some men are known by all. We should always be grateful that society as a rule has a sense of right and wrong, (whether the majority practice it or not), and good is recognized by all men for what it is. No man can continue in "good works" for a period of time without being identified as the source of such. The general admonition of Vs. 24, 25 is to "wait awhile" before appointment of elders—in this period of proving, the character of men will be made known.

Fact Questions 5:17-25

149. What is "the double honor" due some elders? Please remember you are under no obligation to accept our opinion.

150. Should some elders be paid for their work? Explain.
151. When an elder is accused of sin, what is the procedure?
152. Before whom should sinning elders be rebuked? Explain.
153. What should be the good effect of such a rebuke? Explain. Why is it often the reverse?
154. Explain the place and purpose of vs. 21.
155. Explain the total ordination process.
156. Why is it so important that we do not ordain in haste?
157. How are we to understand the little phrase "keep thyself pure"?
158. Attempt to show the connection of vs. 23 with the context.
159. Is there a thought here for the moderate use of wine?
160. How could sins go before unto judgment?
161. Who is doing the "following" in vs. 24?
162. In verse 25 what "cannot be hid", and why?

EXEGETICAL EXAMINATION OVER CHAPTER FIVE OF I TIMOTHY

1. Why would Timothy be tempted to "rebuke an elder"? Explain the proper treatment of the older man.
2. Explain the proper treatment of younger women.
3. Discuss two classes of widows that cannot be enrolled by the church.
4. Give your exegesis of vs. 5.
5. Why would a Christian be worse than an unbeliever if he did not care for "his own"? Explain.
6. Discuss briefly the five qualifications of the enrolled widow.
7. Explain: "washed the saints' feet".
8. What is "the first pledge" of the younger widows?
9. Discuss "the double honor" of certain elders.
10. Give your exegesis of vs. 23.

4. CARE OF SLAVES 6:1,2

Text 6:1,2

1 Let as many as are servants under the yoke count their own masters worthy of all honor, that the name of God and the doctrine be not blasphemed. 2 And they that have believing masters, let them not despise them, because they are brethren; but let them serve them the rather, because they that partake of the benefit are believing and beloved. These things teach and exhort.

Thought Questions 6:1,2

210. Did Paul believe in slavery? If not, why not condemn it?
211. What is "the yoke" of vs. 1? Please attempt an explanation.
212. How could the Christian slave count some masters worthy of honor when they were "despots"?
213. Is Paul suggesting that slaves even take abuse from some masters? If so, why? If not, explain.
214. Why would a Christian slave be tempted to despise a Christian master? What will prevent it?
215. What is "the benefit" of vs. 2? We urge you to advance an opinion.
216. Would the principles here taught, ultimately abolish slavery? If so, explain how.

Paraphrase 6:1,2

1 Let whatever Christian slaves are under the yoke of unbelievers, pay their own masters all respect and obedience, that the character of God whom we worship may not be calumniated, and the doctrine of the gospel may not be evil spoken of, as tending to destroy the political rights of mankind. See Eph. vi. 5.
2 And those Christian slaves who have believing masters, let them not despise them, fancying that they are their equals, because they are their brethren in Christ; for though all Christians are equal as to religious privileges, slaves are inferior to their masters in station. Wherefore, let them serve their masters more diligently, because they who enjoy the benefit of their service are believers and beloved of God. These things teach, and exhort the brethren to practice them.

Comment 6:1,2

Vs. 1. We come now to the final section of the *care of the members of the church;* this would not be complete without instruction for the vast slave population in the churches. Note that the word "honor" runs throughout: 5:3, 5:17, 6:1. Show "all honor"—a high respect—for your master. Paul uses a word for "masters" from which we have "despot". Is this a veiled thrust at the principle of slavery?

The Christian slave is to have a genuine desire to please his master at whatever cost to himself. The name and teaching of God are far more important than the comfort of the slave. "Under the yoke" is simply another way of emphasizing the slave's position. If the Christian bond-servant can maintain an attitude of good-will at all times, however trying the circumstances, he will have a strong influence on his master. If Jehovah God and the gospel do not alter the conduct of slaves for good, then the master will be tempted to speak out against it. If the master can not read the power of the gospel in the life of his Christian slaves, he will have no interest in reading it elsewhere.

Vs. 2. But what of those who have Christian masters? Surely there would be no problem here—but there is—the human heart is indeed "deceitful above all things and desperately wicked". The temptation would be for the Christian slave to take advantage of his relationship to his master, as not only his master, but his brother. Paul suggests that if the Christian slave was faithful to an unbeliever, how much more would he be to a believer; this was a fine expression of wisdom. "They that partake of the benefit" is not a very clear expression. Who is to partake? and what is "the benefit"? It would seem Paul means to say that the believing masters would share in the benefit of the good work of believing slaves. The slave should serve exceptionally well because he loves his master as a Christian brother and wants his brother to prosper as well as himself. The Christian slave is happy to see the success in his master's business as a result of his own good work, because he loves his master as Christ has loved him. Paul suggests that such matters as appear in 5:17-6:2 need to be constantly taught and urged.

Fact Questions 6:1,2

163. What is Paul's veiled thrust at the principles of slavery?
164. The Christian slave is to please his master at whatever cost. Why?
165. Is Paul asking the impossible in some cases? Discuss.
166. Why would there be any problem between Christian slave and Christian master? What is it?
167. How solve the problem?
168. What is "the benefit" of vs. 2?

VI. THE MINISTER HIMSELF. 6:3-21a

1. MOTIVES 3-10

Text 6:3-10

3 If any man teacheth a different doctrine, and consenteth not to sound words, even the words of our Lord Jesus Christ, and to the doctrine which is according to godliness; 4 he is puffed up, knowing nothing, but doting about questionings and disputes of

words, whereof cometh envy, strife, railings, evil surmisings, 5
wranglings of men corrupted in mind and bereft of the truth,
supposing that godliness is a way of gain. 6 But godliness with
contentment is great gain: 7 for we brought nothing into the
world, for neither can we carry anything out; 8 but having food
and covering we shall be therewith content. 9 But they that are
minded to be rich fall into a temptation and a snare and many
foolish and hurtful lusts, such as drown men in destruction and
perdition. 10 For the love of money is a root of all kinds of evil:
which some reaching after have been led astray from the faith,
and have pierced themselves through with many sorrows.

Thought Questions 6:3-10

217. A preacher should "guard his heart with all diligence", that his motives for service be pure—if he deviates from the plain teaching of the Scripture can we say it is because of pride? Read Vs. 3, 4 carefully.
218. Are we to understand from vs. 3 that Paul is speaking of the actual words of Jesus as recorded in the four gospels, or does he refer to something else?
219. What is the meaning of the expression "the doctrine . . . according to godliness". Does this mean the doctrine leads to godliness, or proceeds from godliness?
220. Does Paul mean to say that everyone who teaches false doctrine does so because of pride? Cf. vs. 4.
221. How did such a one become sick? In what sense does he "know nothing"?
222. Why would we naturally expect evil results from false teachings? Cf. vs. 4b.
223. Paul says some men are "corrupted in mind". Explain.
224. How would anyone imagine that godliness was a way of gain?
225. Can we have godliness without contentment? Can we have contentment without godliness? Explain.
226. To believe vs. 7, 8 will produce contentment with our godliness. Explain why.
227. Do you know of anyone who is completely satisfied with only food and covering?
228. Please notice who is discussed in vs. 9. Does this apply to the present day preacher? There are many more who want to be rich than those who are troubled with actual riches. Which is the worst?

229. What is the difference between "the temptation", and "a snare" in vs. 9?
230. Why compare those who are minded to be rich with "drown men in destruction"? Show the points of similarity.
231. Does this verse say (vs. 10) that money is the root of all evil? What does it say?
232. In a very specific manner show how the love of money leads away from "the faith". Remember, this can mean the preacher.
233. What picture is presented to your mind in vs. 10b? i.e.: have pierced themselves through with many sorrows".

Paraphrase 6:3-10

3 If any one teach differently, by affirming, that under the gospel slaves are not bound to serve their masters, but ought to be made free, and does not consent to the wholesome commandments which are our Lord Jesus Christ's, and to the doctrine of the gospel, which in all points is conformable to true morality,

4 He is puffed up with pride, and knoweth nothing either of the Jewish or of the Christian revelation, although he pretends to have great knowledge of both; but is distempered in his mind about idle questions and debates of words, which afford no foundation for such a doctrine, but are the source of envy, contention, evil speakings, unjust suspicions that the truth is not sincerely maintained.

5 Keen disputings carried on contrary to conscience, by men wholly corrupted in their mind, and destitute of the true doctrine of the gospel, who reckon whatever produces most money is the best religion. From all such impious teachers withdraw thyself, and do not dispute with them.

6 But godliness, with a competency of food and raiment, (ver. 8) is great gain, as it makes us happy both in the present life and in that which is to come; neither of which riches can do.

7 For we brought nothing into the world with us; and plain it is, that neither can we carry anything out of it. Things which we must leave behind us, cannot make us happy in the other world.

8 Wherefore, having food and raiment, and lodging, let us therewith be contented; banishing, as godly persons ought, immoderate desires of things not necessary, and which can be enjoyed only in this life.

9 But they who, not contented with food and raiment, are bent on being rich, fall into great temptations and snares in the pursuit; and, in the enjoyment of riches, into many foolish and hurtful lusts, which plunge men into destruction here, and into eternal perdition hereafter.

10 I have spoken thus sharply against covetousness, because the love of money is the root of all the sinful passions and actions of men; as may be seen in the false teachers, some of whom, eagerly desiring money, have wholly corrupted the doctrine of the gospel, and have pierced themselves all around with many sorrows, occasioned by the stings of conscience and the fears of punishment.

Comment 6:3-10

Vs. 3. The concluding section of this letter is addressed to the personal needs of Timothy as a minister. He writes first of the motives of the minister. One wrong motive is pride, which is stated in V. 4. The results of such an unworthy motive are given in V. 3: (1) He will teach a different doctrine. (2) He is not satisfied with the healthy words of the gospel. (3) Nor does he want a teaching that produces godliness. A love for self and position, produces a message to satisfy self and those who would be foolish enough to follow.

To advance self as an authority we must discount God's Word as the only source of authority. When such happens we can be sure such teaching as will be given will not produce healthy, strong Christians, but stunted and diseased heretics. When God and His Son are not the center of our motive for preaching, we can know the products of our preaching will not be godly.

Vs. 4. This verse discusses the *cause* for the results of v. 3: in one word it is *pride*, but in its ramifications it can be described as: (1) Puffed up (2) Knowing nothing (3) Sick on questionings and disputes of words. Further results of such pride: (1) envy (2) strife (3) railing (4) evil surmisings. We shall discuss briefly these words in order: "Puffed up" means to inflate, to besmog. Truly, the inflated ego will put anyone in a fog, "Knowing nothing" is given in the sense of ignorance of the very basic tenets of the Christian faith; such a man has not even started to learn, for a learner or disciple will first "deny himself", and take up his cross to follow Christ. "Doting" or "sick" about questionings and disputes. It is a little difficult to say whether such are sick *because* of such questionings and disputes, or because he is "sick" he disputes and questions. We prefer the former.

How deceptive is error? Neither those who are in error nor those who follow errorists find what they seek. The leader imagines he will find a measure of peace and power—the followers look for security, and a new spiritual insight—what is found?: envy, strife, railings, evil surmisings. Those who do not trust God find it difficult to trust anyone else—even themselves. Such an evil brood keeps coming forth from those in error.

Vs. 5. In the latter half of this verse we have another wrong motive, *avarice.* The rest of this section, i.e. 6-10, carries a discussion of those "who are minded to be rich". The results of pride and avarice are difficult to separate—indeed they overlap one another. Both pride and money-love proceed from a diseased mind. Satan has robbed them of the truth. Could it be that anyone could enter the holy service of God and His Son with the low purpose of making money? To such, acquainted with the history of the church and present circumstances, such a question sounds naive indeed. This is an ever present temptation. When such offers are considered, please remember, to accept such is an admission of mind-corruption and truth-robbery.

Vs. 6. To balance the scale of values, Paul adds that in godliness there is great gain. The principle of gain through godliness is true. But this godliness must be genuine—in it, and in it alone we must find our self-sufficiency. The contentment others seek in money, we must find in fellowship with God through Christ.

Vs. 7. Here is an axiom declared and emphasized by many, ancient and modern, profane and divine—"There are no pockets in a shroud". we shall take out of this world exactly what we brought in—nothing! Why should our time and energies be spent on those things which perish with the using? The very things we have prepared for contentment will not bring it, even if we are afforded the opportunity to try them; which we many times are not. "Happiness is within, not without."

Vs. 8. This verse pre-supposes we have seen the emptiness of striving after soul satisfaction in the husks of material possessions. When once we are thoroughly persuaded that security, peace, and hope, are *not* found in riches, we are ready to be shown just where they can be found. Man never gives up in his search for hope, happiness and security. When these are found in Jesus and His kingdom-service, how shall we balance the natural need for food and shelter? When we have enough to eat, and covering for our body and head, we are satisfied. What were the creature comforts of our blessed Lord? and yet He is our example in successful living. When shall we follow Him?

Vs. 9. There are men driven by various types of desires; but of all the desires, the lust to be rich is at once the most popular and perilous. Such men are here described as an animal who has fallen into a trap from which he cannot escape. The bait is taken, and the trap springs to take its victim. What a sore trial man brings upon himself when once he reaches after the illusive pot of gold. Money was never intended to be an end, only a means. Money can be a wonderful servant, but what a monster for a master! Once we open the door to money-love, there are many related sins to entertain. Pride, honor, power, popularity—all must be considered—all are foolish and hurtful. Paul changes the figure from an animal trap to a struggling swimmer. The swimmer struggles to save himself, but all who watch know he has spent his strength and is drowning. He is about to go down for the last time. What a tragic picture. But when we remember the drowning is in the lake of fire, and the death is eternal, we are indeed sad! How hard it is for a rich man to enter the kingdom of heaven, or for those who are eager to be rich.

Vs. 10. This is a conclusion to the foregoing verse, and a warning to Timothy. At the base of this evil tree of many sorrows, you shall find the root of money-love. To follow after mammon is to leave the faith. We have but one life to invest—when we use it up in the pursuit of money, or what money can give, we have no time or energy left for God. We have not only forsaken the service required of the faithful, but we have forsaken the basic tenet of the Faith—"deny yourself." How gradual and easy it is to be led astray by money-love. What seems to be an advantage becomes a terrible disadvantage—what we intended to use is using us—what we hoped was a bed of ease has become a couch of spears. The love of money will obligate us to fulfill our commitments. One after another, sorrow upon sorrow pierces our hearts. This is spiritual suicide!

Fact Questions 6:3-10

169. What is the general content of this, the closing section of this letter?

170. State two results of pride as a false motive for Christian work.
171. Explain the meaning of "puffed-up", and "doting".
172. Show the deception of error.
173. Both pride and money-love proceed from one source—what is it?
174. Explain how godliness offers great gain.
175. Why mention that we brought nothing into the world and we will take nothing out?
176. How is our Lord an example in the use of "creature comforts"?
177. How desribe those who are "minded to be rich"? Why?
178. Show how the love of money leads to spiritual suicide.

2. PROPER WALK 11-16

Text 6:11-16

11 But thou, O man of God, flee these things; and follow after righteousness, godliness, faith, love, patience, meekness. 12 Fight the good fight of the faith, lay hold on the life eternal, whereunto thou wast called, and didst confess the good confession in the sight of many witnesses. 13 I charge thee in the sight of God, who giveth life to all things, and of Christ Jesus, who before Pontius Pilate witnessed the good confession; 14 that thou keep the commandment, without spot, without reproach, until the appearing of our Lord Jesus Christ: 15 which in its own times he shall show, who is the blessed and only Potentate, the King of kings, and Lord of lords; 16 who only hath immortality, dwelling in light unapproachable, whom no man hath seen, nor can see; to whom be honor and power eternal. Amen.

Thought Questions 6:11-16

234. In what sense was Timothy a "man of God"? Cf. I Sam. 2:27 and II Tim. 3:17 for an answer.
235. Are we to infer that money-lovers do not belong to God?
236. From what is the man of God to flee? Please specify from the text.
237. It is not enough to turn away from sin, we must turn toward God. Look up the Greek tense in which the verbs—"flee" and "follow" appear.
238. How is the word "righteousness" used?
239. Explain in a very practical sense the meaning of "godliness".
240. In what way should we pursue "faith"?

241. Must we work to obtain "love"?
242. Explain the place of patience and meekness in the life of the minister.
243. Does "the fighting spirit" have any place in the life of the preacher?
244. What is "the good fight of the faith"?
245. How could Timothy be in present possession of "eternal life" and yet be admonished to "lay hold" upon it?
246. Who called Timothy to eternal life? Where and when? How?
247. What is "the good confession" made by Timothy? Prove your answer.
248. What makes this confession "good"?
249. Is this a "confession" or a "profession"?
250. Before whom did Timothy make the good confession? Be specific.
251. Why the urgency of the charge given in vs. 13?
252. Show how the one quality of God here given (vs. 13) is appropriate. Do the same with the single quality of Jesus (vs. 13b).
253. What is "the commandment" of vs. 14?
254. What could Timothy do that would bring a "spot" upon the commandment? Who would bring the "reproach"?
255. Did Paul expect the second coming of Christ in the lifetime of Timothy? Explain vs. 14b.
256. Who is to show what in vs. 15?
257. Who is "the blessed and only Potentate"?
258. If Christ or God only hath immortality, how can we say that man is born an immortal being?
259. How could vs. 16 refer to Christ, when it states "whom no man hath seen, nor can see'?

Paraphrase 6:11-16

11 Therefore do thou, O servant of God, flee these things; and pursue justice in all thy dealings, piety towards God, the firmest faith in the gospel, love to the souls of men, patience in afflictions, and meekness under provocations.

12 Since these virtues are not inconsistent with courage, combat the good combat of faith, by boldly maintaining the true doctrine of Christ against infidels and false teachers; and, as a conqueror in this combat, lay hold on eternal life, the prize, to the attainment of which thou wast called; and in particular, confess the

good confession, that Jesus Christ is the Son of God, in the presence of all mankind.

13 I charge thee, in the presence of God, who raiseth all from the dead, to reward every one according to his works, and who, if thou lose thy life in the good combat, will give thee eternal life; and in the presence of Christ Jesus, who witnessed under Pontius Pilate the good confession, and sealed it with his blood.

14 That thou obey this commandment of confessing the good confession, with out spot in respect of the commandment itself, and unblamable in respect of thy performance thereof, which will contribute to preserve the good confession in the world, till the appearing of our Lord Jesus Christ himself, to raise the dead, and judge the whole human race.

15 Which appearing in his own season, the season which he himself hath fixed, the blessed and only Potentate in the universe will shew, even the King of kings, and Lord of lords; the King and Lord who rules with irresistible power all other kings and lords:

16 Who alone hath life without either beginning or ending, and dwelleth in light inaccessible to mortals, which therefore no man hath seen, or can see, in this mortal body; to whom be ascribed honour and might everlasting. And to shew that this is the truth concerning the nature of God, I say Amen.

Comment 6:11-16

Vs. 11. A very powerful positive word is given in this verse. Paul has just discussed certain men of error; he now refers to "The Man of God". The use of this expression is not confined to Timothy alone—all Christians are to be "Men of God." Cf. II Tim. 3:17. We belong to God. Cf. I Cor. 6:19, 20. When once we completely awaken to our ownership, we will be ready as Timothy was to follow out the admonitions of this verse. Please notice that Paul does not say to fight but to flee. We are to fight the good fight of the faith, but in the area of temptation we are to do what Joseph did from Potiphar's house—run! None of us are a match for Satan, "to will is present, but to do that which is good is not." Do not entertain Satan's suggestions, whether they be in the realm of false doctrine, pride, avarice, or whatever, do not tarry with them, *RUN* from them, resist and deny them, do not discuss them! The tense of the verb suggests that this be an attitude of conduct—"keep fleeing". We are not only fleeing from, we are following after. The sad condition of the men described in vs. 3-10 did not develop in one day—neither will the qualities of character here described be ours, without a steadfast pursuit of them. Timothy is admonished to place up before himself, as a runner sets before him a goal, these virtues—and then stretch every nerve to reach them. What are they?:

righteousness:
Put forth every effort to be right before God and man. Righteousness is simply doing that which is right. This is a *virtue* that we must pursue, or we shall never lay hold upon it. This we do by a study and practice of His Word. We then *must* give ourselves to the only Power for right doing. Except He strengthens us by His Spirit in the *inward* man we shall never be righteous.

godliness:
Someone has suggested that the six virtues here listed, i.e.: (1) Righteousness; (2) Godliness; (3) Faith; (4) Love; (5) Patience; (6) Meekness—could be divided into 3 pairs: (1) Righteousness and Godliness: our attitude toward God; (2) Faith and Love: these are the source of righteousness and godliness; (3) Patience and Meekness: the virtues necessary to live righteously and godly. Perhaps this is true—at least the conclusion is a good one. Is it possible to be godlike? Not without a consistent effort on our part. But we are not called upon to do more than our Saviour did—to us are given the same weapons He used in winning the battle of godliness. He "condemned sin in the flesh" and lived a godly life; this He expects us to do.

faith:
Why does Paul admonish Timothy to follow after faith? Didn't Timothy have faith? We are sure that he did. This is an exhortation for the expression and work of the faith already possessed—as we say in our day: "To have the courage of his convictions." Paul wanted Timothy to *live* by faith.

love:
What we have said of faith could also be said of love. Each of these virtues are to be activated. Timothy is never to believe he has loved as he could, there is always a fresh expression to be given. We can always go further in devotion to both God and man: see our Saviour ahead of us, beckoning us onward and upward in the path of love.

patience:
What a great and continual need would be found for this quality of character. In Ephesus there was need for patience with the many problems already described in this letter. We shall only have patience in our problems when we have some hope of solution of them. This we find in Christ and His Way of life. Paul does not say for how long we are to be patient—it must be a continual pursuit on our part.

meekness:
This is never to be equated with weakness. Meekness is strength under control. Moses was the meekest man on earth. Our Lord was meek and lowly in heart. We could not think of either of these as being weak.

Vs. 12. Continuing the thought of the proper walk of the man of God, Timothy is urged to "contend well in the good contest"; or to "fight well in the good battle". There is some disagreement as to which figure is used—the athletic field, or the battle field. In either case Paul's word is the same—he says: Be actively, aggressively engaged in the contest. Feel that you have a personal responsibility in this matter. No one else can take your place. If you hold back, "the faith" will suffer. "The fighting spirit", so much a part of God's man Paul, is so sorely needed today, It would seem that most of God's soldiers are on furlough or most of his athletes have turned "professional".

"Life eternal" is held up as the prize at the end of the race. We are to eagerly reach out to take hold upon it, but not until we have finished the course. Paul exhorts Timothy, that even now he is to stretch forth his hand in eager anticipation of taking hold of the final and highest prize. All during the race, maintain just such an attitude. The prize is well worth the effort; it is unlike the fading leaves of the world's cinder track.

To such a race and to such an attitude, God called you when you became a Christian, when you confessed your faith in the sight of many witnesses. When and where did God call Timothy into the good contest?—at Lystra when Paul first preached the gospel in this pagan town. It was just before his baptism, in the presence of the town-people of Lystra, and possibly Derbe and Iconium, that Timothy declared his faith in Jesus as Lord and Saviour.

Paul is saying: "let the memory of your confession before men now strengthen your resolve to run and to fight for the one whose name you confessed."

Vs. 13. Here is something stronger than an exhortation: Paul solemnly *charges* Timothy with his holy responsibility. In many ways we can consider verses 11-16 as the climax and conclusion to this wonderful letter. In vs. 13-17 we have the top of the climax—"In the light of all I have previously written in this letter about error and truth, about sin and the Saviour, I charge you—". This seems to be the tenor of the thought here. The content of the charge is the central thought, but do not forget the witnesses to it—!: God, who gives and preserves the very life you now have, is watching to welcome you at the end of the race. He is there to approve your good efforts all along the track. Our annointed Saviour is also a witness. He knows what it is to pledge Himself and confess His faith and purpose. He did it under far more trying conditions than you—before Pontius Pilate! Can we fail Him when He did not fail us?

Vs. 14. Here is the content of the charge: "*Keep the commandment without spot, without reproach*". Timothy is personally responsible for preserving intact the whole gospel, or of keeping the gospel whole. Timothy confessed his faith and confidence in Christ and His work. Paul now urges fulfillment of this confession. We take the word "commandment" to refer to "the faith" or "the gospel". "Without spot" refers to any deviation or change, man might make in this perfect message. There are various ways in which our conduct can cast reproach upon the message we preach.

Paul thought of the second coming of Christ as an ever present reality. Should Jesus return while Timothy was preaching in Ephesus, He would find him faithful; ready to give a good account of his stewardship. We like the expression of D. Edmond Hiebert on this point—he says: "While Paul eagerly looked for that event, he never pretended to know the date of the return. The overwhelming magnitude of the Second Coming made it seem near, and shrivel up all intervening time, like some vast mountain, which, as it rears its gigantic peak above the horizon, seems near, though actually is a long distance away." (p. 118, 119)

Vs. 15. The Second Coming will be a great day of revelation, so very many things will then be revealed; things that are now concealed. One which is not usually mentioned is here emphasized: *The Second Coming of Christ will reveal the character of God.* Notice, please: (1) He will be seen as the blessed and only Potentate (2) King of kings (3) Lord of lords (4) Who only hath immortality (5) dwells in an unapproachable light (6) whom no man hath seen, nor can see (7) to whom all honor and power are due.

We take the little expression, "which in its (his) own times he shall show," to refer to the Second Coming as brought about by God. Only the Father knows the time. Here is a reference to when He shall reveal to man "His time and season".

Vs. 16. In what sense are we to understand the expression: "Who only hath immortality"? God is the *only source* of immortality. He only has immortality within Himself. For each of us immortality is given, not so with God (or with "the Word" Cf. Jn. 1:1).

God covers Himself with glory as with a garment. This light is so intense man can not approach God. When Saul of Tarsus beheld but momentarily a little of the effulgence of the presence of God, he was blinded and thrown to the ground. Because God is a Spirit and man can not, while in this body, see a spirit, no man hath seen God, nor can he hope to see Him while man remains in his earthly tabernacle. Men have seen a physical manifestation of the power of God in the form of Angels, or of some other manifestation. This has been only for man's benefit. God in essence is spirit—man cannot see a spirit, therefore indeed "no man hath seen, nor can see".

If such a Being possesses the seven qualities just described, we can say with Paul: "to whom be honor and power eternal." The "amen" seals all that has just been said of this great God.

Fact Questions 6:11-16

179. In what sense was Timothy a "man of God"? In what sense does this term apply to all Christians?
180. Specify two things from which Timothy was to flee.
181. How often is Timothy to flee and follow? Explain in your own words the meaning of the virtues stated in Vs. 11.
182. What is the fight of the faith? Are we to fight a "good" fight or is the fight "good"?
183. If we already possess eternal life, how can we "lay hold" upon it?
184. To what was Timothy called? Cf. 12b. When did Timothy confess the good confession?

185. Why did Paul give Timothy the charge of Vs. 13, 14?
186. What was "the commandment"?
187. Did Paul believe there was a possibility of the second coming of Christ in the time of Timothy? Explain.
188. What is the meaning of the expression: "Which in its own times he shall show".
189. Old Testament references can be found in which each of the seven attributes of God here given are also stated. Cf. (1) Deut. 6:4 (2) Ezek. 26:7 (3) Deut. 10:17 (4) Is. 40:28 (5) Ex. 34:35 (6) Deut. 4:12 (7) Neh. 8:6. Please find and read these.
190. Explain the sense in which God "only hath immortality", and the sense in which "no man hath seen God".

3. FAITHFUL MINISTRY 17-21a

Text 6:17-21a

17 Charge them that are rich in this present world, that they be not highminded, nor have their hope set on the uncertainty of riches, but on God, who giveth us richly all things to enjoy: 18 that they do good, that they be rich in good works, that they be ready to distribute, willing to communicate; 19 laying up in store for themselves a good foundation against the time to come, that they may lay hold on the life which is life indeed. 20 O Timothy, guard that which is committed unto thee, turning away from the profane babblings and oppositions of the knowledge which is falsely so called; 21 which some professing have erred concerning the faith.

Thought Questions 6:17-21a

260. How would Timothy carry out the injunction of Paul as in Vs. 17?
261. In what town were these rich people living?
262. Why would rich folk be especially tempted to be "high minded"?
263. Specify "their hope" in riches—show how deceptive it is.
264. Show in particular, "the uncertainty of riches".
265. How would Timothy know that these rich folk were fulfilling his word?
266. Does Paul say in 17b that God created all things for man's enjoyment? How does this affect pride and materialism?

267. The rich are to be rich in good works—isn't this the responsibility of all? Why specify the rich?
268. Meaning of "ready to distribute, willing to communicate".
269. Can money be used to lay up a good foundation for heaven?
270. Is Paul saying that however good life might be here, it can not compare with the life to come? How does this relate to earthly treasure?
271. What was Timothy to guard?
272. How was Timothy to guard it?
273. Was "the deposit" with Timothy or Christ?
274. What were the "profane babblings"?
275. What is "the knowledge" of vs. 20?
276. There is a false knowledge and a true knowledge—explain the difference.
277. Some professing themselves to be wise become fools—what particular false knowledge was before Paul's mind in vs. 21a?

Paraphrase 6:17-21a

17 Though riches often prove a great snare to the possessors, they may be retained innocently. Therefore, charge the rich in the present world, to beware of pride, and of seeking their happiness from riches, the possession of which is so uncertain: But to trust in God, who ever liveth to make them happy, and who supplieth to us plentifully all things really necessary for enjoyment.

18 And instead of employing their riches merely in gratifying their senses, rather to use them in doing good works, and to be rich in those lovely works whereby the happiness of society is promoted: To be ready to distribute a part of their riches to the poor, communicative of their time and pains for advancing the interests of truth and virtue in the world;

19 Providing for themselves, not money, which can be of no use to them in the other world, but what is infinitely better, a good foundation to stand on in the day of judgment, that they may lay hold on the prize of eternal life.

20 O Timothy, preserve the doctrine committed in trust to thee, avoiding the impious, noisy, senseless talking of the Judaizers, and the oppositions to the gospels, founded on wrong interpretations of the Jewish scriptures, which they dignify with the appellation of knowledge; but it is falsely so named.

21 Which knowledge of the scriptures, some teachers professing,

have erred with respect to the true Christian faith. But may the grace of God be with thee, to preserve thee from error. Amen.

Comment 6:17-21a

Vs. 17. There are those who wish they were rich—with such we have already dealt (Cf. 6:9, 10). Then there are those few who are blessed with material possessions. It is with such persons we are concerned. The gospel has a direct and personal application to every life. To the rich there are certain and particular temptations to avoid. Timothy is to speak with a good deal of urgency to these folk, about the temptation to look down on their less fortunate brothers. They might remember the one who "though He was rich, yet for their sakes He became poor". Or the words of our Lord to the rich young ruler. There is a second temptation of special concern. Do not set your hopes on riches and what they can do. How easy it is for money to fail. Set your hope on God who never fails. There is a play on words in the last half of this verse. Notice that Paul includes himself and all other Christians, in the thought that God has made us rich. All things are of God. We are rich because God has so blessed us—"naught have we gotten but what we received—grace has bestowed it since we believed." What a blessed truth to know that all good things were given for our enjoyment. This surely contradicts the thought that there is evil in matter. God intended our enjoyment of all material possessions, within the framework of His Will.

Vs. 18. The positive advantages of wealth are outlined in this verse. To whom much is given much is required—even in the material realm. Notice the four ways to enjoy riches: (1) To do good—i.e. to find some area where help is needed, and supply the need. This is good and acceptable in the sight of God. (2) Be rich in good works. This would seem to be but an emphasis of the former admonition. It suggests that the satisfaction and pleasure of the rich, will be found in work for Christ through their riches, instead of in the bank account. (3) Be ready to share well and generously with others—find the real meaning of "it is more blessed to give than to receive". This is easily said by those who have but little—but it was originally said by Him who possessed all things (Acts 20:35). (4) Be ready to associate closely with those who have less—feel a real partnership with every other Christian—rich or poor. How pointed and pertinent these words are for the wealthy in Ephesus, and in all other places.

Vs. 19. The words of our Lord come imediately to mind upon reading this verse. Paul suggests that the rich can use their money and influence in such a manner as to lay up for themselves a warm welcome into heaven. This is just what Jesus meant when He said—"make to yourselves friends of the unrighteous mammon, that when it shall fail they may receive you into the eternal tabernacles" (Cf. Luke 16:9). Our money can and should be used to win souls—when it is, then the souls won who have gone on before will be waiting to welcome us into life which is life indeed. An awareness of this truth on the part of the rich, becomes within their consciousness and before God, "a good foundation" for appearing before God on judgment.

Vs. 20. In one verse we have the summation of the whole letter. God and Paul have made an investment in Timothy—they expect returns on their investment. To Timothy was entrusted "the gospel"—by this we mean, that which Paul has written in this letter and all the words of every inspired writer. To guard it, Timothy was not to simply keep it buried in his heart and home, but to keep it like a banker who keeps a great deposit of money. Thus it would not only be intact, but would be used and increased to the owner's advantage.

Positive instructions as to just how such a guarding is done, are found in the latter half of vs. 20. The same instructions with which Paul opened the letter (Cf. 1:4-6) are given to close it. Paul asks Timothy to shun, to ignore, to turn away from all such empty chatter as that which he hears from certain "law teachers". To argue with such persons is to give dignity to their teaching, which it does not deserve. Such false teachers imagine themselves to be full of knowledge, when they are only puffed up with their own ego. If God did not reveal the information in the body of truth called "the faith" (which we know now as the New Testament), then such information is to be treated as "profane" or unclean. "One guards the truth by turning away from all insipid ranting".

Vs. 21. Regardless of how ridiculous the teaching might be, there are always some who will follow it. When such persons leave "the faith" for empty babblings, they do so professing to have some new and better light. They are actually in darkness and have "missed the mark".

Fact Questions 6:17-21a

191. There are two groups associated with riches—name them.
192. What is the meaning of the expression "high minded"? How can we avoid this temptation?
193. Explain the play on words in vs. 17.
194. God has given us richly all things to enjoy—how do we fulfill this purpose of God?
195. What is meant by telling the rich to "do good"?
196. The rich are to be "rich in good works"—specify two or three good works in which they could be rich.
197. Explain: "ready to distribute, willing to communicate".
198. Show how Luke 16:9 and vs. 19 discuss the same subject.
199. What "deposit" did God and Paul have in Timothy?
200. Just how was Timothy to "guard the deposit"?
201. What was the "knowledge which is falsely so called"?
202. Give the meaning of the expression: "erred concerning the faith".

CONCLUSION 6:21b

Text 6:21b

Grace be with you.

Thought Questions 6:21b

278. Just how was the word "grace" used here?
279. Is anyone besides Timothy included in the word "you"? Explain.

Paraphrase 6:21b

21b But may the grace of God be with thee, to preserve thee from error. Amen.

Comment 6:21b

Vs. 21b. This is the briefest of all the conclusions to Paul's letters. This same conclusion is found in Colossians. The word "you" is in the plural form in the Greek text.

EXAMINATION OVER CHAPTER SIX OF I TIMOTHY

1. Give in your own words Paul's instructions concerning slaves who have unbelieving masters, and those with believing ones.
2. Would the instructions of Paul abolish slavery? Explain.

3. What is considered "different doctrine"? What is the result of such teaching?
4. State and explain three of the wrong motives in teaching.
5. In what should the Christian find contentment? Do you accept Paul's estimate of what is sufficient of this world's goods? Explain.
6. State and explain four of the results of desiring to be rich.
7. State and explain three of the virtues after which the man of God is to pursue.
8. Explain: "taking hold of eternal life".
9. Why and how is the second coming of Christ introduced into Paul's exhortation to Timothy?
10. What is the deposit Timothy is to guard, and how is he to guard it? What is the falsely-named knowledge"?

EXAMINATION OVER PAUL'S FIRST LETTER TO TIMOTHY

1. Reproduce the outline of the letter.
2. "Paul, an apostle of Christ Jesus according to the Commandment of God our Saviour" . . . . Explain the "Commandment" in this verse.
3. ". . . . and the goal of the charge is love out of a pure heart" . . . . Explain the charge, and the arrival at the goal, i.e. how the goal is achieved.
4. "But we know that the law is good, if one uses it lawfully . . . ." Explain the lawful use of the law.
5. ". . . . but I received mercy because being ignorant I acted in unbelief . . . ." Show how ignorance relates to mercy—be careful here.
6. ". . . . the prophecies which led the way to you, that you might wage in them the good warfare . . . ." Explain the prophecies, and Timothy's use of them.
7. "In order that we may lead a tranquil and quiet life in all godliness and dignity." What is going to provide this type of life? Explain the cause of which this is a result.
8. "I desire therefore, that men pray in every place, lifting up holy hands, without wrath and disputing." Discuss the connection between prayer, wrath and disputing.
9. Give the two reasons for saying: "I do not permit a woman to teach."
10. "Faithful is the Word: if someone reaches after an overseer-

ship, he desires a good work." Discuss the words: "reaches after" and "good work".

11. Discuss two mental qualifications, and two personality qualifications of the bishop.
12. Would a man who had developed the ability to superintend well by other means than rearing a family, be excluded from the eldership? If so why? If not why not?
13. Explain the following phrase: "And let these first be tested".
14. Is there room for females in the office of deacon? Discuss.
15. Give meaning to the following: "Because every created thing of God is good, and nothing to be thrown away, being received with thanksgiving: *for it is sanctified thru God's word and petition*". Explain especially the last phrase.
16. Explain how godliness is profitable for all things.
17. What gift or gifts did Timothy have? How did he get them? What was he to do with them?
18. Answer the following questions about the enrollment of widows: 1) What is the meaning of the term "enrollment"? 2) For what purpose? 3) What qualifications? (state and explain at least two) 4) Should we practice it now?
19. What is the "double honor" of the elders?
20. Who is the "blessed and only potentate . . . ." Please explain from the context why you answer as you do.

PAUL'S LETTER TO TITUS

INTRODUCTION

PAUL'S LETTER TO TITUS

We refer you to our *introduction* (pp. 19,20) as to the background of both the letter and the one to whom it was addressed.

It is very important that you have an analytical grasp of this epistle.

Here are four outlines of the letter. Please read through the epistle of Titus using these outlines as guides. Read the epistle *four* times, once for each outline—notice the points of the outline as you read.

1. E. K. Simpson: (*The Pastoral Epistles*, the Greek Text with Introduction and Commentary, Wm. B. Eerdmans Pub. Co., Grand Rapids, Michigan.)
   1. Salutation 1:1-4
   2. Ministerial Qualifications 1:5-9
   3. The Cretan Character 1:10-16
   4. Admonitions to Seniors and Juniors 2:1-8
   5. Directions to Servants 2:9,10
   6. The Life Consonant With the Dispensation of Grace 2:11-15
   7. Demeanor to the Outside World 3:1, 2
   8. The Contrast between Past and Present 3:3
   9. The Glory of the Gospel of God's Grace 3:4-7
   10. Epitome of Counsels 3:8-11
   11. Personalia 3:12-15
2. Victor E. Hoven (*The New Testament Epistles* — Analysis and Notes. Baker Book House. Grand Rapids 6, Michigan)

INTRODUCTION 1:1-4

1. The writer, 1-3. In service Paul is God's "bondservant"; in office he is Christ's "apostle." His activity is "according to," or with a view to, producing "faith," by preaching the gospel; "knowledge," by teaching the gospel; "godliness" by exhortation to live the gospel—all of which is "in hope of eternal life," promised "before times eternal" and "intrusted" to Paul. This enabled Titus to speak by divine authority to false teachers in Crete.

2. Greeting to Titus, 4. He was Paul's convert by "a common faith," a faith for everybody and for all time; was encouraged by benediction of divine "grace" and "peace".

PART I. WHY PAUL LEFT TITUS IN CRETE, 1:5-16.

1. To set things in order, 5. The whole island his parish; every church his responsibility; Paul's teaching his rule of faith and practice. Cp. Gal. 6:16; Phil. 3:16.

2. To appoint elders, 5-9. Cp. I Tim. 3:1-7. They were to be "blameless" (a) in family life, 6, (b) in personal life, 7, 8, (c) in teaching, 9.

3. To stop destructive teachers, 10-16. Not only Titus, but the elders must do this (9). Verses 10-14 describe their character and conduct, confirmed by the Greek poet Epimenides and accepted by Paul. In 15, 16, the state of their heart and conscience is given. See Matt. 15:19-20. What a field of labor!

PART II. THE TEACHING TITUS WAS TO ENFORCE. 2:1-3:11

1. Christian character in relation to the church, 2:1-15.

a. Conduct which befits sound doctrine, 1-10. "Sound" means healthful uncorrupted teaching, opposed to doctrine of false teachers which had made the church mentally and morally sick. Christians of all age levels, men and women, are enrolled as learners. In order to be effective, Titus himself must be model in speech and behavior.

b. Motives for such conduct, 11-14. They are: (1) The grace of God, 11, 12. It has "appeared," become visible, in Christ, John 1:14, bringing salvation, recorded for instruction of right living in three directions: "soberly" as to self, "righteously" as of fellow-man, "godly" in relation to God. (2) The return of Christ, 13. This also motivates right living, for He is our only "hope" of life eternal, 1:2, and He returns for judgment, Matt. 25:31ff. (3) The death of Christ, 14. He gave Himself on our behalf that He might redeem, purify and possess us. These things Titus was to teach and enforce, backed by all authority of Christ.

2. Christian character in relation to the world, 3:1-7.

a. Duties to civil authority, 1, 2. Judaizers held that worshipers of Jehovah need not obey pagan magistrates, not so Paul, cp. Rom. 13:1-7.

b. Reasons for subjection, 3-7. First, there is recollection of the old life, 3; next, transition from the old to the new, 4-7.

It is motivated by "the kindness of God," accomplished, not by man's moral goodness, but by two agencies—"washing of regeneration" (laver, bath of rebirth, or immersion into Christ) "and renewing of the Holy Spirit," that is, renewing of the human spirit by the Spirit of God. Cp. Ps. 51:10. In conversion the Spirit presents to the human mind what to do to be saved from past sins, I Pet. 1:23; Jas. 1:18; the result is a new person. After conversion the Spirit continually renews the mind of a Christian by His word, II Cor. 4:16; Eph. 4:22-24. The result is a new life. The final objective is "eternal life".

3. Duty of Titus concerning these things, 8-11. He is to affirm confidently, shun all that is unprofitable and maintain discipline.

CONCLUSION, 3:12-15

1. Directions to Titus, 12-14. When Paul sent either Artemas or Tychicus to succeed Titus in Crete, he was to hasten to Paul at Nicopolis; Zenas and Apollos were to be set forward by supplying their needs for travel; the Cretans, who were "idle gluttons," 1:12, were to apply themselves to some honest occupation.

2. Salutations and benediction, 15. Salutations come from Paul and his fellow-workers, include all in the "faith" and exclude the false teachers. The benediction of "grace" is not for Titus alone, but for all the churches in Crete.

3. William Hendriksen *(New Testament Commentary*—Exposition of the Pastoral Epistles, Baker Book House, Grand Rapids 6, Michigan).

Theme: The Apostle Paul, Writing to Titus, Gives Directions for the Promotion of the Spirit of Sanctification.

Chapter 1: In Congregational Life.

- A. The Address and Salutation.
- B. Well-qualified elders must be appointed in every town.
- C. Reason: Crete is not lacking in disreputable people who must be sternly rebuked.

Chapter 2: In Family and Individual Life.

- A. All classes of individuals that compose the home—circle should conduct themselves in such a manner that by their life they may adorn the doctrine of God, their Savior.

B. Reason: to all, the grace of God has appeared unto sanctification and joyful expectation of the appearing in glory of our great God and Savior, Jesus Christ.

Chapter 3: In Social (i.e. Public) Life.

A. Believers should be obedient to the authorities. They should be kind to all men, since it was the kindness of God our Savior—not our own works! —which brought salvation.

B. On the other hand, foolish questions should be shunned, and factious men who refuse to heed admonition should be rejected.

C. Concluding directions with respect to kingdom-travelers (Artemas or Tychicus, Titus, Zenas, Apollos) and Cretan believers in general. Greetings.

4. John H. Bratt (*Back to God Hour*, 10858 Michigan Ave., Chicago 28, Ill.)

Contents

Greetings — 1:1-4
Theme: Pastoral Directions

I. Concerning Elders and Errorists 1:5-16.
   A. The Kind of Elders to be Ordained 1:5-9.
   B. Dangerous Errorists 1:10-16.

II. Concerning Various Groups in the Congregation 2:1-15.
   A. The elderly men 2:1-2.
   B. The elderly women 2:3-5.
   C. The young men 2:6-8.
   D. The slaves 2:9-10.

III. Concerning the position of Christians generally 3:1-11.
   A. Their citizenship 3:1-2.
   B. Their past and present status 3:3-8.
   C. Who and what to shun 3:9-11.

Conclusion 3:12-15.

Please originate your own outline of this short letter — if you must make a composite of the four we have given — do so. The important point of learning here is that you think through the analysis of the whole letter. *Do it.*

Here is the outline we shall follow in our study of the letter:

PAUL'S LETTER TO TITUS

Greetings 1:1-4.

I. The care of the church 1:5-16.
   1. The selection and qualifications of elders 1:5-9.
   2. The description and refutation of false teachers 1:10-16.

II. The conduct of church members 2:1-15.
   1. Older men 2:1-2.
   2. Older women 2:3.
   3. Young women 2:4-5.
   4. Young men 2:6-8.
   5. Slaves 2:9-10.
   6. The motives for conduct 2:11-15.

III. Church members in society 3:1-11.
   1. As citizens 3:1-2.
   2. The motive for proper conduct 3:3-7.
   3. Truth and error 3:8-11.

Conclusion3:12-15.

GREETINGS 1:1-4

Text 1:1-4

1 Paul, a servant of God, and an apostle of Jesus Christ, according to the faith of God's elect, and the knowledge of the truth which is according to godliness, 2 in hope of eternal life, which God, who cannot lie, promised before times eternal; 3 but in his own seasons manifested his word in the message, wherewith I was intrusted according to the commandment of God our Saviour; 4 to Titus, my true child after a common faith: Grace and peace from God the Father and Christ Jesus our Saviour.

Thought Questions 1:1-4

1. Someone said, "the expression 'God's bond servant' occurs nowhere else at the head of his Epistles.". Is this true? Please take time and thought enough to answer.
2. Give the meaning of the name "apostle"; show how it has special reference to Paul.
3. How could "the faith of God's elect" regulate the apostleship of Paul?
4. Is "the faith" in vs. 1 subjective or objective? Explain why you answer as you do.
5. How does one become one of God's "elect"?
6. Does Paul say here that he was appointed an apostle for the purpose of leading "the elect" into a knowledge of the truth? How did you arrive at your conclusion?

7. Does "the truth" lead to godliness or proceed from it?
8. Are we to understand the hope of eternal life is a part of "the truth" into which Paul was to lead the elect?
9. Are we to equate "eternal life" with heaven? Is eternal life an extension of this present life? Explain.
10. Is Paul saying here (vs. 2) that God had provisions made for the eternal life of His elect even before He created the world?
11. What has been manifested in due season? (Cf. Gal. 4:4). Please be careful in your answer to this question — did God manifest His Son — His gospel — or His purpose?
12. What is "the command"—or "commandment"—of vs. 3?
13. In what sense was Titus Paul's "true child"?
14. Explain the phrase "common faith."
15. Show the distinction in the use of the words "grace" and peace."

Paraphrase 1:1-4

1 Paul, a servant of God, and an apostle of Jesus Christ, sent forth by him in order to promote the faith of the Gentiles, the elected people of God, and to persuade them to acknowledge the gospel, whose end is to make men godly and virtuous in every respect;
2 In hope that they shall also obtain that resurrection to eternal life, which God, who cannot lie, promised to believers of all nations in the persons of Adam and Abraham, long before the Jewish dispensation began.
3 The knowledge of God's promise was long confined to the Jews; but He hath manifested to all, in its proper season, his promise, by the preaching of the gospel, with which I am entrusted by Christ, according to the commandment of God, the original contriver of the method of our salvation:
4 To Titus, my genuine son by the common faith, the faith in Christ which the Gentiles are permitted to have in common with the Jews, I wish gracious assistances, merciful deliverances, and eternal life, from God the Father, and the Lord Jesus Christ, the accomplisher of our salvation.

Comment 1:1-4

Vs. 1. Paul refers to himself as a slave to Jesus Christ in Rom. 1:1, Gal. 1:10, Phil. 1:1; but here and only here he identifies himself as a "slave of God." Actually there are two characteristics of the Apostle given by himself to himself:

(1) Slave of God, (2) Apostle of Jesus Christ. Paul says he is a slave and an apostle, with thte approval of and in agreement with "the faith" known and believed by the Christians of his day. Such Christians are here called "the elect."

Those believers on the isle of Crete, who knew the revealed truth as given by the inspired writers of that day, would immediately accept Paul's apostleship as from Christ, and his service as to God.

Such revealed truth leads to being like God, or godly.

We are aware that the above interpretation is not acceptable to some; however, after a very careful study of both sides of the issue, we feel Paul was saying his service to God and his apostleship from Christ was "in agreement with" *the faith* of God's elect, and not for the purpose of inducing faith in "the elect." Of course, we believe that elsewhere Paul states that his apostleship was for the purpose of producing faith—but not here.

We refer you to another book in *The Bible Study Textbook Series* for a study of the expression "God's elect": *Romans Realized*, pp. 155-158. Suffice it to say here that God elects those who elect to follow Him. The choice of election is in the sure knowledge of God and the free will of man at the same time, with no conflict to either.

The use made of this epistle by Titus on the isle of Crete must not be forgotten. Whenever the teaching of Titus is called into question he can refer immediately to this letter, which is in perfect harmony with *the faith* or the truth. The elect of God who have a knowledge of the truth will accept the message of Paul through Titus—those who do not accept it are in error.

Vs. 2. Paul was called to be an apostle of Jesus Christ in the hope of eternal life. Paul served God as a slave serves his master in the hope of reward. He will not be disappointed, for the never-lying-God has made this promise of eternal life; indeed, this promise has been in preparation for ages past.

How are we to understand the little expression "eternal life"? Is this to be equated with heaven? We believe it is. However, it carries the same overtones as the expression of the rich young ruler; (Mark 10:17) he inquired, "what must I do that I might inherit *eternal life*?" This young man wanted life that could not be found in morality. The rich young man came to the right source. Jesus came to give us life (John 10:10) and life that is life indeed. Paul found this life here and now; but he knew, as we do, that the largest share of it is yet to come. Enjoying the benefits of life here; having promise of continuing such life in ideal conditions in the new earth; such promise issuing from the unlying-God is enough to give incentive to anyone!

How shall we understand the expression "before times eternal"? Shall we look in the Old Testament for the promise of "eternal life"? In other words—does the expression refer to the Old Testament age? We rather prefer the thought that God promised to His Son "before the foundation of the world," that all who would come through His death would have eternal life.

Vs. 3. It is through the good news that life and immortality are brought to light. Whereas the offer and hope of eternal life had been in the mind of God "before times eternal," He did not announce it until the fullness of time (Gal. 4:4). "His word" mentioned in vs. 3 is to be understood as a synonym for "Gospel," in which the promise of eternal life is embodied. To Paul was this message entrusted. What a fearful responsibility; what a high and holy privilege. It was on the Damascus road, Saul of Tarsus was confronted with the subject and object of this message: the subject was Jesus of Nazareth—the object was to herald forth the message that "Christ Jesus died to save sinners." This commission by Christ Jesus is called here "the commandment of God our Saviour." Paul could never forget "the heavenly vision" and to it he could not be disobedient. Six times in Paul's letters to Timothy and Titus he uses the expression "God our Saviour" (Cf. I Tim. 1:1; 2:3; 4:10; Titus 1:3; 2:10; 3:4). Since God is the ultimate source of all that relates to our salvation, it seems appropriate to refer to Him as "our Saviour." Paul felt his personal relationship to God as indicated by his use of "our" Saviour.

Vs. 4. It has been suggested by some that, since the name of Titus does not appear in the Book of Acts, perhaps Luke left him out for personal reasons. Maybe Titus was Luke's brother, and through a desire to be humble he was not mentioned. The above is only an opinion, but it is a fact that the name of Titus occurs only in the Pauline epistles.

Titus is a true child after a common faith. Was Titus a convert of Paul? We believe he was, but it is only a matter of conjecture. It can not be asserted from this reference. The expression "my true child" could be one of endearment, as Paul thought of the age of Titus as compared with himself. Paul's hope and life proceeded from the same source as Titus—faith in the Lord Jesus Christ; thus "a common faith." We believe, however, that the emphasis here should be on the objective quality of "the faith." "As measured by the common faith held by all Christians, Titus is a genuine child of God." (Kent)

The greeting here given to Titus is the same as given to Timothy, minus the thought of "mercy." It was the sincere concern and prayer of Paul that Titus have the favor and peace of God the Father and Christ Jesus "our" Saviour. In verse three God is called Saviour, here Christ Jesus is called by the same name. This is not strange, since both are the source of our salvation. Since the Holy Spirit brought the message of salvation, we could also refer to Him as "our Saviour."

Fact Questions 1:1-4

1. Only in this letter does Paul use an expression of his relationship to God. What is it?
2. Explain the expression "according to the faith of God's elect."
3. What is "the truth" as in 1b?
4. Who are "the elect"—how were they elected?
5. What was " in the hope of eternal life"—God's elect or Paul? i.e., to whom does this expression refer?
6. Discuss the meaning of "eternal life."
7. To what does the expression "eternal life" refer?
8. How shall we understand the use of the expression "His word" in vs. 3?
9. Why was Paul so willing to obey the heavenly vision?
10. Was Titus related to Luke? Why suggest such?
11. Doesn't the use of the term "my true child" indicate that Titus was a convert of Paul? Discuss.

I. THE CARE OF THE CHURCH
1:5-16

1. THE SELECTION AND QUALIFICATIONS OF ELDERS 1:5-9.

Text 1:5-9

5 For this cause left I thee in Crete, that thou shouldest set in order the things that were wanting, and appoint elders in every city, as

I gave thee charge; 6 if any man is blameless, the husband of one wife, having children that believe, who are not accused of riot or unruly. 7 For the bishop must be blameless, as God's steward; not self-willed, not soon angry, no brawler, no striker, not greedy of filthy lucre; 8 but given to hospitality, a lover of good, sober-minded, just, holy, self-controlled; 9 holding to the faithful word which is according to the teaching, that he may be able both to exhort in the sound doctrine, and to convict the gainsayers.

Thought Questions 1:5-9

16. When had Paul left Titus on the isle of Crete? Can we refer to the Acts account for the time mentioned here?
17. Did Paul begin the work on Crete? Give a reason for your answer.
18. Was Titus invested with apostolic authority for straightening out the difficulties in the Cretan churches?
19. Do we have men today with the same authority and responsibility?
20. Was Titus to accomplish the selection as well as the appointment? How?
21. Are we to understand that since Titus was to appoint elders in "every city" there were several churches in each city over which one set of elders ruled? What are we to understand by the expression "every city"?
22. What is "a charge"—as in vs. 5b?
23. Someone is always ready to cast blame upon the elder—how, then, could a man be blameless?
24. Are the men to be considered all older men—i.e., in age? How old?
25. What if the prospective elder is a widower, does this exclude him?
26. If the children are grown before a man becomes a Christian and such children fail to become believers, does this eliminate the father from the eldership?
27. Are we to understand the terms "elder" and "bishop" are here used to refer to the same office? Why use two terms?
28. The elder is also called "God's steward." Show how this is true.
29. Isn't everyone "self-willed"? What is meant by this expression?

30. Wasn't Jesus "soon angry" at all sin? Explain.
31. What is a "brawler"?
32. There must be some distinction between "a brawler" and "a striker"—what is it?
33. How could Titus or the church decide if a man was or was not "greedy of filthy lucre"?
34. What are the indications of hospitality?
35. The elder is to be a "lover of good"—does this refer to persons? i.e., "a lover of good men"?
36. What are the indications of the lack of a sober mind? Are we to equate this with wisdom?
37. In what matters would an elder need to be "just"?
38. If the elder met all of the qualifications so far stated, wouldn't he already be "holy"? Explain.
39. Show how the qualifications of self-control would be particularly pertinent to the Cretans.
40. What is "the faithful word according to the teaching" in vs. 9?
41. Show the distinction between "exhorting in the sound doctrine" and "convicting the gainsayers."

Paraphrase 1:5-9

5 For this purpose I left thee in Crete, that thou mightest supply the things wanting in the churches there, and in particular ordain, in every city where there are churches, elders, as I commanded thee. I will, therefore, describe the character and qualifications of the persons thou oughtest to make elders.

6 If anyone be in the eye of the world blameless, the husband of one wife at a time, having children who are Christians, and who are not accused of riotous living, nor are disobedient to their parents; persons of this character ordain bishops, that they may assist thee in opposing the Judaizers,

7 For a bishop should be free from blame, as becomes the steward of the mysteries of God. He should not be headstrong nor ready to fall into a passion, nor addicted to wine; not a striker of those who displease him; not one who loves money so much that he makes gain by base methods;

8 But, instead of loving money, hospitable, a lover of good men, prudent in conduct, just in his dealings, holy in speech, and temperate in the use of every sensual pleasure.

9 He should hold fast the true Christian doctrine as he hath been taught it by the apostles, that he may be able, by wholesale teaching, both to instruct them who desire instruction, and to confute false teachers who speak against the truth to overturn it.

Comment 1:5-9

Vs. 5. Paul now takes up the burden of the letter. Paul had been on the isle of Crete working for Christ. What he had not completed he now wanted Titus to complete. To "set in order" means to set straight as a doctor would set a broken bone. This is a general expression having reference to any and all needs of the congregations on the isle of Crete. "This verse gives us the historical setting for the Epistle. Titus is working on the island of Crete when Paul writes to him. Crete is one of the largest islands in the Mediterranean, situated almost equidistant from Europe, Asia, and Africa. A high state of civilization once flourished there, but by New Testament times the moral level of its inhabitants was deplorable. Their ferocity and fraud were widely attested; their falsehood was proverbial; the wine of Crete was famous and drunkenness prevailed." (D. Edmond Heibert)

By reading Titus 3:12 we can know Paul was leaving Titus on a temporary basis. He planned on sending another worker to replace him.

We can not imagine there was anything of an arbitrary nature in the work of Titus. Correction was done by the means of instruction and example. But let us not forget that deficiencies and dislocations *were* corrected by Titus.

The appointment of elders is a specific work to be carried out in every church in every city on the island. As to the method of appointment, we refer you to our special study on the subject. We are particularly concerned with the qualifications of the elders.

Vs. 6. We shall follow the same procedure here as in our study in I Timothy—i.e., a consideration of the qualifications in the order given by Paul, with no attempt on our part to group them (not that we have any objection to such grouping—see Special Studies).

"*blameless*": This word means to be "unaccused." It will soon be known by those who are concerned in selecting candidates for the office, whether such persons are accused or not. Has the prospective elder conducted himself in such a manner that no ugly stories concerning him are circulating in the community?

"*the husband of one wife.*" We have a special study upon this subject; to this study we refer all those who wish to pursue this theme further. Suffice it to say that there are several views on this verse: (1) that the elder must be married; (2) that he must remain a widower if his wife dies; (3) that he must not have more than one wife at a time. We ask you to thoughtfully decide which view is correct. Read I Timothy 5:14; Romans 7:2, 3; I Cor. 7:39 as to second marriages.

"*having children that believe.*" Since elders would be chosen from older men, it would be natural to assume that most of them would have children; and that such children would be old enough to be Christians. It is not right or healthy for the elder to have pagan children. If the prospective elder accepted Christ late in life, he might not be at fault for the unbelief of his children, but he can not ignore his relationship to them. If his children are pagan in their attitude and conduct, it will reflect on him and his service to Christ.

"*who are not accused of riot or unruly.*" If the elder can not win his own children to Christ, how could he instruct others? "The family is the nursery of the church, and these two act and react upon each other so that a bad or weak father can never be an elder." (Lipscomb)

The word "riot" means "inability to save"; the second word suggests insubordination. A father who has a prodigal son under his roof will have a very difficult, yea, impossible time in attempting to lead others into a life of self-discipline and holiness.

Vs. 7. The terms "bishop" and "elder" are used interchangeably as seen from the use of the word "for" in this verse. Verse seven is a conclusion to verses five and six. In verse five the term "elder" is used, then in reference to the same office the term "bishop" is used in verse seven. The men who hold this office are to be older in the faith and are to exercise oversight for the flock of God. The word "blameless" appears twice because of its inclusive quality.

"God's steward" would seem a bit strange inasmuch as his service is to and for the church—one would imagine the elder would be called "the church's steward." The church is the household of God. The elder serves in this household as a steward. In such a responsible position he must be without blame; moreover, it is required of a steward that he give an account of his stewardship.

In verse seven we have five negative qualifications:

"*not self-willed*": This has reference to pride. The elder must not be arrogant. The self-loving man will have little regard for others, except when they enhance his estimate of himself.

"*not soon angry*": There is no place in the eldership for a "hothead." The wrath of man never did work the righteousness of God (Jas. 1:20). In the eldership the wrath of man will work havoc with His saints.

"*no brawler*": Literally, "not one who sits along side wine." Of course, the reference here is to the influence of wine. The bishop must leave wine alone.

"*no striker*": The bishop must not be a pugilist. Discussions are never settled when fists are used to settle them. Corporal punishment should be confined to small children who have not reached the age where other types of reasoning can be used. The elder who would resort to physical violence is himself immature, and is using tactics reserved for his younger children.

"*not greedy of filthy lucre*": "Not eager of shameful gain." Here is some hint as to the payment of elders for their service. Perhaps we should say that Paul assumed Titus knew that elders would, in their office, have opportunity to mishandle funds and thus included this comment. We should say this quality of greediness should be no part of a Christian's life in or out of the office of overseer.

Vs. 8. In contrast to the five negative qualifications in verse seven are the six positive qualifications in verse eight:

"*given to hospitality*": The elder is to be generous to guests; to entertain strangers with kindness and without reward. No one sets a stronger example than the overseers of the church. A general friendly and out-going attitude should prevail in the assembly and in the personal contact of each member. Let the elder set the pace in this regard. I Peter 4:9 and Galatians 6:10 indicate that such an attitude is the responsibility and privilege of every Christian.

"*a lover of good*": The elder must not only be a lover of strangers—as inferred in the preceding qualification—but also a lover of all that is good and holy. This is a cultivated quality not often found. It is obtained by setting the mind upon those things which are good, and lovely, and just, and of good report (Cf. Phil. 4:8). It is a fruit of love which "taketh not account of evil, but rejoiceth with the truth" (Cf. I Cor. 13:5, 6).

"*sober-minded*": The overseer should resist mind intoxication. Balanced judgment is such a needed quality in carrying out the important work of feeding and protecting the flock of God. There are some men who are compulsive drinkers and others who, under the influence of ambition, are compulsive thinkers—from both may the kingdom be delivered!

"*just*": To be fair at all times with all people is such a commendable quality. How tragic it is when elders are partial and prejudiced instead of just and fair in their judgment. Many a congregation has been split asunder for lack of this important quality.

"*holy*": The steward of God must be "unpolluted"; no man is worthy of the office who can be corrupted by Satan. The elder is to so keep his heart that no corrupt speech would come from his mouth—that no sensual thoughts would stain his mind. When examined by God or man, the elder should be pure in character. There is a wonderful beauty in holiness, such beauty should be seen in the life of the overseer.

"*self-controlled*": This is literally, "in control of strength." The elder is a strong man—this is one thing—but to be in control of this strength is quite another. There are many men who possess great capacities, but mastering such and marshaling them into the service of Christ, is the need of the church. Joseph is a good example of "self-control." He did not allow men, circumstance or lust, to control him—he controlled them!

Vs. 9. This verse has been taken by many to be a commentary of I Tim. 3:2—in which Paul states that the elder is to be "apt to teach." There must be some purpose or object in the qualifications. We believe such a purpose is stated here: "holding to the faithful word . . . that he may be able both to exhort in the sound doctrine, and to convict the gainsayers."

The expression "faithful word" is to be understood as a synonym for "the gospel" or "the faith." The elder is to both live and teach "the faithful word." He is to hold to it as a pattern for teaching and as a philosophy of life.

How shall we understand the phrase "which is according to the teaching"? Is this a reference to the teaching of the elder— "thus meaning that the elder must hold on to the teaching which was imparted to him. Or are we to understand that Paul is saying that 'the elder must hold to God's Word which is in accordance with the recognized body of truth taught by the apostles' (cf. Acts 2:42)?" (Kent) We much prefer the latter interpretation.

In so handling God's Word he will be prepared to encourage the saints and refute false teachers. To "exhort" means to encourage or to incite to action. The "gainsayers" are those who would speak against the truth of God, or in any way oppose the teachings of the Gospel.

Fact Questions 1:5-9

12. What is the meaning of the expression "set in order"?
13. Give two facts about the isle of Crete.
14. Why do we say that the stay of Titus on Crete was only of a temporary nature?
15. What do we mean by saying that we do not believe Titus was arbitrary in his appointing of elders?
16. Explain in your own words three of the negative qualifications.
17. What is the meaning of "riot or unruly"?
18. Prove that the term "bishop" and "elder" refer to the same office.
19. In what sense is the elder "God's steward"?
20. Explain in your own words four of the positive qualifications.
21. What is "the faithful word" of vs. 9?
22. What is the two-fold task in the teaching of the elder?

2. THE DESCRIPTION AND REFUTATION OF FALSE TEACHERS 1:10-16.

Text 1:10-16

10 For there are many unruly men, vain talkers and deceivers, specially they of the circumcision, 11 whose mouths must be stopped; men who overthrow whole houses, teaching things which they ought not, for filthy lucre's sake. 12 One of themselves, a prophet of their own, said,

Cretans are always liars, evil beasts, idle gluttons.

13 This testimony is true. For which cause reprove them sharply, that they may be sound in the faith, 14 not giving heed to Jewish fables, and commandments of men who turn away from the truth.

15 To the pure all things are pure: but to them that are defiled and unbelieving nothing is pure; but both their mind and their conscience are defiled. 16 They profess that they know God; but by their works they deny Him, being abominable, and disobedient, and unto every good work reprobate.

Thought Questions 1:10-16

42. Please show the connection of verse ten with the preceding verses.
43. In what sense would the men described in verse ten be "unruly" or "vain talkers"?
44. Is Paul discussing the Jews in vs. 10?
45. Just how was Titus going to gag such false teachers?
46. Is Paul discussing a problem in the churches of Crete? Prove your answer.
47. Why would anyone be willing to pay to hear such false teaching?
48. Why quote from one of the Cretan prophets? Can we identify him?
49. Why would Cretans be tempted above others to be liars, evil beasts, idle gluttons?
50. Who is to be "reproved sharply"?
51. From verse 13 it would seem the ones to be reproved sharply are Cretan Christians—is this true?—are they also the "unruly men"?
52. A discussion of "Jewish fables" has already been considered —where? Discuss.
53. Show how verse 15 relates to the context.
54. Discuss a very basic principle of psychology involved in verse 15.
55. How are the words "mind and conscience" used in verse 15?
56. How was God denied in the works of certain men?
57. What is the meaning and use of the word "abominable" in verse 16?
58. Discuss the term "reprobate."

Paraphrase 1:10-16

10 For there are many teachers, who, being unsubjected to us, talk in a foolish manner concerning genealogies and fables, and deceive others; of this sort especially are the Jewish teachers,
11 Whose mouths must be stopped, neither by persecution nor force, but by clear and strong reasoning, because they carry off whole families to Judaism, teaching things which they ought not,

for the sordid purpose of drawing money from their disciples.
12 The Judaizers in this are true Cretians, agreeably to what one of themselves, a prophet of their own, hath said, The Cretians are exceedingly addicted to lying, and of a savage noxious disposition, and lazy gluttons.
13 This testimony concerning the Cretians is just; for which cause I order thee to rebuke them and their disciples sharply, that, laying aside their wicked principles and practices, they may be healthy in the faith;
14 Not giving heed to Jewish fables concerning the law, and to precepts concerning meats, enjoined by men who turn away true doctrine from themselves and others as a thing noxious.
15 All meats indeed are pure to the well-informed and well-disposed: but to those who are polluted by intemperance, and who are unfaithful to Christ, no kind of meat is pure; for both their understanding and conscience is polluted by their intemperate use of the meats which the law reckons clean.
16 They of the circumcision profess to know the will of God better than others; but by their works they deny him—being abominable on account of their sensuality, and disobedient to the express commands of God, and to every good work without discernment: They neither know nor approve of any good work.

Comment 1:10-16

Vs. 10. We are now introduced to the "gainsayers" or those who contradict. Paul says four things about them: (1) they are insubordinate, (2) they are empty talkers, (3) they are deceivers, (4) they are Jewish.

Such men were very numerous on the isle of Crete. Are we to understand that they were Christians? If they were not members of the church they were very closely associated, because they were upsetting "whole houses" in the church.

Timothy had the same problem in Ephesus—and must deal with it in the same manner (Cf. I Tim. 1:6-8). The admonition to "gag" such persons can be understood when we look at their character: insubordinate, proud, and deceitful or dishonest. Such persons are not all Jews, but most of them are. The elders are to be so taught that they could recognize such teachers.

Vs. 11. With some heretics it is better to ignore them than to challenge their teaching; not so with these teachers. They must be muzzled! A simple authoritative charge to cease teaching, backed up with an apostolic letter, would stop such mouths.

It does make a vast difference what is taught! It is always a constant wonder why there are some among the saints who will hear and heed a false teacher. Paul knew of whole families who were being infected by this diseased doctrine. The deceived members of the churches on Crete were paying money to be duped! Such a tragic condition must be changed; elders were to be appointed for this purpose.

Vs. 12. Paul characterizes the Cretans by the words of Epimenides, one of the prophets of this people. Epimenides lived about 600 B.C. and was held in almost divine regard. His testimony concerning his own countrymen was anything but complimentary. Three things are said of Cretans: (1) they are habitual liars, (2) evil, brute-like people, (3) indolent belly-worshippers. What is known from all sources confirms this testimony. A special expression was coined to describe the lying of the Cretans. "The expression 'to Cretize' meant 'to lie,' and 'to play the Cretan with a Cretan' meant 'to out-trick a trickster.' " (Hiebert) The expression "evil beasts" indicated the level on which they were living—their lower natures were in full control. No attempt was made to curb any selfish, sensual or vengeful desire. The expression "lumpish greedy-guts" is used by Simpson to describe the third quality of such persons. When no attempt is made to control the appetites of the body, such a person will carry around an advertisement of his lack of self-control. It will be a large stomach!

Vs. 13. Paul used the words of a respected prophet—not that he believed in the prophetic powers of such—to say with sharper meaning and condemnation what he also wanted to say. It is not to be imagined that all Cretans were under such condemnation, for some of them were "new creatures in Christ Jesus," but some among the believers were being influenced. To such members of the churches, Titus was to deliver a charge with the force and cutting power of a sharp ax. Such diseased teaching must be cut off with an accurate clean stroke! The result will be very good: health and vigor will return and they will be strong in the grace that is in Christ Jesus.

Vs. 14. The Jewish fables have been discussed before in I Timothy. Please notice Paul's estimate of such teaching—"fables, and commandments of men." There is no foundation in reality, and no divine authority behind such teachings. The expression "turn away" means that they continue turning away. Such men are willful and do not want to follow the truth. There is Satanic influence at work in these men to blind their eyes to the truth; such influence is to be avoided at all costs, hence the urgency of the admonition.

Vs. 15. Paul states in this verse a principle that will both cure and condemn. "To the pure all things are pure." Please keep this principle in its context. The distinctions made by the Jewish law to clean and unclean meats and men, is probably in view. The apostle is saying that such distinctions have been removed, and therefore, such teaching is to be ignored. The point implicit in Paul's principle is: *You*, not the meats, are impure! When the heart is clean, then all nonmoral objects are clean, but when your heart is polluted, then all you use is also unclean.

To such law teachers in Crete (even as in Ephesus) Paul has no hesitancy in saying they are "defiled and unbelieving." When we will not believe the truth, we must look deeper than an intellectual difficulty. The defilement of the heart precedes the disbelief of the mind. The effects of moral dishonesty are tragic: "nothing is pure—mind diseased—conscience seared." Only in humble acceptance of God's word is there moral and intellectual purity.

Vs. 16. Profession without possession spells condemnation. To claim a knowledge and association with the infinitely holy God, while we live the loose life of the self-indulgent, is to make ourselves liars and to deny the very one we profess to follow. Such persons are seen by God as detestible and loathsome. The hypocricy of those who declare their faith, and live in denial of it, are plainly willful in their conduct; such men are not sick or maladjusted, they are "disobedient." The word "reprobate" has reference to the testing of coins for genuineness. The errorists have been tested and have been found spurious. Their works have been examined and have been found worthless.

Fact Questions 1:10-16

23. Show the distinction in the use of the words "unruly—vain talkers—deceivers."
24. How was Titus going to carry out the injunctions of Paul to "gag" or "muzzle" certain men?

25. Were the false teachers on the inside, or the outside of the church? Explain.
26. Try to reconstruct the situation in which certain men would be paid to deceive.
27. Wouldn't Paul antagonize the very ones he was trying to help, in citing the very critical comment of Epimenides? Discuss.
28. Who was to be reproved sharply? Why?
29. Are "Jewish fables, and the commandments of men" the same thing? Explain.
30. Give your exegesis of vs. 15. Please relate this verse to the context.
31. Show how the principle stated in vs. 15 relates to our life.
32. Is it possible to defile the conscience beyond repair? Discuss.
33. If professing we know God will not make it so—what will?
34. Is Paul saying in 16b that the works of such men are worthless, or that they are worthless regardless of their works?

EXEGETICAL EXAMINATION OVER CHAPTER ONE

1. What is the meaning of the expression: "according to the faith of God's elect"?
2. Give your own exegesis of verse three.
3. Write from memory your own outline of this chapter.
4. Explain the responsibility of Titus in appointing elders.
5. Discuss the qualifications of the elder as found in verse eight.
6. Show the connection of verse ten with the preceding verses.
7. Discuss the force of verse twelve.
8. Explain how to "reprove them sharply," and yet not lose them quickly.
9. How shall we develop the capacity to be those persons to whom "all things are pure"?
10. Discuss the supposed reasons for the prevalence of false teachers on Crete.

II. THE CONDUCT OF CHURCH MEMBERS 2:1-15

1. OLDER MEN 2:1, 2.

Text 2:1, 2

1 But speak thou the things which befit the sound doctrine: 2 that aged men be temperate, grave, sober-minded, sound in faith, in love, in patience:

Thought Questions 2:1, 2

59. Evidently a contrast was intended, since the word "but" is used; what is the contrast? Please think this through—it will be worth your time.
60. The speaking of Titus in this particular context refers to ordinary conversation. How would Titus fulfill this admonition? Show examples of circumstances in which Titus would fulfill the instructions here given.
61. In what particulars would some aged men be "intemperate"?
62. There are two extremes on either side of this word "grave" —what are they?
63. Show some distinction in the use of the word "sober-minded" as contrasted or compared with "temperate" and "grave."
64. Older men are to be sound or healthy in three particulars—discuss each of them.

Paraphrase 2:1, 2

1 The fables and commandments of men taught by the Judaizers sicken the soul; But do thou inculcate the practices which are suitable to the wholesome doctrine of the gospel:
2 That aged men, who hold sacred offices, be attentive to the behaviour of their people, venerable in their own manners, prudent in their behaviour, spiritually healthy by faith, love, patience.

Comment 2:1, 2

Vs. 1. The care of the congregation in its eldership and faith, was the subject of chapter one. The care of individual members of the church, is the subject of chapter two. Paul is concerned about the family. If the family is holy, the whole church will be holy. There are five members of the Christian family before the mind of the apostle. Perhaps we should say there are five classes: aged men, aged women, young married women, young men, and slaves.

In sharp contrast to the disease-spreading talk of the "empty-talkers," Titus is to spread in his ordinary conversation, the health-giving word of the faith.

Vs. 2. When visiting in the homes; when conversing in the market-place; when helping with a personal problem—instruct the older men in the following attitudes: let them be *temperate* or moderate. Older men are tempted to lose patience and be carried away with exasperation. Some are prone to other extremes of attitude. Titus is to teach them by word and example to curb these tendencies.

grave: The same qualities to be found in elders and deacons, are here applied to the older men of the congregation. It should be said that all the qualities of character necessary for the elder and deacon, are also to be a part of the Christians' conduct. To be "grave" means to be "serious, dignified, or respectable."

sober-minded: This has reference to being sensible, balanced in judgment.

The older men are to be strong and healthy in three areas: (1) in *the* faith, (2) in *the* love, (3) in *the* patience.

Hendrikson wisely suggests that the older men have a threefold obligation: (1) To God—to be sound in their faith, (2) To others—sound in love, (3) Toward trials—sound in patience.

Fact Questions 2:1, 2

35. How are chapters one and two alike, yet different in content and purpose?
36. "But speak thou the things which befit the sound doctrine" —what type of speaking is here involved—i.e., public? private? etc.
37. Show how the instructions for the aged men are appropriate to their needs.
38. Discuss the threefold obligation of the aged men.

2. OLDER WOMEN 2:3.

Text 2:3

3 That aged women likewise be reverent in demeanor, not slanderers nor enslaved to much wine, teachers of that which is good;

Thought Questions 2:3

65. To what does the word "likewise" in vs. 3 refer?
66. Define the word "demeanor" in vs. 3.
67. Would older women be especially tempted to be "slanderers"? Discuss.
68. Why were aged women "enslaved to much wine"? Is this a problem today?
69. Where and when would the older women teach? Define the use of the word "good" in vs. 3b.

Paraphrase 2:3

3 That the aged women, whom the church employs to teach the young of their own sex, in like manner, be in speech and be-

haviour as becometh persons employed in sacred offices; not slanderers, not enslaved to much wine, but good teachers:

Comment 2:3

Vs. 3. Titus has an urgent and large responsibility: he must prompt action on the part of the older and younger members of the churches to fullfil the qualities of character and conduct here described. To the aged women: they should be first of all concerned with their general impression on the public. What is the first, as well as the total impression, given by the older women? Is it one of holiness and reverence?

Older women are sometimes especially tempted in two areas. Because they many times are alone—and sometimes in poor health—they are open to the temptation to seek solace in wine instead of worship. While thus addicted to wine they can become the tool of the great accuser, and begin to slander the various members of the church.

In contrast to the idle, slandering, wine-filled life, the reverent older woman will seek out some avenue of service in which she can be a teacher of good. The particular areas are specified in vs. 4.

Fact Questions 2:3

39. Just how was Titus going to fulfill the admonitions of these verses? i.e., how was he to obtain co-operation from the older men and women?
40. Show how the first quality of character is inclusive of all the others.
41. Explain how and why older women would be tempted to be slanderers and addicted to much wine.
42. Is there anything for an older woman to do in the church? What is it?

3. YOUNGER WOMEN 2:4, 5.

Text 2:4, 5

4 that they may train the young women to love their husbands, to love their children, 5 to be sober-minded, chaste, workers at home, kind, being in subjection to their own husbands, that the word of God be not blasphemed:

Thought Questions 2:4, 5

70. When would a young woman become an older woman? How young is young?

71. Would young women need special training in loving their husbands? Explain.
72. Isn't it natural for mothers to love their children? Why the need for training?
73. "Sober-minded" seems to be a very needed qualification—explain. Show how this quality is especially related to young married women.
74. If a young woman was a Christian, would she need special training to be chaste?
75. With whom would the young married women be tempted to be unkind?
76. Does the expression "workers at home" suggest that they should not work away from home?
77. Just what is involved in "being in subjection to their own husbands"?
78. The spiritual education of the young married women was for a very worth-while purpose—what was it? Discuss the meaning of the expression "the word of God."

Paraphrase 2:4, 5

4 That they may persuade the younger women under their care to be lovers of their husbands, performing the duties of marriage from affection, and lovers of their children, by bringing them up religiously;
5 To be of a calm disposition, chaste, attentive to the affairs of their families, good to their domestics, obedient to their own husbands, that the gospel may not be evil spoken of, as encouraging wives to neglect their husbands and children, on pretence of their attending on the offices of religion.

Comment 2:4, 5

Vs. 4 & 5. Neither Titus nor the elders are given the responsibility of training the young married women. This is the responsibility of the older women. Who would be better qualified? This, of course, presupposes that such older women have themselves learned the lessons they are to teach the younger women. Much of this training can and does take place before the daughter leaves home. The best lesson is a good example. There are seven qualities to be instilled by the older women (whether it be the mother or someone else):

(1) Husband-lovers, (2) Children-lovers, (3) sober-minded, (4) chaste, (5) worker at home, (6) kind, (7) in subjection to her own husband.

Paul has more to say about this group than any other; and well he might, for if failure is found here, it will affect all other groups. The one big lesson is the lesson of love: *love* your husband, your children, your home, your Lord—and we might add, your position as help-meet. When the proper motive is used to obtain these virtues (Cf. 2:11-14) they seem but a natural outgrowth of the Christian life.

Conduct and character have never been divorced either in the mind of God or in the eyes of the world. If the young married women are examples in the above particulars, the word of God will be honored!

Fact Questions 2:4-5

43. Why is the training of young married women given to the older women?
44. Who are these older women? How shall they teach? i.e., by a class, by private lessons, or just how?
45. Mention from memory four of the seven areas in which the older women are to give instruction.
46. Why so much to say about this group?
47. How does the proper motive relate to this teaching?
48. When will the word of God be honored?

4. THE YOUNG MEN 2:6-8.

Text 2:6-8

6 the younger men likewise exhort to be sober-minded; 7 in all things showing thyself an example of good works; in thy doctrine showing uncorruptness, gravity, 8 sound speech, that cannot be condemned; that he that is of the contrary part may be ashamed, having no evil thing to say of us.

Thought Questions 2:6-8

79. Would it be right to assume that all men who are not called "older men" would be classified as "younger men"?
80. Give the meaning of the word "exhort."
81. Please notice the repetition of the term "sober-minded" (Cf. 1:8; 2:2, 4, 5). Give the meaning and application of this word.
82. Show how Paul's word to Titus was prompted by the context.

83. To what, in previous verses, does the expression "all things" (vs. 7) refer?
84. Is there some difference in an "ensample" and an "example"? If so, what?
85. Read Matt. 23:3 and relate this to Titus, and then to present day preachers.
86. To what do the two words, "uncorruptness" and "gravity" refer? Do they relate to the content of the teaching, or to the manner in which it is taught? Discuss.
87. The content of the message is the subject of vs. 8. Give the meaning of the word "sound." What will be the evidence of sound speech?
88. Who would criticize the teaching of Titus? Explain the use of the word "condemnation" in vs. 8.
89. Who is "he that is of the contrary part"?
90. Describe the possible circumstances under which someone would be "ashamed."

Paraphrase 2:6-8

6 The young men, in like manner, exhort to govern their passions, that they may behave soberly in the giddy season of youth. 7 To give weight to thy exhortations, in all things make thyself a pattern of those good works which thou enjoinest to others. In teaching, shew incorruptness of doctrine, gravity of speech, and sincerity with respect to the motives by which thou art influenced.

8 In conversation, and in proving offenders, use clear and strong, but temperate speech, which cannot be found fault with even by the offenders themselves; that he who is not a Christian may be ashamed of his opposition to thee, and to the elders, thy assistants, having nothing bad to say concerning you as teachers.

Comment 2:6-8

Vs. 6. Paul has but one word to give the young men, and it should be sufficient:—"be sensible"! Exercise control over yourself, think through your decisions and words. Some commentators would place the phrase "in all things" with verse six instead of verse seven. In such a case Paul would be asking the young men to be balanced in judgement in every area of life. Morals and doctrine have both been discussed in these verses. Let the young men be prompted to exercise self-mastery in both areas.

Vs. 7. Both Timothy and Titus are urged by the Apostle to set the example for those who are being taught (Cf. I Tim. 4:12).

The word "pattern" literally means "an impress of a die", and hence in a metaphorical sense an "example." This pattern is to be presented in all things—or for all things. If the elders of Crete or Ephesus wanted to know the meaning of any of the teaching given, they could see a living translation of it in the conduct of Titus or Timothy. What an awesome responsibility!—"who is sufficient for these things?"—"our sufficiency is in God."

Are we to understand the words: "in thy doctrine showing uncorruptness, gravity," to refer to the content of teaching, or to the manner in which the teaching (or doctrine) is given? We prefer the latter. So much depends on the manner of presentation. Two words are used: "uncorruptness" and "gravity"—let the man of God so speak as to pursuade men by his manner as well as by his material, that he could not be corrupted by those who would seek to influence him by base gain—whether it be for money or popularity. Let the man of God desist from all clowning and tom-foolery while teaching and preaching the Word of God. If seriousness can be turned off and on like a faucet, the preacher becomes suspect in his manner of teaching. This is a serious matter—"be serious" about it!

Vs. 8. This verse discusses the content of teaching—"healthy speech"—the word speech could relate to all speaking whether publicly or in private. There are preachers who destroy by their unhealthy speech in private, all they have built up by their healthy speech in public. This MUST NOT be! There is no way to produce strong, profitable servants on a mixed diet of flesh and Spirit.

Those on the outside are always waiting and watching for something evil to say of the man of God. Paul personifies the opposition by the use of the pronoun "he." It should be "he that is of the contrary part" who is ashamed—not the preacher. When word is spread around the community concerning some inconsistency of word or action, let the life of the evangelist be so exemplary that when the truth is known, those who doubted him would be ashamed they ever entertained such thoughts. When the trial is over, there is no evil thing to be said against God's man.

Fact Questions 2:6-8

49. Give the meaning and application of the one word to young men.
50. When Paul instructed Titus to be "an example" what did he mean?

51. To what do the words "uncorruptness" and "gravity" refer?
52. Explain the use of the word "speech" in vs. 8.
53. Who is the one "of the contrary part"? What is our responsibility to him?

SLAVES 2:9, 10

Text 2:9, 10

9 Exhort servants to be in subjection to their own masters, and to be well-pleasing to them in all things; not gainsaying; 10 not purloining, but showing all good fidelity; that they may adorn the doctrine of God our Saviour in all things.

Thought Questions 2:9, 10

91. Does Paul condone slavery by his reference to it in vs. 9a?
92. Are these slaves Christians? How shall we decide this question?
93. How could a slave be well-pleasing to his master if the master was a despot?
94. What is "gainsaying"?
95. Explain "purloining."
96. Give a synonym for the word "fidelity." Show how it is used here.
97. Slaves are to provide the clothing for the teaching of God—explain.

Paraphrase 2:9, 10

9 Slaves exhort to continue subject to their own masters, and, in all things, lawful, to be careful to please; especially by performing their service cheerfully; not insolently answering again, even though they may be reproved unjustly or with too much severity. (See I Pet. ii. 18). 10 Not secretly stealing any part of their master's goods, but shewing the greatest fidelity and honesty in every thing committed to them; that, by the whole of their behaviour in their low station, they may render the doctrine of the gospel amiable, even in the eyes of their heathen lords.

Comment 2:9, 10

Vs. 9. There are five groups with whom Titus is to work. Each of the preceding four have been in the church. We believe the slaves are also members of the church. The instructions given could not be followed by less than a Christian. The latter part of verse 10 settles the matter: slaves are to conduct themselves in the manner here prescribed so as to offer attractive testimony to the non-Christian of the doctrine of God.

The thought of Christian slaves becoming restive because of their position, has been discussed in Paul's first letter to Timothy (Cf. I Tim. 6:1,2). The word "exhort" is supplied by the translators of the American Standard Version, for smooth reading —Please do not overlook the fact that the whole section (i.e. vss. 9, 10) is given not as suggestions, but as imperatives of Christian conduct.

The Christian slave will serve with a purpose. His purposes will be to serve Christ in his service for man. In doing this, he will accomplish the lesser but nonetheless important purpose of pleasing his Master. Such service is to be given "in all things." In those tasks where human choice and preference enter—put the desires of your Master above those of yourself.

Two very common faults (shall we call them "sins") of slaves are here brought to light. The Christian slave should not "sass-back"—offer no "back-talk." Do your work without murmuring or complaining. Paul does not discuss *who* is right—he points out *what* is right.

Vs. 10. "Not taking things for themselves" (Lenski). This has a broader scope than petty thievery. The reference here is to embezzlement in any and all forms. Slaves held very responsible positions in the society of the first century. Opportunity of appropriating that which belonged to another was very great. The master of the Christian slave should be able to trust the slave implicitly. It would not be easy to serve as a Christian slave. To know that all men are created equal in the sight of God, and yet to be bound as property to another man, would indeed be difficult. For this reason, there must be a higher and holier purpose in the service of the slave than mere free labor for another man—even if he is a Christian brother. That higher, holier purpose is to provide luster and beauty to the teaching of God. The slave could exemplify in his service the beauty and power of the teaching he professed. The doctrine of God is only attractive to others if we make it so by our lives. If God can save the slave in his lowly, unpaid position, He is, indeed, in truth—the Saviour.

Fact Questions 2:9, 10

54. What is the conclusive point indicating that the slaves were Christians?

55. In what manner was Titus to deliver these instructions to slaves?
56. What attitude must prevail in the heart of the slave before he could "please his Master in all things"?
57. The Christian slave is to serve without "gainsaying"—exlain.
58. "Purloining" is more than petty thievery. Discuss it's broader applications.
59. How could the slave become "an adornment for the doctrine of God"?

6. THE MOTIVES FOR CONDUCT 2:11-15

Text 2:11-15

11 For the grace of God hath appeared, bringing salvation to all men, 12 instructing us, to the intent that, denying ungodliness and worldly lusts, we should live soberly and righteously and godly in this present world; 13 looking for the blessed hope and appearing of the glory of the great God and our Saviour Jesus Christ; 14 who gave himself for us, that he might redeem us from all iniquity, and purify unto himself a people for his own possession, zealous of good works. 15 These things speak and exhort and reprove with all authority. Let no man despise thee.

Thought Questions 2:11-15

98. The word "for" in vs. 11 connects this new section with the one just concluded. Show how.
99. Discuss the meaning of the expression "the grace of God."
100. When and where did the grace of God appear?
101. How shall we understand the phrase "bringing salvation to all men"—all men are not saved. How is this true?
102. Please think carefully and personally as to just how the grace of God becomes a great teacher or instructor. Express the truth in your own words.
103. Read Rom. 1:18-32 for a definition of ungodliness and worldly lusts. Is it enough to just "deny" these things? Explain.
104. Show the distinction in the words: "soberly - righteously - godly."
105. How are Paul's words applicable to us in-as-much as our word or age is somewhat different than his?
106. What is our blessed hope? In what way is this hope blessed?
107. How is the word "glory" used in vs. 13?
108. Does the text here say that Jesus is our Saviour and great God? Discuss.

109. In what sense did Jesus give Himself for us?
110. Since Christ redeemed us from our iniquity, does this excuse our continued sinning?
111. When, where and how does Jesus purify a people?
112. If certain people are not zealous of good works, does it follow that such persons do not belong to Christ?
113. How much of chapter two is included in the 15th verse?

Paraphrase 2:11-15

11 These things I command, because the gospel of God, which bringeth both the knowledge and the means of salvation, hath shone forth to all men, to Jews and Gentiles, rich and poor, masters and slaves, without distinction, 12 teaching us, that renouncing ungodliness, especially atheism and idolatry, and putting away worldly lusts, we should live temperately, righteously, and godly in this present world, 13 expecting not any temporal rewards, such as the law promised, but the accomplishment of the blessed hope of the appearing of the glory of the great God, and our Saviour Jesus Christ, who will bestow eternal life on all who deny ungodliness and worldly lusts; 14 who, during his first appearing on earth, gave himself to death for us, that he might redeem us from the power, as well as from the punishment, of all iniquity, and purify to himself a peculiar people, not by circumcision and other ceremonial observances, but by being zealous of good works. 15 These things inculcate as necessary to be believed, and exhort all who profess the gospel to live suitably to them. And such as teach otherwise, confute with all the authority which is due to truth, and to thee as a teacher commissioned by Christ. Let no one have reason to despise thee.

Comment 2:11-15

Vs. 11. The well-springs of action are here discussed. Paul has instructed Titus to speak to five groups of Christians about some very important and difficult matters. He is here to discuss the motives for translating into life such admonitions.

The "grace of God" is a great instructor. What is the grace of God? It is the unearned, unmerited favor God has toward sinful man. We are constrained to exclaim with Paul elsewhere: surely "the goodness of God leadeth thee to repentance." (Ro. 2:4)

The love of God for the lost world, was made flesh in the person of His own Son. God's grace appeared in Christ from His birth to His ascension; and even more, in the establishment of His church on Pentecost.

In what way did the grace of God bring salvation to all men? Or should we ask: In what manner did the grace of God appear to all men to bring Salvation? We much prefer the first translation, which states that the grace of God in the person of His Son came to provide salvation for all men. We cannot see how it has been true, or is now true, that all men have heard of the grace of God in Christ. We are sure God intended that all men should hear of His love in the person of His Son, but for 1900 years we have failed to fulfill this intention.

God intended, and does now intend, that none should perish, but all come to salvation and a knowledge of the truth. (II Pet. 3:9) (I Tim. 2:1)

Vs. 12. The grace of God is a wonderful pedagogue. The word is stronger and broader than the term "teacher"—it quite literally means "to train a child, to bring up a child." Instruction is a part of child training, and God's love toward us has provided such instruction in His word. But such training includes far more than mere instruction or information. "He scourgeth every Son whom He receiveth." The loving concern of God provides discipline as well as instruction. In what way will God our Father lead us to deny ungodliness and worldly lusts? There are so many ways best known to Him, but all of them have their basis in a knowledge of His will. It is one thing to know that we should deny ungodliness and worldly lusts, it is quite another thing to have the desire to do so. But the grace of God will see to it that each child of His will have reasons to decide in favor of doing so. The fruitless, frustrating experience of indulging in ungodliness and worldly lusts could be a strong reason for denying them. A clear and full view of the punishment of the ungodly and lustful, would also turn us to the side of righteousness. This is a school from which we never graduate. The loving concern of our Father continues while life shall last.

Now appears the positive side of the instructive power of grace. We are not only to be repulsed by sin, but we are to learn to love righteousness. Three qualities are here discussed: (1) Soberly or "sensibly." Five times this word is used in this short letter: (Cf 1:8, 2:2, 4, 5, 6). Refer to these other instances for a more detailed explanation (2) "Righteously." In our relationship to our fellow man, we must live a life above reproach. May our lives be a translation of the virtues we espouse. (3) "Godly."

The thought here is to include God in all your plans. God too often becomes "the third man out," with the average church member. It is too easy to leave God at home or at church. The Christian who allows God's grace to instruct him aright, will be ever conscious of the Omnipresent God.

Please remember Titus was on the wild wicked isle of Crete when he received such instructions. Paul expected the Cretans to live out in their daily associations the implications of this instruction. "In the present course of things" let the grace of God so teach us. Surely if the Cretans were expected to do this, we have little excuse for less.

Vs. 13. The motives for holy living—what are they? The unearned concern of God is one motive—this we have discussed. In vs. 13 we are introduced to another motive: "the blessed hope and appearing of the glory of the great God and our Saviour Jesus Christ." We know that one day all our aspirations of triumph over sin, Satan and the grave will find fulfillment.

The second coming of Christ will vindicate all our efforts to live for Him. It will also be a vindication of His own claims. It is a blessed hope to us. It shall be a glorious appearing for Him. He appeared once for sin. He shall appear the second time apart from sin for those who wait (hope) for Him. D. Edmond Hiebert has asked very pertinently, "When He thus returns 'in glory,' whose glory is it?" Is Paul referring to one person or to two persons? There is a great deal of divided opinion over this question. We prefer to believe this is a reference to the diety of Jesus. However, the term could be applied to either God or Jesus with almost equal reason, as will be noted from the alternate reading given in the American Standard version. Reference to Christ as God can be found in other Scriptures: Cf. John 20:28; Rom. 9:5; Heb. 1:8; II Pet. 1:1. We do suggest that you read one of the many discussions on this interesting point.

On that day when He comes He will come as "our Saviour." On that day we shall be delivered from all that thwarts and hinders the full expression of His rule among men.

Vs. 14. Yet another motive for holiness is seen in recognizing the purpose of God and Christ in the redemption of the cross. Why did Christ die? To "redeem us from all iniquity, and purify unto Himself a people for His own possession, zealous of good works."

Our blessed Lord voluntarily "gave Himself for us." No man took His life—He freely laid it down as payment for the guilt of our sin. In a grand sense, Jesus gave Himself to us, all during His earthly life. But in a unique sense, He gave Himself at Calvary for us. If the thought of substitution is not in this expression, then it is meaningless.

We were taken captive unto the will of Satan—such captivity must be broken. It was broken by payment of the redemption price. He has redeemed us—but to what intent? There is both a negative and a positive answer to this question. (1) That He might redeem us from all iniquity—that He might purify unto Himself a people for His own possession.

If we do not turn from iniquity or "lawlessness," what shall we say of the purpose of redemption? We must say that in our understanding of the death of Christ for us, we have missed the point. Christ did *NOT* come to save us *in* our sins but *from* them. How can we continue in sin while beholding what it cost God and His son? Our acceptance of Christ's redemption is fatally faulty, if it fails to include a turning from all our iniquity.

"We were not only guilty, but dirty." We are also delivered and purified. We immediately think of the sanctifying services of the Old Covenant. The purifying of the priests was but a shadow, of which we are the substance. We are cleansed from the inside, by our acceptance of God's Lamb, and His Sacrifice for us. This is true if we understand the power of the cross in our hearts, and meet the requirements of cleansing as stated in His Word. Cf. Rom. 6:1-6 for a discussion of where and when we meet the death of Christ for the inward cleansing.

The King James version uses the expression "peculiar people" where the American Standard has "a people for his own possession." The thought of the word is in reference to something that "belongs in a special sense to oneself." The word "particular" is better understood by us today, instead of "peculiar." We belong to Christ in a "particular" sense; we are His very own.

(2) Christ redeemed us to the intent that we should be "zealous of good works." This is the positive aspect of redemption. Once again we must say, that if we are not eager and urgent in our living the Christian life and communicating the good news to others, we have not a clear view of the purpose of Calvary.

Vs. 15. This is a fitting conclusion to the chapter. We refer the expression "these things" to the instructions and admonitions of chapter two. But we could as well include chapter one, or even allow this to stand at the head of chapter three, as applying to it.

Someone has said, the words here given to Titus outline the preaching and teaching ministry of the evangelist:
speak: "talk" would be a good synonym. In ordinary conversation with the persons mentioned, do not hesitate to discuss these important matters. Let others discuss the weather and relatives, but do not forget to "talk" about these more important subjects discussed in this letter.
exhort: Some will need help in applying the truth to life. This is your place in God's program. It is always easier to see the implications of the truth, when pointed out by someone else. We are reluctant to apply it by ourselves to ourselves.
reprove: Others will need chastening. The man of God has the holy responsibility of indicating short-comings in reference to God's laws for living. He must remind the Christian that God has punishment for violators.

Titus is to do this with "all authority." He is to be aware that God speaks through him. This letter will confirm the importance and source of what he says.

"*Let no man despise thee.*" The word "depise" means "to think around."

Among the older men, older women, younger men, or the slaves, there will be those who seem to continue in their error in spite of your words. Do not ignore this attitude! Be sure each one faces squarely and personally the will of God for his life. Stand boldly in the pathway of those in need.

Fact Questions 2:11-15

60. Give the central thought of vss. 11-15.
61. When and where was the grace of God manifested?
62. In what way did the grace of God bring salvation to all men?
63. The grace of God is a great "pedagogue." Explain.
64. How do we learn from the "grace of God" to deny ungodliness and worldly lusts?
65. Explain the meaning of the three words: soberly, righteously and godly, as in vs. 12.
66. Show how the Second Coming of Christ becomes a motive for holy living.

67. When He returns "in glory" whose glory is it? Discuss.
68. Explain in your own words how the cross becomes a motive for holy living.
69. To what intent has Christ redeemed us? Give both the negative and the positive answer to this question.
70. Show how we are sanctified by our acceptance of the death of Christ.
71. In what sense are we a "peculiar people"?
72. If we are not eager and urgent in living the Christian life, what is the difficulty according to vs. 14b?
73. What are the "things" of vs. 15a?
74. How is the word "speak" used here?
75. Explain how the word "reprove" is used in vs. 15.
76. Give the meaning of the phrase, "Let no one despise thee."

EXEGETICAL EXAMINATION OVER CHAPTER TWO OF THE EPISTLE TO TITUS

1. Give from memory your own outline of this chapter.
2. Present an explanation as to how to help older men, young women and young men.
3. Explain the responsibilities of the older women.
4. Give your own exegesis of vs. 8.
5. Show the pertinency of the instructions to slaves.
6. How can we "adorn the gospel"?
7. What is "the grace of God" as in vs. 11?
8. What is the powerful incentive for denying ungodliness and worldly lusts?
9. Show the relationship of holiness and the second coming.
10. Give your own exegesis of vs. 15.

III. CHURCH MEMBERS IN SOCIETY 3:1-11

1. AS CITIZENS 3:1, 2

Text 3:1, 2

1 Put them in mind to be in subjection to rulers, to authorities, to be obedient, to be ready unto every good work,
2 to speak evil of no man, not to be contentious, to be gentle, showing all meekness toward all men.

Thought Questions 3:1, 2

114. Had the Cretans been instructed before on the matter of their relationship to civil authorities? When, and by whom?

115. Is there some distinction between rulers and authorities? Specify.
116. Why say "to be obedient" when they are already reminded to be "in subjection"?
117. What "good work" would be open to Christians on Crete? Please note that this "good work" is civil in nature.
118. In what sense are we "to speak evil of no man"? Paul outlined and itemized the evil works of many men.
119. How can we "contend for the faith" and yet not be contentious?
120. Discuss the strength of gentleness.
121. Surely "showing all meekness toward all men" is an overstatement. Show how such an injunction could be translated into life.

Paraphrase 3:1, 2

1 Put the Cretians in mind of what I have taught them; namely, to be subject to the governments and powers established in Crete; to obey magistrates though they be heathens; to be ready to perform every good work enjoined by the laws of their country;
2 To speak evil of no one on account of his nation or religion, to be no fighters, but of an equitable disposition, (Phil. 4:5, note), and to show the greatest meekness to all men, even to enemies.

Comment 3:1, 2

Vs. 1 Here are some of the "good works" for which the Christians on Crete are to be zealous. Evidently Paul had spoken to the Cretans about this before—it now remains for Titus to "put them in mind" of these things, for the truth to be carried out. If we are to believe historians of the time (and we have no reason to doubt them), Cretans were very dissatisfied with the Roman rule, and showed signs of revolt. So says Polybius and Plutarch. In the light of this situation, the Christians leave a testimony to present to the world.

Adopt a willingness to subject yourselves to your rulers. Even if such rulers live evil lives, yet God has ordained law and order. As long as the laws of the land do not contradict the laws of God, we should be perfectly willing to obey men (Cf. Acts 5:29). The word "authorities" as coupled with "rulers" simply enlarges on one thought, that is, rulers have authority. Romans 13:1-6 indicates such authority is from God.

The Christian is not only to be willing, but when called upon to act, he will obey. How easy it is to justify disobedience when we feel the ones who command obedience are themselves disobedient—most especially is this true when the laws are apparently but a matter of opinion or interpretation. Such attitudes cannot be indulged in by the Christian, for his example is watched and followed. To those looking for an opportunity to criticize The Way, he has provided it. To those looking for occasion to rebel, he has unwillingly given excuse.

In what "good work" would the civil authorities engage, to which we could lend assistance? We can think of a number of community projects to which we could pledge our support if we would. Is the donation of blood a "good work"? Would the relief of war victims be a "good work"? Would appeal to our public officials for righteous legislation, or support of some who are attempting to persuade such legislation, be a "good work"? What are we doing about it?

Vs. 2. There are in vss. 1, 2 seven responsibilities for the believer. Three are in vs. 1 and four in vs. 2: (1) Be in subjection to rulers and authorities; (2) Be obedient; (3) Be ready unto every good work; (4) Speak evil of no man; (5) Do not be contentious; (6) Be gentle; (7) Show all meekness toward all men.

Vs. 2 seems to relate to those on the outside of the church, whereas verse one discusses those on the inside. To "speak evil of no man" in the midst of a wicked world, is no easy injunction. The word used is stronger than criticism; it means "to heap curses upon" or "to blaspheme." No good is accomplished by such words—our attitude of "good will toward all men," is hardly upheld by such outbursts.

Someone has humorously said, "Some church members are born in the objective case and the kickative mood." Such a one might be designated as "contentious." Such persons are also very poor witnesses for Christ, to say nothing of being poor neighbors and citizens.

The word "gentle" is a good one as relating to its root meaning—one filled with a positive good will—"ready to yield personal advantage, eager to help the needy, kind to the weak, considerate toward the fallen, always filled with the spirit of sweet reasonableness" (Hendriksen). We could easily say of the thought here, that a true Christian will be a true *gentleman*.

How did Paul imagine believers would be able to show "*all* meekness (or mildness) to *all* men"? Was this the attitude needed with these "liars, evil brutes, and lazy bellies"? (Cf. 1:12) We have no right to ask such a question. We do not want to overcome evil with good. We somehow imagine we shall overcome evil with force or demanded respect. Until the world can see some of the *humility* and *meekness* (which is but strength under control) of our Lord, we shall have but little progress in making the kingdoms of this world the kingdom of our Lord and of His Christ.

Please do not shrug off this word as an ideal. It is more—it is God's answer to a lost world.

Fact Questions 3:1, 2

77. How was Titus finishing a work started by Paul?
78. Timothy was told to pray for rulers. Titus was told to command obedience to them. Is this a fair comparison? If not, why not? If so, why so?
79. When, and only when, should the Christian rebel against authority?
80. Is there some distinction in the use of the terms, "rulers and authorities"?
81. Since many laws are only a matter of opinion, why should we bother to obey them? (Especially when we are in a hurry to keep an important appointment.)
82. In what "good work" could the believers help?
83. List the four responsibilities of vs. 2, and give a specific, personal example of how they are fulfilled in daily life.

2. THE MOTIVE FOR PROPER CONDUCT 3:3-7

Text 3:3-7

3 For we also once were foolish, disobedient, deceived, serving divers lusts and pleasures, living in malice and envy, hateful, hating one another.

4 But when the kindness of God our Saviour, and his love toward man, appeared,

5 not by works done in righteousness, which we did ourselves, but according to his mercy he saved us, through the washing of regeneration and renewing of the Holy Spirit,

6 which he poured out upon us richly, through Jesus Christ our Saviour;

7 that, being justified by his grace, we might be made heirs according to the hope of eternal life.

Thought Questions 3:3-7

122. Just who is included in the "we" of vs. 3?
123. If all such actions as those described in vs. 3 are in the past tense, why the need for the injunctions of vs. 1 and 2?
124. In what context is the word "foolish" used in vs. 3a?
125. Is there some order of progress in the sins described in vs. 3? Please examine them carefully.
126. In what sense is the word "deceived" used?
127. Why would anyone actually serve something that offers so little, if any, benefit as "divers lusts and pleasures"?
128. Is there any genuine "pleasure" in serving Satan? Discuss.
129. Show the distinction between: malice and envy—hateful and hating one another.
130. Point out the difference in the use of the words "kindness" and "love" as in vs. 4.
131. Is Paul discussing the conversion of the Cretans, in vs. 4, or is this a reference to the first advent of Christ?
132. We are not saved by works—or are we? Please explain.
133. Paul plainly states that the Cretans were saved from the power and penalty of the sins mentioned in vs. 3. If we as church members continue to practice some of these sins, can we say we are saved? Discuss.
134. We are saved "by the means of" the "washing of regeneration and renewing of the Holy Spirit." Please explain just what experience this describes.
135. What did God pour out upon us richly?
136. Explain the phrase, "justified by his grace."
137. Is eternal life the inheritance of the "heirs" of vs. 7b? Please note the marginal reading.

Paraphrase 3:3-7

3 This behavior, towards those who profess false religions, becometh us Jews: For even we ourselves were formerly foolish in our notions of religion, and in observing the traditions of the fathers; disobedient to God, erring from the truth, slavishly serving divers inordinate desires and pleasures, living in malice and envy, hated by the Gentiles, and hating one another.

4 But when the goodness and philanthropy of God our Saviour (Chap. 2:11), shone forth to all mankind, through the preaching of the gospel,

5 He saved us Jews from the miserable and wicked state in which we were living, not on account of any works of righteousness which we had done under the law to merit such a deliverance, but in prosecution of his own merciful purpose, which he accomplished through the bath of regeneration, and the renewing of the Holy Ghost,
6 Which he poured out on us richly, in his various gifts at our conversion, through Jesus Christ our Saviour, who procurred these gifts for men;
7 That being delivered, by the mere favor of God, from the wickedness and misery of our former state, we might be made children and heirs, agreeably to the hope of eternal life given us by the promise of God.

Comment 3:3-7

Vs. 3. Paul is to say, that since the Cretans were Christians, it should not be difficult to follow out the seven points of instruction in vss. 1, 2. But what a grand way to approach the subject! Surely the incentive to act as Paul asks will be developed by his approach.

Notice the inclusion of himself and Titus in what he says: "For *we* also were once foolish." It will be observed that whereas there were seven areas of obedience (vss. 1, 2) there are here seven areas of disobedience (vs. 3): (1) Foolish; (2) Disobedient; (3) Deceived; (4) Serving divers lusts and pleasures; (5) Living in malice and envy; (6) Hateful; (7) Hating one another.

This is also a description of the former life of the Christians on Crete. We were once this way, but from these things we were delivered—the strong inference being "we cannot fall back into the pit from whence we were digged"! It will be greatly profitable to meditate a moment on each of these descriptive terms.

Foolish: Sin is foolishness. It is not that the unregenerate is not intelligent, but rather that he walks in the vanity of his own understanding which has been perverted by Satan. The philosophy of the unregenerated is not cohesive; he has left out the one who holds all things together.

Disobedient: This is an outgrowth of foolishness. The sinner is not only disobedient to God, but to his own better self; to will to do right is present, but the power to carry it out is not.

Deceived: We could say with Paul elsewhere "deceived and being deceived." Those who offer no resistance to Satan are helpless victims of his wiles. Those who walk not according to the truth, inevitably walk in error. Sin is an illusion of worth—those who pursue it for reality are deceived.

Serving divers lusts and pleasures: The strong drives of human nature have become their masters. They are no better than animals who live only for the sensations of the body. When control is not exercised in the area of appetites, we become the unhappy and almost unwilling slaves. How fleeting the pleasure offered—how empty is all the satisfaction our heart desires.

Living in malice and envy: Perhaps envy is an outgrowth of malice. Malice is a desire for evil directed toward another person. In contrast to the one who would want good for his neighbor, the one living in malice would wish him every misfortune. It could be that envy was one of the reasons for such an attitude developing.

Hateful: Detestable or abominable would be a better word. From God's viewpoint, such a person has become loathsome. The strange part of the whole life of indulgent living is, that we can never quite understand why people do not like us—except to their own advantage. Ingrown selfishness produces an impossible associate.

Hating one another: The selfish man is never wrong, that is, in his own eyes. Such an attitude develops hatred for those who disagree with us. When two or two dozen such people associate together, the expression "hating one another" is an accurate description of their attitude.

Vs. 4 God made an appearance on the stage of our life. When He came, He was full of kindness and love. We did not deserve kindness—indeed, our repulsive conduct would call for punishment! There was nothing loveable about us. But God came to stretch out arms of love to us, even if He must stretch them on the cross of Golgotha. There is a whole vista of understanding in the little expression, "the kindness and love toward man." As Hendriksen states, "The expression—is *one* concept; hence, the verb in the original is singular." It is one thing to love—and God can do no other, for He is love—but to be kind, one must have a personal interest and concern. God not only loved us, but sought to personalize His love in speaking to our individual needs. How did the preacher know what you needed when first you heard the good news? It was the kindness of God adapting His love to your deepest need through the man of God.

Vs. 5 We can have patience with persons yet in sin, when we remember our deliverance or salvation. We cannot look down on them, inasmuch as we also remember it was out of God's mercy and grace we were saved, and not by or because of any merit of our own.

Our salvation was obtained by or through the means of "the washing of regeneration and renewing of the Holy Spirit." The alternate reading in the American Standard version reads: "*laver* of regeneration and *through* renewing of the Holy Spirit." The means by which our salvation or regeneration was affected is here described. What is the import and meaning of the expression, "the washing of regeneration and the renewing of the Holy Spirit"? We shall discuss these two phrases separately.

Washing or laver of regeneration: To be regenerated is to be born again. We were given birth once by our earthly parents; we are given a new or second birth by our heavenly Parent. We are almost constrained to ask with Nicodemus—"How can a man be born when he is old?" The answer is here—it is through the *laver* or *washing* and through the *renewing of the Holy Spirit*. Let us not overemphasize one to the exclusion of the other. We shall call in a few witnesses as to the meaning and application of the term "washing or laver."

Hendriksen: "It is clear from such passages as John 3:3,5 and especially Ephesians 5:26 (Cf. Heb. 10:22) that this 'washing of regeneration and renewing' stands in some relation to the rite of baptism." (Ibid., p. 392)

Lenski: "God saved us by means of baptism. Baptism is a bath of regeneration and renewing, in both of which the Holy Spirit is the actor. That is why God could use baptism as such a means; by baptism, is by no means a mere symbol or picture, but a true means of divine grace. It is not an *opus operatom* as when a crowbar turns over a stone, but as when spiritual grace operates spiritually by the Holy Spirit's entering the heart with his grace and kindling the new life" (Ibid.).

Hoven: "It is motivated by 'the kindness of God'; accomplished, not by man's moral goodness, but by two agencies—'washing of regeneration' (laver, bath of rebirth, or immersion into Christ) and 'renewing of the Holy Spirit,' that is, renewing of the human spirit by the Spirit of God. (Cf. Psalms 51:10) In conversion, the Spirit presents to the human mind what to do to be saved from past sins, I Peter 1:23; James 1:18; the result is *a new person*. After conversion, the Spirit continually renews the mind of the Christian by His word, II Corinthians 4:16; Ephesians 4:22,24. The result is *a new life*. The final objective is eternal life." (Ibid., p. 99)

W. J. Conybeare: "Laver—the word does not mean "washing", (A.V.), but *laver*, that is, a vessel in which washing takes place." (*The Epistles of Paul*, p. 188.)

Fairbairn: "And the only question is, how the expression, when coupled here with regeneration, is to be explained. Some have taken it in an altogether figurative sense, as emblematically representing the spiritual change; some, again, of the Holy Spirit, or of the word—the one as the efficient, the other as the instrumental cause of regeneration. But these cannot be termed quite natural explanations; and neither here nor in Eph. 5:26 do they seem to have occurred to the ancient interpreters. They all apply the expression to the baptismal ordinance." (Ibid., p. 294)

Thus we have a good company of witnesses when we relate the washing or laver of regeneration to the waters of baptism. It is not to say there is something magical in the water of baptism. But we *do* intend to say that it is here we are buried *into the death of Christ*. (Cf. Rom. 6:1-3). It is here we appropriate the cleansing power of His blood. It is here we receive in our watery grave the gift of God which is the Holy Spirit (Acts 2:38). It might be significant to point out that Christ received the renewing of His spirit in Joseph's tomb. We do not know *why* God ordained that in baptism man finds the "bath of regeneration" but that He did, we cannot ignore. We are also aware that to many, baptism is no more than "going down a dry sinner and coming up a wet one", but this does not negate God's teaching on the bath of regeneration. When one comes to baptism in wholehearted faith and repentance, it becomes just what God intended —a "new birth."

Renewing of the Holy Spirit: Is this a renewing of the Holy Spirit Himself, or a renewing accomplished by the Holy Spirit? From what we have already written, one could conclude we believe this has reference to the renewing of the spirit of man by the Holy Spirit. Just how is this accomplished? The Holy Spirit presents His transforming — life-giving truth to the mind of man. When man is ready to accept such truth, our minds or spirits are renewed, and we are transformed into His likeness. (Cf. Rom. 12:1, 2).

Vs. 6 What is it that is "poured out upon us"? Is this in reference to the Holy Spirit? We believe that it is. The figure of pouring out in reference to the Holy Spirit, is a very familiar one. The reception of the Holy Spirit on the part of all Christians, is not expressed with any frequency. God has been no respector of persons in this expression of His love; He has given the Holy Spirit to all who obey Him. (Cf. Acts 5:32). This is the sense in which the word "abundantly" or "richly" is used. Of course, Paul had received the outpouring of the Holy Spirit in the baptism of the Holy Spirit: many of the leaders of the churches had received special gifts of the Spirit from the hands of Paul undoubtedly including Titus. But this is a reference to the general reception of the Holy Spirit by all Christians, as an expression of God's love and mercy.

Vs. 7 The final objective of the new life in Christ—"eternal life." "The process of reasoning which we find in these verses (3-7) is familiar to the student of Paul's epistles. Note the three stages: We *were* by nature children of wrath—we *have been made alive*—we *now look* forward by faith to the ages to come when we shall receive even greater glory (Eph. 2:1-10); We *were* idol-worshippers—we *now* serve the true and living God—we *await* the coming of the Son of God from heaven (I Thess. 1:9,10) and our everlasting fellowship with Him (I Thess. 4:13-18). We *were* ungodly and ruled by worldly passions— we *have renounced* all this and are now living lives of self-mastery, fairness and devotion—we *are waiting* for the realization of the blessed hope (Titus 2:11-13." (Hendriksen, Ibid., pp. 392, 393.) The concluding thought in the motive for holy loving, is the hope of reward. We are now heirs of the eternal life to come.

Fact Questions 3:3-7

84. Explain the purpose of Paul's approach to the instructions for Christian living.
85. Define in your own words three of the seven words describing the former state in sin.
86. What distinction was made between "kindness" and "love"? Do you agree? Explain.

87. What is "the laver or bath of regeneration"? Please do not accept our conclusion unless you have good reason to do so. Discuss.
88. What is "the renewing of the Holy Spirit"?
89. What has God poured out upon us richly?
90. Show how this whole section, i.e., vss. 3-7, relates to the heading, "The motive for proper conduct."

3. TRUTH AND ERROR 3:8-11

Text 3:8-11

8 Faithful is the saying, and concerning these things I desire that thou affirm confidently, to the end that they who have believed God may be careful to maintain good works. These things are good and profitable unto men:

9 but shun foolish questions, and geneaologies, and strifes, and fightings about the law; for they are unprofitable and vain.

10 A factious man after a first and second admonition refuse;

11 knowing that such a one is perverted, and sinneth, being self-condemned.

Thought Questions 3:8-11

138 What is the "faithful saying"?
139 Concerning what things is Titus to "affirm confidently"?
140. Were the saints on Crete so weak that they needed constant help? Explain.
141. What things are good and profitable to all men? Who is included in "all men"?
142. Try to approximate the circumstances prevailing with Titus, as he followed out the command to "shun foolish questionings", etc., i.e. just how would he accomplish it?
143. Are "foolish questionings and genealogies" the same as "strifes and fightings about the law"? Discuss possible distinctions.
144. In what sense "unprofitable" and in what sense "vain"?
145. Who is to determine when a man is factious? It could be done with the churches on Crete—it can be done now—how?
146. Just what is involved in "the first and second admonition"?
147. Is this a discussion of "disfellowship"?
148. How could Titus be so confident that certain men were "perverted", "self-condemned"?
149. Define the word "perverted", i.e. in its context.

Paraphrase 3:8-11

8 This doctrine, that men are justified and made heirs merely by God's grace, is true; yet, concerning these heirs, I command thee strongly to affirm, that they who have believed in God should take care to promote good works. These are the things honourable and profitable to men: They are good for others, as making them happy; and most profitable to one's self, as productive of happiness both here and hereafter.
9 But the frivolous questions proposed by the Judaizers, and the genealogies by which they pretend to prove individuals rightly descended from Abraham, and their strifes and fighting about the law, resist; for they are unprofitable, and destitute of foundation.
10 An heretical teacher, who, after a first and second admonition, continues in his evil courses, cast out of the church, and have no further communication with him, because he is irreclaimable;
11 Knowing that such a teacher is utterly depraved, and in teaching false doctrine from worldly motives, sinneth, being self-condemned.

Comment 3:8-11

Vs. 8 As near as we can conclude the "faithful saying" is contained in verses four through seven. It is with the content of this word, Paul is concerned. He urges Titus to speak with all confidence and assurance. Unlike the law teachers who knew not of the things they so confidently affirmed, Titus can speak with the confidence of inspired and experimental knowledge. There is a grand purpose in such continual instruction; "that they who have believed may be careful to maintain good works." Unless men are often reminded of their duties and privileges, they soon forget. Titus had been heralding forth the good news. Paul urges him to keep it up and to look for the fruit in the lives of the saints in the form of "good works."

To what does the little phrase: "These things are good and profitable to all men" refer? What are "the things" and who are "the men"? We cannot relate this to only the faithful saying of the verses immediately preceding. We believe it has a wider application—indeed to all that is written in the letter. All the advice and doctrine here written is good and profitable, not alone to the Christians, but to "all men"—believers or unbelievers. If the world wants a good and profitable philosophy of life, they cannot do better than to follow Paul.

Vs. 9 Now to the negative side of the work of Titus! As Titus was to continue to teach the whole council of God, he was also urged to continue to ignore silly questions and discussions about genealogies. When strife and word-battles arise, turn your back upon them. Do not enter into a discussion as to who is right or wrong. Neither is right—they are both wrong. Here is the place for contempt. Lenski describes such persons as, ". . . full of a lot of silly stuff that was unworthy of serious attention and created nothing but fussing and fighting with true Christians, and deceived those Christians who were not yet well grounded." (Ibid., p. 941). Such advice is very much like that given by Paul to Timothy (Cf. I Tim. 1:4-7).

Vs. 10. How shall we relate vs. 10 with vs. 9? Or should we see a connection between the two verses? We believe the heretical man of vs. 10 is one who has been beguiled from the faith by the teachers of vs. 9. If such treatment as described in vs. 10 is accorded the disciples of false doctrine, what shall be the action taken against the teacher? It will be the same. A factious man is *any* man who holds *any* opinion different from the Scriptures. It makes little difference if the opinion be considered important or unimportant. If he teaches it as from God and it is not in accord with the Word of God, he is a heretic! He should be treated in the manner here described. Please notice that a factious man and a heretic are the same man—*a heretic is one who holds his own opinion in the realm of faith.*

Vs. 11. This verse indicates the seriousness of the sin committed, from the viewpoint of the one committing the sin. Such a one is "perverted" or "turned out from" the true doctrine of Christ. When the elders from the church attempt to lead him back into the path of truth, he rejects both attempts. Yet all the while his conscience condemns him. This is no pagan unbeliever; this is a prominent member of the Church. Even while loudly and energetically promoting his own opinion, he is yet aware that he is wrong and is, therefore, sinning. But because of the popularity, the money or the prestige, he will not listen; he will not change—it costs him too much by human values. No one need condemn him; he is self-condemned. What a havoc such a one can cause both to himself and to those who heed him. Let all the members of the churches give such a one the cold shoulder of indifference.

Fact Questions 3:8-11

91. What is it Titus is to "affirm confidently"? Show how his effort would be like, yet different from, the law-teachers of I Tim. 1-4-7.
92. Who are the persons involved in the little phrase, "all men" of vs. 8b? What is profitable to them?
93. What is to be done when strife and word-battles arise? Is there a present day application of this situation? If so, discuss.
94. Show how Matt. 18:15-17 relates to vs. 10.
95. How does one become a heretic? Is there an admonition here to public disfellowship? Discuss.
96. What is the meaning and use of the term "perverted" as used in vs. 11?
97. Explain how such a one as the heretic is "self-condemned." Do you believe this applies to all factious men and women? Discuss.
98. What are some of the comparisons and contrasts of Cretan churches and those today?

CONCLUSION 3:12-15

Text 3:12-15

12 When I shall send Artemas unto thee, or Tychicus, give diligence to come unto me to Nicopolis: for there I have determined to winter.

13 Set forward Zenas the lawyer and Apollos on their journey diligently, that nothing be wanting unto them.

14 And let our people also learn to maintain good works for necessary uses, that they be not unfruitful.

15 All that are with me salute thee. Salute them that love us in faith. Grace be with you all.

Thought Questions 3:12-15

150. Why was Paul sending Artemas or Tychicus to Titus?
151. Where is Nicopolis? (Do not shrug this question off with a "I do not know"—you have a map; *look it up!*)
152. Why spend the winter in Nicopolis? That is, why not move on to other fields?
153. What is the meaning of the expression, "set forward," in vs. 13?
154. How is the word, "diligently," used in vs. 13?
155. Is Paul asking Titus or the churches to pay the traveling expenses of Zenas and Apollos? Where are these men going?
156. What are the "good works" and the "necessary uses" of vs. 14?

157. In what sense would the Cretans be "unfruitful," as used in vs. 14b?
158. From where was this epistle to Titus written? Please refer to the introduction for your answer. Who are some of the possble persons to be with Paul?
159. Just what was the "salute" mentioned in vs. 15?
160. How is the word "faith" used in vs. 15b?

Paraphrase 3:12-15

12 When I shall send either Artemas to thee, or Tychicus, to supply thy place in Crete, leave the churches to his management, and as speedily as possible, come to me at Nicopolis, for there I have determined to winter.
13 Diligently supply Zenas the lawyer, and Appolos (see Acts 18:24-28), with whatever is necessary for their journey, that, in coming to me, nothing which they need may be wanting to them.
14 And, that the expense necessary to such offices may be defrayed, let our disciples in Crete also learn to follow honest trades for supplying what is necessary to themselves, and that they may not be unfruitful in good offices to others.
15 All my fellow-labourers who are with me in Colosse wish thee health. Present my good wishes to them in Crete, who shew their love to me by maintaining the true faith of Christ. The favour and blessing of God be with all of you. Amen.

Comment 3:12-15

Vs. 12. A few closing and personal words from Paul to Titus. It is vain to speculate as to the identity of Artemas. Attempts at identification have been made, and if you wish to read them, we refer you to our bibliography. Tychicus is well-known to us; see: Acts 20:4; Eph. 6:21; Col. 4:7; II Tim. 4:12. We do know Paul trusted these men and intended for one of them to carry out the work after Titus left. There must have been, for Titus, further plans for evangelism and the establishment of churches. We prefer to locate Nicopolis on the coast of Greece. There were a good number of cities with the name, Nicopolis (city of victory), so-called because of some military triumph. Paul refers to the one at Epirus, founded by Augustus in 30 B.C. in honor of his victory at Actium, four miles from Nicopolis. Paul had not yet arrived in this city, but planned to be here for work and plans during the winter. Surely he selected an excellent place by way of climate.

Vs. 13. Perhaps we have here a reference to those who carried the letter from Paul to Titus. Was Zenas a "law expert" or "jurist" in the Roman sense, or with the Old Testament? His name is Roman, but then, so is "Paul" a Roman name, and so is the name "Apollos." We prefer to think of him as referred to in Acts 18:24 and last mentioned in I Cor. 16:12. Titus is here instructed to "outfit and expedite for a journey" (Lenski) these faithful men. They are not on Crete as yet, but are on their way (perhaps with this letter), and when they arrive they are to be helped on this way, and this is to be done in a diligent manner.

Vs. 14. Titus could not himself provide the funds necessary for Zenas and Apollos. He is to lead in obtaining from the churches the necessary provisions. But Titus is not alone responsible for such leadership in good works. "Our people" are to lead out in such cases of necessity, that at other times of less obvious need they will not be unfruitful. Paul looked upon the matter of helping one another as an opportunity for Christian growth, not a burdensome duty.

Vs. 15. Where was Paul when he wrote this letter? We have suggested he was probably in some part of Macedonia—possibly Philippi. Those traveling companions of Paul (which seem always to be with him) send greetings to Titus who probably at other times were co-labourers with Titus and the apostle. Paul assumes that many, if not all, of the saints of the churches on Crete will feel warmly toward him as an apostle and servant of Christ Jesus. On this basis he greets each of those who read or hear this letter read.

May all be constantly aware of God's favor toward us in Christ Jesus.

Fact Questions 3:12-15

99 Give two facts about Artemas and Tychicus.
100. Give two facts about Nicopolis.
101. What did Paul plan to do while in Nicopolis?
102. State two facts about Zenas and Apollos.
103. Just what was Titus' responsibility for Zenas and Apollos?
104. The churches on Crete were going to have an opportunity to be fruitful in Christian service—what was this opportunity?
105. Where was Paul when he wrote this letter? Who sends greetings to whom?

EXEGETICAL EXAMINATION OVER CHAPTER THREE

1. Give from memory an outline of this chapter.
2. Define and discuss in context the following words: "every good work"; foolish"; "not to be contentious"; "living in malice and envy.
3. Show the distinction and application of the words "kindness" and "grace" in vs. 4.
4. Discuss in your own words, "The renewing of the Holy Spirit."
5. What has been "poured out upon us richly"?
6. In what sense are verses four through seven a "faithful saying"?
7. Give your own exegesis of vs. 9.
8. Who is the "factious man"? How applied to present day situation?
9. Is every factious man perverted and self-condemned? Explain.
10. Give your own exegesis of vs. 14.

EXAMINATION ON PAUL'S EPISTLE TO TITUS

1. When and where and why was the epistle to Titus written?
2. Give the outline of the epistle.
3. In the introduction the writer gives his position—his standard—his commission—what are they?
4. What responsibility did Titus have to the elders on Crete?
5. Give and explain three qualifications of the eldership.
6. Give and explain two characteristics of the false teachers.
7. Give the meaning of the expression: "All things are clean to the clean."
8. State and explain one point of instruction to the older men.
9. Give two responsibilities of the younger women.
10. Explain the two sins slaves were to especially avoid. How?
11. Give and explain two things the grace of God teaches us.
12. How does the second coming of Christ provide a desire for Christian conduct?
13. Give the meaning of the expression "toward every good work to be ready." Give the explanation in the context.
14. Why not be a "slave of desires and pleasures of various kinds"?
15. Can you put any water into "the washing of regeneration"? Explain.

PAUL'S SECOND LETTER TO TIMOTHY

We once again refer you to our introduction for a preparation in understanding the circumstances of the writing of this letter. Suffice it to say here that this epistle is far more personal in style and content than Paul's first letter, and that it was written from Rome in the year A.D. 67. It is a letter written under the long shadow of death; probably not more than a few months before Paul's martyrdom. Paul wants once more to see his son in the faith. He urges him to make haste to his side—we like to believe Timothy reached Paul before he died.

Without analysis, there can be no synthesis. In other words, if you do not understand the structure of this letter, you will have great difficulty with any conclusions from it. It is *imperative* that you have a useable outline of this letter.

Here are four outlines from men who have thought through the structure of the letter. Read Paul's second letter to Timothy once for each outline—notice carefully each outline as you read.

1. Russell Bradley Jones — from *The Epistles To Timothy* — A Study Manual — Baker Book House, 1959.

INTRODUCTION (1:1-5)
- A. The Writer (1:1).
- B. The Addressee (1:2a).
- C. The Blessing (1:2b).
- D. The Thanksgiving (1:3-5).

I. EXHORTATIONS (1:6—2:26)
- A. "Stir Up the Gift of God" (1:6-10).
  1. The Exhortation.
  2. The Reason for this Exhortation.
  3. The Basis of the Exhortation.
- B. "That Good Thing . . . Guard" (1:11-14).
  1. The Example of Paul.
  2. The Duty of Timothy.
- C. "Suffer Hardship with Me" (1:15—2:13).
  1. Paul's Experience with Fellow-workers.
     - a. The Failures.
     - b. The Faithful.
  2. Paul's Appeal to Timothy.
     - a. The Urgent Duty.
     - b. The Glorious Example.
     - c. The Saving Purpose.
     - d. The Faithful Saying.

D. Be an Unashamed Workman (2:14-26).
  1. Reminding Others.
  2. Seeking Approval.
  3. Shunning Babblings.
  4. Confident in the Lord.
  5. Forsaking Unrighteousness.
  6. Exercising a Restrained Gentleness.
  7. Correcting Others.

II. WARNINGS (3:1—4:5)
  A. Perilous Times Shall Come (3:1-13).
    1. Decadent Men.
      a. Characteristics.
      b. Actions.
      c. End.
    2. Delivered Men.
      a. Paul.
      b. All the Godly.
    3. Deception's Power.
  B. "Fulfill Thy Ministry" (3:14—4:5).
    1. Abide in the Things Learned.
      a. From the Apostle.
      b. From the Sacred Writings.
    2. "Preach the Word."
      a. The Charge.
      b. The Manner.
      c. The Need.
      d. The Duty.

III. TESTIMONY (4-6-18)
  A. Paul's Confidence as He Faces Death (4:6-8).
    1. The End.
    2. The Record.
    3. The Reward.
  B. Paul's Request that Timothy Come to Him (4:9-15).
    1. Paul and His Fellow-workers.
      a. Timothy
      b. Demas

c. Crescens
d. Titus
e. Luke
f. Mark
g. Tychicus

2. Paul and His Cloak, Books, and Parchments.
3. Paul and an Enemy.

C. Paul's Praise of His Faithful Lord (4:16-18).

1. The Lord Delivered.
2. The Lord Will Deliver.

CONCLUSION (4:19-22)

A. Added Personal References (4:19-21).

1. Salutations.
2. News.
3. Renewed Appeal.
4. Greetings.

B. Benediction (4:22).

2. David Lipscomb and J. W. Shepherd, *New Testament Commentaries*—Gospel Advocate, 1942.

PERSONAL APPEAL FOR LOYALTY TO THE GOSPEL (1:1—2:13)

1. Apostolic Greeting.
2. Thanksgiving for Timothy's Past and Exhortation That He May Be Zealous and Willing, Like Paul, to Suffer for the Gospel.
3. Deserters and Loyal Friends.
4. Renewed Appeal to Transmit to Others the Gospel, Even at the Cost of Suffering.

THE MINISTERS OF GOD AND FALSE TEACHERS (2:14—4:8)

1. He Dissuades from Unprofitable Discussion.
2. Grievous Times Impending.
3. Charge to Timothy to Fulfill His Ministry.
4. Requests and Personal Details.
5. Salutations and Benedictions.

3. Leslie G. Thomas, *An Introduction To the Epistles of Paul*, Gospel Advocate, 1955.

SALUTATION (1:1,2)

I. A PERSONAL PLEA FOR LOYALTY TO THE GOSPEL IN THE FACE OF A GRAVE CRISIS (1:3-18).

A. Thanksgiving for Timothy's Past (1:3-5).
B. An Exhortation to follow Paul's Example in Suffering, Willingly, and Zealously, for the Gospel (1:6-14).
C. Deserters and Loyal Friends (1:15-18).

II. DETAILED APPEAL FOR A COURAGEOUS EFFORT IN PERPETUATING THE GOSPEL, AND THE TEMPER NEEDED FOR THE TASK (2:1-26).

A. The Need for Faithfulness, even at the Cost of Suffering (2:1-13).
B. The Spirit of the True Workman for God in the Church (2:14-26).

III. THE LAST DAYS WILL BE TESTING ONES, BUT TIMOTHY IS PREPARED FOR THEM (3:1-17).

A. The Principle Features of the Days of Trial (3:1-9).
B. Timothy's Divine Resources for Meeting Them (3:10-17).

IV. FINAL SUMMARY OF THE CHARGE TO TIMOTHY (4:1-8)

V. PERSONAL REQUESTS AND PAUL'S ASSURANCE OF ABIDING FAITH IN THE LORD (4:9-18).

SALUTATIONS AND BENEDICTIONS (4:19-22).

4. W. B. Taylor, *Studies in the Epistles and Revelation*, Standard Publishing Company, 1910.

I. INTRODUCTION (1:1-5)

A. Apostleship declared.
   1. An apostle to Christ.
   2. By divine approval, through the will of God, according to the promise in Christ Jesus.
B. Personal greeting.
C. Thanksgiving: for service, friendship, and faith.

II. DUTY OF A MINISTER (1:6—2:13)

A. Gifts to God.
   1. Charges to.
   2. Duty to the saved.
B. According to grace: the grace of hearing, suffering, endurance, understanding, memory, salvation, and of the new life.

III. DUTY OF THE CHURCH (2:14—3:13)
   A. In the present crisis.
   B. In the coming apostasy.
IV. DUTY TO THE SCRIPTURES (3:14—4:8)
   A. The preacher's duty toward.
   B. The preacher's work in connection with the Scriptures. preach the Word.
   C. Enforced by Paul's experience.
      1. His service.
      2. His reward.
   D. A crown for all who love.
V. CONCLUSION (4:9-22)
   A. His associates.
   B. His enemies.
   C. Salutation.
   D. Final benediction: "The Lord be with thy spirit, grace be with thee."

Read the letter one more time. This time work out your own outline of the letter. This is *very important*—please do it.

Here is the outline we shall follow in our study of this epistle:

INTRODUCTION 1:1-5

1. Salutation 1:1,2
2. Paul's gratitude 1:3-5

PART ONE

Exhortations 1:6—2:26

1. DO NOT BE ASHAMED 1:6-18
   a. Timothy 6-11
   b. Paul 12-14
   c. Onesiphorus 15-18
2. BE STRONG IN THE SERVICE OF CHRIST 2:1-26
   a. As a child 1,2
   b. As a soldier 3,4
   c. As an athlete 5
   d. As a farmer 6-13
   e. As a workman 14-19
   f. As a utensil 20-23
   g. As a bondservant 24-26

PART TWO

Warnings 3:1—4:5

1. Recognize the coming apostasy 3:1-9

2. Withstand the apostasy 3:10-17
3. Preach the Word 4:1-5

PART THREE

Testimony 4:6-18

1. Assurance in the face of death 4:6-8
2. Request for Timothy to come to Paul 4:9-15
3. Praise for his Lord 4:16-18

CONCLUSION 4:19-22

1. Personal References 4:19-21
2. Benediction 4:22

INTRODUCTION 1:1-5

SALUTATION 1:1,2

Text 1:1,2

1 Paul, an apostle of Christ Jesus through the will of God, according to the promise of the life which is in Christ Jesus, 2 to Timothy, my beloved child: Grace, mercy, peace, from God the Father and Christ Jesus our Lord.

Thought Questions 1:1,2

1. Show how the will of God related to Paul's apostleship.
2. Who made the promise of life? To whom? When? Why?
3. In what sense was this "life" in Christ Jesus?
4. Show *two differences* in the salutations of I and II Timothy.
5. Is "beloved child" different from "genuine child"? Explain.
6. Define each word: (1) grace; (2) mercy; (3) peace.

Paraphrase 1:1,2

1 Paul, an apostle of Jesus Christ by the will of God, on account of publishing the promise of eternal life, which, being made to believers of all nations in the covenant with Abraham, is to be obtained, not by obeying Moses, but Christ Jesus.
2 To Timothy, my beloved son in the faith: May gracious dispositions, merciful deliverance, and inward peace, be yours, from God the Father of Jews and Gentiles, and from Christ Jesus our common Lord.

Comment 1:1,2

Vs. 1. Perhaps the opening of this letter sounds a bit formal to our western understanding. Besides the difference in letter style, let us not forget that this epistle was to be read, like the first one, by many in the church at Ephesus, and perhaps in some of the other churches of Asia. This is a personal letter, but it contains inspired, apostolic instruction.

In this salutation, Paul speaks of *himself* in the following terms: (1) an apostle of Jesus Christ; (2) called to the office by the will of God; (3) called into the office for the purpose of announcing the promise of life in Christ Jesus. He next speaks of *Timothy* in the following terms: (1) beloved son; (2) he "invokes" on him the threefold blessings of grace, mercy, and peace from God the Father and the Lord Jesus Christ.

Paul is in prison, about to be beheaded, and yet he says his calling and work were according to, and directed by, the will of God. Such complete commitment enabled him to "rejoice always" (Phil. 4:4). As to the meaning and use of the term "apostle," we refer you to our comment on I Timothy 1:1.

Jesus came to give life and life more abundantly (John 10:10). Paul felt his responsibility as an apostle was to tell about this Life. Without Christ we are existing, but not living. God promises life to all those who will accept it in His Son who is The Life (John 14:6).

Vs. 2. The greeting here has but little variation from the one found in Paul's first letter. Here Timothy is addressed as "beloved child"; in the first letter, he is called "genuine child." There is a very good reason for this term of endearment: Paul was facing death—as he recalled those with whom he had labored, none were nearer or dearer to him than Timothy. Paul had the same heart-satisfaction as a father with an obedient, faithful son. Paul could not have thought more of Timothy if he had been of his own flesh and blood. Indeed, he was his child in The Faith.

Fact Questions 1:1,2

1. Explain how such a formal greeting appears in an informal letter.
2. Was it the will of God that Paul suffer execution at the hand of Nero? Explain.
3. What is "the life" which is in Christ Jesus?
4. In what sense was Timothy "beloved" by Paul?
5. What is "mercy," as here used by Paul?

2. PAUL'S GRATITUDE, 1:3-5

Text 1:3-5

3 I thank God, whom I serve from my forefathers in a pure conscience, how unceasing is my remembrance of thee in my supplications, night and day 4 longing to see thee, remembering thy tears, that I may be filled with joy; 5 having been reminded of the

unfeigned faith that is in thee; which dwelt first in thy grandmother Lois, and thy mother Eunice; and, I am persuaded, in thee also.

Thought Questions 1:3-5

7. Who were the "forefathers" of vs. 3?
8. Is Paul discussing his previous life while a persecutor of the church, when he speaks of a "pure conscience"? Be sure and consider this point carefully.
9. For what was Paul thankful?
10. What does Paul say was unceasing, his remembrance, or his prayers?
11. What tears of Timothy were remembered by Paul?
12. How would the presence of Timothy fill Paul with joy?
13. How was Paul reminded of the faith of Timothy? What is "unfeigned faith"?
14. Is Paul saying here that Lois and Eunice became Christians before Timothy? Explain.

Paraphrase 1:3-5

3 I give thanks to God (whom, according to the knowledge received from my forefathers, I serve with a pure conscience, when I preach to all the promise of life through Christ), that I have unceasing remembrance of thee in my prayers, evening and morning, as a faithful minister of Christ.

4 Remembering thy tears, I greatly desire to see thee, that I may be filled with joy in conversing with thee, and in giving thee my dying charge and blessing.

5 This desire is increased by my calling to remembrance also, the unfeigned faith in the gospel which is in thee since I instructed thee, which dwelt first in thy grandmother, Lois, and in thy mother, Eunice, and I am persuaded that it dwelleth firmly fixed in thee also, through the instructions of thy pious parents, as well as through my care.

Comment 1:3-5

Vs. 3. Students of Paul's letters will see a pattern established in the opening expression of a good many of his epistles. A greeting is given, followed by an expression of thanksgiving or praise. Such is the case here. But we must hasten to say that such a mode of expression was far more than just a custom. Every word of the thanksgiving is sincere and appropriate.

Notice this brief outline of Paul's gratitude: (1) Paul thanks God for his unceasing remembrance of Timothy in prayer; (2)

He has a great desire to see Timothy—especially as he remembers his tears—if he could but see him, his joy would be full; (3) Someone or something reminds Paul of the sincere faith of Timothy. Such faith was first in Lois, then Eunice, and is now in Timothy.

The service of Paul to God was "from" his forefathers. Are we to understand by this expression that there was a constant succession of servants in the family of Paul from Benjamin, the son of Jacob, to Saul of Tarsus? We think not. The word, "from," could be translated, "after the example of" his forefathers. It could be that he has reference to some of his more immediate ancestors, such as parents and grandparents.

The word, "service," used by Paul, is just as well translated "worship." The apostle is not discussing his previous service or worship, but rather, his present efforts as a Christian. Paul's parents prepared him with a sincere attitude toward his relationship to God, which is now reflected in his apostleship for Christ. Paul served God with a "clean conscience." What a bulwark of strength for service. No service can either be sustained or strong without a pure conscience.

We are not unaware of the problem of understanding, present in the translation of vss. 3-5, but we do not feel any advantage is gained by discussing it here. We are satisfied with the American Standard translation of the text. If any are interested in pursuing the subject further, *Lenski*, *Hendriksen*, or *Hiebert* would be good authorities to consult.

Why is it that Paul thanks God that he can unceasingly pray both night and day for Timothy? It must have arisen out of the need Timothy had for such supplication. Paul and Timothy knew of the need; we do not, but it must have been a great source of comfort and encouragement to Timothy to know that his particular needs were being held up night and day before the throne of grace by the Apostle Paul!

Vs. 4. Please remember that vss. 3-5 are all contained in one sentence; read these verses again as one sentence. In Paul's prayers there arises not only the needs of Timothy, which frame the content of his supplications, but also a strong desire to see him one more time before he finished the race. This intense desire is prompted by a recollection of the tears of Timothy on behalf of Paul. Just where and when, or why these tears were shed, we do not know. Was it in Lystra when Timothy and others stood over the bruised and broken body of Paul? We know that God raised Paul up to continue his work, but it would not keep back the tears of those who loved him. Perhaps Paul's remembrance had to do with the tears shed at the parting of Paul and Timothy. The presence of Timothy with Paul would assure the Apostle that his trusted son was safe. No letter can ever take the place of speaking face to face. Paul was at peace with a pure conscience, but he did want the assurance that all was well with Timothy.

Vs. 5 Something happened in Paul to remind him of the faithfulness of Timothy. Did someone visit Paul to tell him of the early childhood of Timothy? Did something else remind him of the blessing Timothy had in Lois and Eunice? We do not know who or what it was, but the first half of this verse states that he was reminded. Does such a remembrance need outside stimuli?

There was no pretense in the faith of Lois and Eunice. Transparent sincerity is such a blessing—to the possessor and to all who associate with him. The faith of Lois and Eunice, as well as Timothy, was first in the Old Testament Scriptures and the God there revealed. This same attitude was transferred to Jesus Christ when the good news was announced by Paul.

The heart condition of these two women reminds us of the good and honest heart of Lydia. Wherever such conditions prevail, the seed of the kingdom grows to produce its glorious harvest.

Fact Questions 1:3-5

6. What style-pattern of writing is discovered in the opening section of Paul's letters?
7. For what does Paul thank God? Why?
8. In what sense was Paul's service to God "from" his forefathers?
9. Was Paul's service to God always given from a pure conscience? Remember "the goad" of Acts 9:1-6.
10. Did Paul have specific times for prayer?
11. When were the tears shed that Paul remembered?
12. What caused Paul to remember the unhypocritical faith of Timothy?
13. What pre-disposition of heart prevailed with Lois and Eunice?

PART ONE

Exhortations 1:6—2:26

1. DO NOT BE ASHAMED 1:6-18
   a. Timothy 6-11

Text 1:6-11

**6 For which cause I put thee in remembrance that thou stir up the
gift of God, which is in thee through the laying on of my hands.**

**7 For God gave us not a spirit of fearfulness; but of power and
love and discipline. 8 Be not ashamed therefore of the testimony
of our Lord, nor of me his prisoner: but suffer hardship with the
gospel according to the power of God; 9 who saved us, and called
us with a holy calling, not according to our works, but according
to his own purpose and grace, which was given us in Christ Jesus
before times eternal, 10 but hath now been manifested by the appearing of our Saviour Christ Jesus, who abolished death, and
brought life and immortality to light through the gospel, 11 whereunto I was appointed a preacher, and an apostle, and a teacher.**

Thought Questions 1:6-11

15. What "cause" does Paul have in mind in vs. 6a?
16. Had Timothy forgotten he had a gift from God? Why the use of the term, "remembrance"?
17. What was "the gift of God" possessed by Timothy?
18. What would Timothy need to do in order to "stir into a flame" the gift of God?
19. When and where did Paul give Timothy this gift? Is there a discrepancy when we compare I Tim. 4:14 with II Tim. 1:6?
20. Was Timothy "fearful," as indicated in vs. 8?
21. In what realm of life is the power of God to be exercised?
22. What is the meaning and application of the word, "discipline"?
23. What is, "the testimony of our Lord"?
24. In what regard would Timothy be tempted to be ashamed of Paul?
25. Paul was a prisoner, but he felt he was not held first by Rome, but by whom?
26. Paul suffered hardship with the gospel according to the power of God. Specify at least two instances of such.
27. In what sense are we to understand the phrase, "who saved us"? Are we saved, or in the process of being saved? Explain.
28. What is the "holy calling" by which we have been called?
29. What "works" are before the mind of the apostle, as in vs. 9b?

30. There is some distinction between "purpose" and "grace"—what is it? In whom do we have our purpose and grace?
31. Explain in context the phrase, "before times eternal" (vs. 9b).
32. What has now been manifested? How?
33. In what sense did Christ abolish death?
34. Give your own explanation as to just how Christ brought "life and immortality to light through the gospel." I thought we were, by nature, immortal beings.
35. To what was Paul appointed as "a preacher, and an apostle, and a teacher"?

Paraphrase 1:6-11

6 Because I believe thy faith to be unfeigned, I put thee in mind to stir up the spiritual gift of God which thou possessest through the imposition of my hands: Improve thy gift, by boldly exercising it in preaching and defending the doctrines of the gospel against all false teachers.

7 For God hath not infused into us a spirit of cowardice which shrinks at danger, but of courage, such as becometh those who possess the gifts of inspiration and miracles, and of benevolence, which disposes us to communicate the Gospel to all mankind, and of self-government, to behave with prudence on every occasion.

8 Wherefore, be not thou, like many in this city, ashamed of testifying the things which concern our Lord Jesus, neither be thou ashamed of me who am a prisoner on his account: But do thou come and jointly suffer evil with me for the gospel which I preach to the Gentiles, according to the power of God bestowed on thee;

9 Who hath resolved to save us, and for that purpose hath called us into his kingdom with an holy calling; a calling whose object is to make us holy; and hath thus called us, not on account of our works as meriting it, but in accomplishment of his own purpose and gift, which was given us through Christ Jesus in the covenant made with mankind at the fall, long before the times of the Mosaic dispensation.

10 And this gift of salvation is now made manifest by the appearing of our Saviour Jesus Christ in the flesh, who, through His own death and resurrection, hath indeed made death ineffectual, and hath made an immortal life after death, and the nature of that life, clear through the gospel, which assures us that we shall live forever in the body, after the resurrection.

11 For proclaiming which good news I am appointed an herald, and an apostle, and furnished with spiritual gifts to make me a successful teacher of the Gentiles.

Comment 1:6-11

Vs. 6. Paul says, in essence: "Because of your unhypocritical faith, you should be able to stir unto a flame the gift of God within you." This gift was supernatural in nature. It was given by the instrumentality of Paul's hands.

We believe Timothy was the possessor of two gifts: (1) The gift given by the hands of the elders, i.e., the office of the evangelist (Cf. I Tim. 4:14); (2) The gift of supernatural ability given by Paul, as stated in this verse. Both gifts could have been bestowed at the same time. In such a case, Paul would have been present at Timothy's ordination to grant, along with the gift of the office of evangelist by the elders, the divine equipment for the office.

The exercise of such supernatural ability was not without the faith and surrender of the possessor. Peter and John healed a lame man by the power of God, but it was not without the exercise of faith on their part (Cf. Acts 3:16). There were many factors present in Ephesus to quench the faith of Timothy. In the face of such difficulties, Timothy is to reassert his confidence in the power of God. Evidently there were conditions present that would cause Timothy to actually question the outcome. Paul's request was to believe in God's power for every problem.

Vs. 7. Verse seven is a description of the results of exercising the gift of God. When we are strengthened by His Spirit in the inward man, we are able to face all the changing circumstances of life without fear, full of power and love. Such inward assistance creates a mastery of self.

Whereas we do not have the supernatural powers from the hands of the Apostle, yet the disposition just described as relating to Timothy and the Apostles does also apply to us. "Greater is He who is in us than he who is in the world." God has given to us the same attitude toward life.

Vs. 8. A word concerning the mode of expression in the phrase, "stir up"; it needs to be said here, as the same thought relates to "be not ashamed." The words of Homer Kent are very helpful just here: "This present infinitive emphasizes the continual stirring up into a flame which is necessary . . . There is no intimation here that Timothy has been failing. Rather, he is told to continue doing what he has been doing . . ." (*Ibid*, p. 258). Once again, on the present phrase, "The mode of expression in the phrase, 'be not ashamed' (Aorist Subjunctive), offers clear evidence that Timothy was not at fault along this line" (*Ibid*. p. 259).

Timothy had not been ashamed, and he was encouraged not to start it.

In July of 64 A.D., Nero set Rome on fire! By October of the same year he had succeeded in transferring the blame to the Christians. A most terrible persecution began against all followers of The Way. Christianity became an illegal religion. Under such conditions, there would be some temptations to be quiet about the testimony of the Lord, or any relationship to one of the Apostles of this illegal faith.

"The testimony of (or for) *our* Lord" has reference to the good news as outlined by Paul in I Cor. 15:1-4. What a beautiful play on words and circumstances to say that he was not a prisoner of Nero, but rather, of Christ. Nero could not imprison Paul's spirit, but Jesus could and did. Paul had been apprehended by Christ and now was His willing prisoner.

When the time and occasion comes—as it most assuredly will—take your share of the persecution for your preaching of the good tidings. You will not be able to stand up to such persecution by your own strength. You will be enabled by Him who is able. Indeed, "He is able to do far abundantly above anything that we ask or think according to the power that worketh in us."

Vs. 9. Someone has called verses 9 through 11, Paul's "beautiful digression"; we feel this is very apt. Verse 8 ends with the word, "God"; thus introducing a description of God. Note please:

I. He saved us and called us.
   1. This salvation and calling was not according to our works.
   2. This salvation and calling was according to His own purpose and grace.
      a. This purpose and grace was given us in Christ Jesus before times eternal.
      b. This purpose and grace hath now been manifested by the appearing of our Saviour, Christ Jesus.
         1) Christ Jesus abolished death.

2) Christ Jesus brought life and immortality to light through the Gospel.
   a) Unto the Gospel, Paul was appointed a preacher, and an apostle, and a teacher.

Please notice the structure of these verses: We are saved and called, this is modified with two thoughts. The second of these thoughts is modified with two thoughts. The second of these thoughts is modified with two thoughts, etc.

Who is saved and called? We take this to refer to Timothy, Paul and all Christians. In what sense, "saved"? God has provided the salvation through His Son. It is up to man to appropriate what God has so graciously provided. In this context, it is looking back to the time when Paul, Timothy, and the saints in Ephesus had appropriated such salvation. Is the "calling" subsequent to salvation? If so, then we would connect this with Paul's call to service on the road to Damascus; in Paul's case, his salvation and calling were almost simultaneous.

The thought that we did not merit or earn such salvation and calling is typically Pauline. He emphasizes this point again and again (Cf. Eph. 2:8,9).

It is glorious to know God has a purpose in His grace, and indeed, grace in His purpose.

God's whole purpose for man is to bring man to His Son. When once we are in Christ Jesus, we are complete—"He is our life." "In Him we are full." "In Him are all the treasures of wisdom and knowledge hidden." God has no other purpose; to look elsewhere is vain. This has been God's purpose from eternity to eternity!

Vs. 10. Something of the completeness of God's purpose in Christ can be seen in what Christ provides for man. Death is abolished! Life and immortality are brought to light! This is all accomplished when the good news is preached and believed.

The word "abolished," does not mean to make nonexistant, but rather, to render ineffective or impotent. By Christ's death and resurrection, He has removed the sting from death. Death becomes but a gateway to life. Oh, glorious victory! Let us *not* imagine that life and immortality were *created* by Christ's death and resurrection. One cannot bring into the light that which did not already exist.

Christ brought life eternal and the incorruptable body out into the full view of man. This He did by His own resurrection.

Man's eternal life and immortal body are now visible to all. Before Christ came, eternal life and the incorruptible body were present, but they were hidden by the shadows of man's understanding. Now they are distinctly seen and understood.

This glorious knowledge is made known when we announce it through the good news. What a priceless privilege — to be a preacher!

Vs. 11. Paul has but *one* task, and that is, to preach The Word. But in this task, or office, he thinks of himself in relation to his message and he says, "*I am a herald*"—one who announces, as a king's messenger, the king's message. He thinks of himself in relation to his preparation for the office and he says, "*I am one sent.* I am doing this because Christ has commissioned me." Finally, he thinks of himself in relation to those with whom he must work and he says, "*I am a teacher.* The persons with whom I labor do not know; they must be informed, and it is my blessed privilege to instruct them."

Fact Questions 1:6-11

14. What is "the cause" of vs. 6?
15. Please explain just how the gift of God can be stirred up.
16. What was the gift of God given to Timothy?
17. Compare 1:6 with I Tim. 4:14 and explain.
18. How is the word, "spirit," used in vs. 7? Explain this word in relationship to the "gift of God."
19. Why would Timothy be tempted to be ashamed?
20. How does the power of God enable us to suffer hardships?
21. Show the connection of vss. 9-11 with vss. 6-8.
22. Who is the "us" of vs. 9?
23. What is meant by "a holy calling"?
24. What is God's purpose and grace?
25. When and where did God manifest His purpose and grace?
26. What is the meaning of the expression, "abolished death"?
27. In what sense are we to understand that Christ brought life and immortality to light?
28. Give your own exegesis of vs. 11.

b. Paul 12-14

Text 1:12-14

12 For which cause I suffer also these things: yet I am not ashamed; for I know him whom I have believed, and I am persuaded that he is able to guard that which I have committed unto him against that day. 13 Hold the pattern of sound words which thou hast heard from me, in faith and love which is in Christ Jesus. 14 That good thing which was committed unto thee, guard through the Holy Spirit which dwelleth in us.

Thought Questions 1:12-14

36. For what cause did Paul suffer? Specify some of his sufferings.
37. There must have been a genuine danger of being ashamed, or it would not have been mentioned so often. Please offer some particular possibilities for being ashamed.
38. Because he knew Christ, Paul was not embarrassed or confused. Explain how such a knowledge relates to being ashamed or embarrassed.
39. In what particular sense would you say Paul "knew" Christ?
40. What was it Paul committed to Christ?
41. What was it Christ committed to Paul?
42. How will Christ guard the deposit? Please be specific and personal.
43. What is "the day" against which the commitment is made?
44. How is the word, "pattern," used in vs. 13?
45. For whom, and against whom, was the pattern of sound words to be held?
46. Is Paul asking Timothy to hold to the healthy words in the spirit of faith and love, or because of his faith and love?
47. What was "the deposit" committed to Timothy?
48. Explain in your own words, with your present knowledge, just how the Holy Spirit would aid in guarding the deposit.
49. In what sense does the Holy Spirit dwell in us?

Paraphrase 1:12-14

12 For publishing the promise of eternal life through Jesus Christ to the Gentiles, I suffer even such things as have now befallen me. Nevertheless, I am not ashamed either of my doctrine or of my sufferings. For I know in whom I have believed, that he is the Son of God; and I am persuaded He is able to guard the doctrine of the Gospel which is committed in trust to me, against infidels and false teachers, till the end of the world.

13 The form of wholesome words in which thou hast heard from me the doctrines of the Gospel, hold fast with that fidelity to Christ, and that love to those who err, which become a minister of Christ.

14 Also, the good deposit of the Gospel doctrine itself, guard by the assistance of the Holy Ghost, who dwelleth in us.

Comment 1:12-14

Vs. 12. "Because I am a preacher, apostle and teacher, I am suffering." Paul's sufferings are minimized by the use of the phrase, "these things," but Timothy knew well to what Paul alluded. In immediate context, they refer to all he is suffering in Rome. For a larger reference, we should read his account in II Cor. 11:23-28. The thought of Job's friends is back of all references to being ashamed, i.e., "if you are doing God's will, why are you suffering?" Paul's answer is the same as Job's. It is found in a person, not in a dogma. I know Christ and Christ knows me; I am perfectly willing to commit my case to Him. I do not understand or enjoy this chain, but I am not embarrassed or discouraged by it. My life is under the direction of my Lord. He is able to work something good out of every circumstance.

There is no small discussion among commentators as to what is committed to whom. Has Paul committed something to God, or has God committed something to Paul? In either case, the emphasis is upon Paul's dependence upon Christ.

If Paul has committed something to God, what is it? His soul, his work, or what? Are not all of these true?

If God has committed something to Paul (and we know from other references that He has), we know what it is—his Apostleship and the Gospel.

We much prefer the thought that God is guarding that which He has committed to Paul. This interpretation fits the context. Paul is suffering now, but the work will yet be carried on. What Paul has kept will be passed on to others and to yet others. How good to know we have living proof of God's power to guard and keep, in the Gospel which we proclaim. When Paul is called upon to give an account of his stewardship, he will be able to show a grand profit for the owner. Will we be able to say as much?

Vs. 13. What is the meaning of the word, "pattern," as here used? The word means "outline" or "sketch." Paul has given the outline; Timothy is to fill it in. Let us not minimize the force of this expression. To go beyond the pattern would be to produce another Gospel, and suffer the condemnation of God (Cf. Gal. 1:7-9). Timothy knew what Paul taught, and what he did not teach, on the matters that pertained to salvation and edification. Such teaching from the words of Paul was healthy and life-giving. Any deviation from such teaching was diseased and deadly.

The attitude in holding the faith is almost as important as the thing held. However orthodox we might be, our orthodoxy will be odious to God and man if not held in faith and love. Please read again I Corinthians, chapter thirteen, to keep the balance between sound doctrine and the essential element. This faith and love for man and God is held "in Christ Jesus"; i.e., it is the outworking of Christ in us.

Vs. 14. We have no hesitancy in saying that the deposit Timothy is to guard is the Gospel committed to him. It is easy to detect the concern of Paul for the continuance of the work after his death. How true this has been for every sincere preacher since his day.

Paul had "kept the faith," so he wanted Timothy to keep intact the sacred message committed unto him. Timothy was to see to it that no change by way of addition, substitution or subtraction, should occur. Such a task is too great for man by himself. Satan is too clever—evil is too near—temptation too strong. We *must* have supernatural aid. This we have through the Holy Spirit which indwells each Christian (Cf. Rom. 8:11). This is a subjective matter which almost defies explanation. Perhaps we are to claim the power without asking for an explanation of His method of operation. I am sure we are.

Fact Questions 1:12-14

29. How did Paul minimize his sufferings?
30. How does Paul's answer to the problem of suffering compare with the answer of Job?
31. Why is the thought that God is guarding what He has committed to Paul, preferred above the other view?
32. In what sense did Paul deliver "a sketch" to Timothy?
33. In what way is the attitude in holding the faith important?
34. How can we detect Paul's concern for the continuance of the Gospel, even after his death?
35. In what particulars was Timothy to guard the Gospel?
36. Explain how the Holy Spirit helps us to guard the deposit.

c. Onesiphorus 15-18

Text 1:15-18

15 This thou knowest, that all that are in Asia turned away from me; of whom are Phygelus and Hermogenes. 16 The Lord grant mercy unto the house of Onesiphorus: for he oft refreshed me, and was not ashamed of my chain; 17 but, when he was in Rome, he sought me diligently, and found me, 18 (the Lord grant unto him to find mercy of the Lord in that day); and in how many things he ministered at Ephesus, thou knowest very well.

Thought Questions 1:15-18

50. Why would it be true that Timothy would know of conditions in Asia?
51. Why did so many turn away from Paul? Why name two of them?
52. Why mention "the house" of Onesiphorus? Why not just mention the man?
53. Give your explanation as to just how Onesiphorus refreshed Paul.
54. Why would it be difficult to find Paul?
55. Is there a play on the word, "find," in vss. 17 and 18?
56. Timothy knew very well what Onesiphorus did in Ephesus, but we do not. Try to imagine two or three of the things he did.

Paraphrase 1:15-18

15 To guard the good deposit among the Ephesians is the more necessary, because thou knowest this, that all the Judaizing teachers who are in Asia have turned me off, denying that I am an apostle; of whom are Phygellus and Hermogenes.

16 May the Lord grant mercy to the family of Onesiphorus. For he continued his attachment to me, and often comforted me in my imprisonment, by his visits and friendly offices, and was not ashamed of me, though chained as a malefactor;

17 But being come to Rome, he searched for me with great diligence among the different prisons in the city, and at last found me.

18 For that good man himself I pray, may the Lord reward him for his kindness to me, and grant to him to find pardon from the Lord Jesus in the day of judgment. Besides, how many things he supplied to me while I abode in Ephesus, thou, being a witness thereof, knewest well.

Comment 1:15-18

Vs. 15. In what manner had those in the district of Asia turned away from Paul? The answer perhaps can be found in noticing the way at least one turned toward Paul. Onesiphorus came to Rome to visit Paul. We cannot believe it was only for a visit. He came to testify in defense of the Apostle. When others in Asia were asked to appear in Rome on Paul's behalf, they turned away. Two prominent members are mentioned—Phygelus and Hermogenes. It was common knowledge to Timothy and the saints of Ephesus, and indeed, throughout the seven churches of Asia, that Paul could find many who talked of their love for him and the Gospel, but when it cost them money, time, and standing in the community, and even their own lives, they turned aside to serve themselves. Paul was not having an easy time. No wonder the thought of "being ashamed" reoccurs so often.

Vs. 16. But there are encouraging and refreshing times. Against the dark background stands the bright form of Onesiphorus. The name of this one would immediately remind Timothy of where he lived and of the family left behind. It was not easy for Onesiphorus to leave Ephesus and travel all the way to Rome; not when Rome was on fire with hatred against all Christians. Would the loved ones of Onesiphorus ever see him again? If they didn't, they could find comfort in knowing his mission was accomplished. He did arrive in Rome; he did find Paul; he did live up to his name, *Onesiphorus*, which means "profit-bringer."

Just how this one "oft refreshed" Paul, we cannot say. There are several possibilities: just his presence would help; news of the blessing of God upon the works begun by Paul; in bringing with him personal messages of concern from those who loved God; perhaps in some literature brought to the Apostle. It is good to know, that even under the most trying of conditions, one can be refreshed.

The fact that Paul was a prisoner did not hinder Onesiphorus in his encouraging ministry. Pleast note that Onesiphorus did this often; he did not come to call on the prisoner in a perfunctory manner and leave having "done his duty."

Vs. 17. When Onesiphorus arrived in Rome, it had been largely destroyed by fire. Christians were scattered and were living in constant fear of being arrested and taken to the Arena. When he inquired concerning the whereabouts of Paul, he had the greatest difficulty in finding those who would identify themselves as friends of a condemned criminal. Such comments are only imaginative. We do not know why he had difficulty in finding Paul. The conditions described could very well have been present.

Can we detect a note of suppressed joy in the little expression. "and found me"? We believe we can.

Vs. 18. There is a beautiful play on words in this verse—what I *found*, may the house of Onesiphorus *find*. I was brought comfort and strength in my hour of need; may the household of this good man find such comfort and strength in the day of judgment.

There is quite an effort made by some to show that Onesiphorus was dead, and that Paul was praying for the dead when he said, "The Lord grant unto him to find mercy of the Lord in that day." Someone must be desperate for Scriptural proofs for a presupposition, to so misuse a text. Is it possible to desire God's blessing upon a man at the judgment before the man dies? Who would say that it isn't?

Reference is made to the mention of Paul's commendation of the "house of Onesiphorus" with no reference to him. We simply ask, "Where was Onesiphorus when this letter was written?" If he was in Rome, and Paul was writing from Rome to Ephesus, how could Paul greet someone who wasn't there? Does this prove he was dead? How ridiculous!

Timothy would appreciate Paul's approval of Onesiphorus, inasmuch as Timothy had observed the good works of this one in Ephesus.

Fact Questions 1:15-18

37. Why couldn't Onesiphorus find Paul? Give your own explanation.
38. Where is the note of "suppressed joy"?
39. Point out the play on words in vs. 18.
40. How do some persons use vs. 18 as a proof text for praying for the dead? How do you answer such a charge?

EXEGETICAL EXAMINATION OVER CHAPTER ONE OF II TIMOTHY

1. Give the time and place, as well as purpose, of the letter.
2. Give from memory your own outline of Chapter One.
3. Discuss two things that Paul remembered about Timothy that were a blessed memory to Paul.

4. What is meant by "unfeigned faith"? How is it obtained? How is it sustained? Who had it?
5. Discuss two ways Timothy was to avoid being ashamed of the testimony of Christ.
6. What was the "gift of God" within Timothy? How was it to be stirred up?
7. Explain two reasons for Paul not being ashamed.
8. Give your own exegesis of vs. 10.
9. What good thing had Onesiphorus done for Paul?
10. Give your own exegesis of vs. 12.

2. BE STRONG IN THE SERVICE OF CHRIST 2:1-26
   a. As a child 1, 2

Text 2:1,2

1 Thou, therefore, my child, be strengthened in the grace that is in Christ Jesus. 2 And the things which thou hast heard from me among many witnesses, the same commit thou to faithful men, who shall be able to teach others also.

Thought Questions 2:1,2

57. What is the connective in chapter one with what is stated here in chapter two? Notice the word, "therefore."
58. Why use the word, "child," in this particular place?
59. Is Paul asking Timothy to be strong, or to receive strength?
60. Specify just how are we strengthened by the grace that is in Jesus Christ.
61. Do we know some of the "things" Timothy heard from Paul? Name three.
62. Give the meaning of the expression, "among many witnesses."
63. Thinking of the circumstances under which this letter was received, who do you imagine were "the faithful men" of vs. 2?
64. Is there some type of apostolic succession in vs. 2b? What is it?

Paraphrase 2:1,2

1 Because there has been such a general defection among the teachers in Asia, my son, be strong in preaching the grace which is bestowed on mankind through Christ Jesus.

2 And what things thou hast heard from me concerning Christ, confirmed by many witnesses who saw and conversed with Him both before and after His Resurrection, these commit in trust to

men of approved fidelity, who shall be fit, also, to teach them to others, that the knowledge of them may be continued in the world to the end.

Comment 2:1,2

Vs. 1. Lenski cannot see a connecting thought in chapter one. Perhaps this is true, and we should eliminate the word, "therefore." But others feel that the defection of those in Asia could be the connection for the exhortation here. If Phygelus and Hermogenes had been strong in the grace of Christ Jesus, they would not have turned aside. Paul could be saying to Timothy, "Be not like them, but be strengthened by the grace that is in Christ Jesus."

The term of endearment, "child," comes from the heart of one about to lay down his life for the gospel. Timothy would not only heed the word of Paul, but would be touched by the love and concern Paul had for him.

Just how did Paul imagine the grace that is in Christ Jesus would be a source of strength for Timothy?

In Christ Jesus is the favor and approval of God. An awareness that we are "in Christ Jesus," and thus in the favor of God, would be a great source of strength to our sometimes fainting heart.

Timothy is to receive strength from his keen consciousness of being "in Christ Jesus."

Vs. 2. The second admonition to his child in the faith, is a most important and far-reaching one. Paul was a teacher and Timothy was his student. Paul's sermons and letters were heard and read for a much larger purpose than the fact that they were inspired and inspiring information. Timothy was listening and learning, so as to be able to teach others. Those taught by Timothy, in turn, were learning to teach others, and so has the inspired succession proceeded down the centuries.

The witnesses here mentioned are best understood to refer to those persons who made up the audiences while Paul spoke. Timothy was in that audience, but so were many others. Paul was preaching the Gospel. Timothy is here instructed to commit the Gospel to able and faithful men who shall in turn commit it to others. This verse is the basis for preacher-training today. Every generation must receive from faithful men the faithful Word.

Fact Questions 2:1,2

41. Is there a connecting thought in chapter one for what follows in chapter two? If so, what is it? If not, why not?
42. What effect would the term, "child," have upon Timothy?
43. Explain how the grace that is in Christ Jesus supplies strength to us.
44. What was it Timothy was to commit to others? Who were these "faithful men"?
45. Who were "the many witnesses"?
46. How does verse two become the basis for present day preacher-training?
47. Is the method of commitment described?

b. As a Soldier 3, 4

Text 2:3,4

3 Suffer hardship with me, as a good soldier of Christ Jesus. 4 No soldier on service entangleth himself in the affairs of this life; that he may please him who enrolled him as a soldier.

Thought Questions 2:3,4

65. Why inform Timothy that he was to take his place in suffering persecution? Was Timothy reluctant to do so?
66. In what way would the sufferings of Timothy be associated with those of Paul?
67. Why use the figure of a soldier? Show two or three comparisons.
68. As a soldier of Christ Jesus, was Paul thinking of Christ as in this army? What position?
69. Why mention possible entangling alliances?
70. When does the Christian soldier get his "furlough"?
71. Specify some of the "affairs of this life" in which the soldier of Christ Jesus could become entangled.
72. How shall we understand the expression, "enrolled him as a soldier"?
73. Is Christ actually affected with our conduct of life on earth; i.e., does He, personally, respond to our good and bad decisions? Explain.

Paraphrase 2:3,4

3 Since thou must maintain the doctrine of Christ, and commit it in purity to others, do thou endure with constancy the evils attending that service as a good soldier of Jesus Christ, that the teachers whom thou appointest may imitate thee.

4 No soldier engages in any of the businesses of this life, that, being constantly ready for action, he may please Him who hath chosen him to be a soldier. The same rule ought a minister of the gospel to follow, that he may please Christ who hath called him.

Comment 2:3,4

Vs. 3. Timothy is not only Paul's child (or God's child), but he is also Christ's soldier.

As a soldier of Christ, he must expect his share in the suffering that accompanies this service. No good soldier of Nero would leave the army or refuse the service because of hardships. Shall we do less for Christ than the soldier does for the emperor?

Are you a good soldier of Christ Jesus? Then expect to suffer—it came with your enlistment.

Vs. 4. Continuing the metaphor, Paul reminds Timothy of the complete dedication required by army service. When there is a choice of activities, all that would hinder obedience to orders from the superior officer, *must* be eliminated.

The expression, "on service," can also be translated ,"warring." The preacher is in a holy war! He must give his part in the battle priority over all else. How very many perfectly legitimate "affairs of this life" have taken up the time, thought and energy (to say nothing of money) that should have been given in winning the battle for King Jesus!

Someone immediately thinks of Paul's "making tents" as a hindering alliance with the affairs of this life. We do not know just how extensive such "tent making" was, or just what he did when working at such a task. But *one thing we do know,* it did not encumber him from warring the good warfare. Another thing we can know is that much "tent making" today *does hinder and entangle* God's soldier—how much time, thought, energy and talents can we devote to our captain when it has been spent elsewhere? Please do not forget that our captain is touched with the feeling of our infirmities, both for good and for evil (Heb. 4:12). He is pleased or hurt by our service. The use of the term "enrolled," as here used, is of one who has mustered an army and is calling for volunteers; for those who will enlist. We have enlisted at the call of our Commander. Let's give Him a full measure of service—He deserves it.

Fact Questions 2:3,4

48. What is the meaning of the expression, "suffer hardships"?
49. Read Heb. 13:23 and discuss its possible application to "suffer hardships with me."
50. How is the complete dedication required of Christ's soldiers here indicated?
51. What is the meaning and application of the expression "on service"?
52. How can it be determined when we have become entangled in "the affairs of this life"?
53. Didn't Paul make tents? Wasn't this an association with "the affairs of this life"?
54. Can we be sure that Jesus is pleased or hurt by our service? How?

c. As an athlete 5

Text 2:5

5 And if also a man contend in the games, he is not crowned, except he have contended lawfully.

Thought Questions 2:5

74. Isn't there a rather abrupt change from vs. 4 to vs. 5? Is there any connecting thought?
75. What "games" does Paul have in mind?
76. What is the purpose of such an analogy?
77. What is the "crown of the contest"?
78. Paul does *not* say the man will be "crowned" if he has won, but rather if he has "contended lawfully." Why this emphasis?

Paraphrase 2:5

5 And also, if one contend in the Grecian games, he is not crowned unless he contend according to the laws of the combat. As little can thou expect to be rewarded, unless thou fulfill thy ministry in the manner prescribed by Christ.

Comment 2:5

Vs. 5. The element of reward is the point of emphasis in this illustration for Christian service. The connective is the reference to the rules. There are rules in the army and there are rules in athletics. The prize is given to those who keep the rules. This thought pre-supposes the contender would excel in the contest.

But even when excelling, rigid rules must be observed. How does this relate to the preacher? There are three qualities of character to be found in the man of God: (1) as a soldier, willingness to suffer; (2) as an athlete, willingness to discipline himself; (3) as a farmer, patience for the harvest.

Absolute self-discipline is taught by the example of the Greek athlete. Instances have been produced where the athlete swore under oath that he had practiced ten months before the games (Lock).

Please notice that there is only one participator in this contest. Each is contending by himself, against himself, and the established record.

What are the rules for the contest of the faith? They are set up by the Lord Jesus. Our Lord "condemned sin in the flesh" (Romans 8:3); i.e., He demonstrated perfect self-discipline. The weapons used by our Lord, in His self-control, are open to all of us. Prayer, meditation, and fasting are yet the greatest needs of the present day self-indulgent, instead of self-disciplined, minister.

Fact Questions 2:5

55. What is the point of emphasis in the illustration of vs. 5?
56. Is there some connection between the illustration of the soldier and the athlete? If so, explain.
57. Something more than excellence in contending is required before a crown is given. What is it? How does this relate to the preacher?
58. What is meant by the expression that Jesus "condemned sin in the flesh"? (Rom. 8:3)
59. What weapons shall we use in the battle of self-mastery? Are they adequate? How do we know?

d. As a farmer 6-13

Text 2:6-13

6 The husbandman that laboreth must be the first to partake of the fruits. 7 Consider what I say; for the Lord shall give thee understanding in all things. 8 Remember Jesus Christ, risen from the dead, of the seed of David, according to my Gospel: 9 wherein I suffer hardship unto bonds, as a malefactor; but the word of God is not bound. 10 Therefore I endure all things for the elect's sake, that they may also obtain the salvation which is in Christ Jesus with eternal glory. 11 Faithful is the saying: For if we died with Him, we shall also live with Him: 12 if we endure, we shall also

reign with Him: if we shall deny Him, He also will deny us: 13 if we are faithless, He abideth faithful; for He cannot deny Himself.

Thought Questions 2:6-13

79. Who is the husbandman in this reference?
80. Why is the word, "must," used in vs. 6?
81. Are we to make a comparison here between the farmer who labors and the lazy farmer who does not? What is the emphasis?
82. What are "the fruits" of which the farmer partakes?
83. In what sense does the farmer "partake" of the fruits?
84. Why consider what Paul is saying, if the Lord will supply the understanding?
85. Why insert this admonition at this place?
86. Why suggest just here that Timothy "remember Jesus Christ"?
87. Jesus is not dead, but alive. Jesus is of the royal line of David. How does this relate to the context?
88. In what sense was the good news—"my gospel"; i.e., belonging to Paul?
89. What is Paul's purpose in describing his persecutions and imprisonment?
90. What is a "malefactor"?
91. In what sense is "the Word of God not bound"?
92. Show the immediate reason Paul could endure all things.
93. In what sense was Paul's imprisonment for the "elect's sake"?
94. If certain persons are "the elect," wouldn't they obtain the salvation which is in Christ Jesus without Paul's efforts?
95. Show how the two above thoughts relate.
96. What is the "eternal glory" mentioned here?
97. Why use the expression, "Faithful is the saying"?
98. When did "we die with Him"?
99. "We shall also live with Him"—is this referring to heaven? Explain.
100. When shall we reign with Him?
101. Name three ways in which we can "deny Him." When, and where, and how will He deny us?
102. Is there some difference in being faithless, and denying Him? Explain.
103. In what respects does Christ remain irrevocably faithful?
104. Christ cannot deny Himself. Does this rise from inability to do so? Explain.

Paraphrase 2:6-13

6 It becometh the husbandman to labour his field before he partakes of the fruits of it. How much more oughtest thou to labour in the ministry before thou art rewarded?

7 Consider what I say concerning the necessity of devoting thyself wholly to the ministry, and of enduring evil, and may the Lord Jesus give thee a just discernment in all religious matters.

8 Often recollect and preach, that Jesus Christ really descended from David, was raised from the dead, and thereby demonstrated to be the true Messiah, according to the Gospel which I preach.

9 For which Gospel I suffer evil even to bonds, as a malefactor. But though my enemies may bind me, they cannot bind the Word of God. It will spread itself in spite of all opposition.

10 For this cause I patiently bear all things on account of the Gentiles elected to be the people of God, that they also may obtain the salvation from sin and death, which is procured by Christ Jesus, and which will be accompanied with eternal glory.

11 Suffering for Christ is not so great a misfortune as the world imagines: For this affirmation is true, that if we die with Christ, as martyrs for religion, we shall also live with him eternally.

12 If, like Christ, we suffer persecution patiently, we shall also reign with Him: But if, when brought before kings and councils, we from fear deny our relation to Him, He will, at the judgment, deny that He knows us.

13 Though we be unfaithful in denying Him, He abideth faithful to all His promises and threatenings. He cannot act contrary to His own essential perfections.

Comment 2:6-13

Vs. 6. Continuing the thought of reward, Paul uses the illustration of the farmer. Is the emphasis upon the effort, or work, of the farmer, or upon the reward he receives from this labor? There is a good deal of discussion among commentators as to which thought should receive the emphasis. It is comparatively easy to say, with the soldier, the point is endurance. In the case of the athlete, it is discipline, or compliance with the rules for the crown. It would seem that both thoughts of hard labor and reward are here used with the farmer, as self-control and reward are used with the athlete.

The faithful minister will work as hard as a hard-working farmer. When he does, he has the assurance that he will be the first to share in the benefits of his labor. What are these benefits? The preacher who does not first preach his sermon to himself is not worthy of the name. "Thou that teachest another, teachest thou not thyself?" The preacher should become the first convert to every sermon. Thus he is first to partake of the benefit of his labors.

In another sense, the preacher is to "live of the Gospel" which he preaches. As he sows spiritual things, he can expect a return in material things. This same thought is emphasized several times by Paul elsewhere.

Vs. 7. Since Paul has compressed three figures of speech into so few words, he feels a word of warning is necessary lest Timothy read the words without a grasp of their full meaning. Ponder, meditate, think upon what I have written. It is written to you, about you; consider it very carefully. Remember also, that the Lord has promised wisdom and grace adequate for our understanding. There would be no mistakes as to points of emphasis with Timothy.

Vs. 8. Verses eight through thirteen are a summary of the principle stated in the previous verses; i.e., we must endure before we can reap, or that hardship precedes victory. Two illustrations are given: Jesus Christ, and Paul. Finally, the subject is concluded with the "faithful saying"; which restates the same principle of, "no cross, no crown."

Timothy is urged to "remember Jesus Christ." But to what purpose? Reading this in its context we would answer, "Because Jesus Christ well illustrates the point, 'He is our grand example.' " "He is risen from the dead . . ." but only after He had suffered at the hands of sinners and was crucified.

Paul adds two modifying thoughts: first, that our Lord was of the royal line of David—thus adding insult to injury by crucifying the heir to the throne of David. Second, that the death, burial, and resurrection of Christ was the heart of the message he preached.

Vs. 9. Because of the good news I preach, I am suffering the present persecution. Knowing of Paul's reluctance to say anything about his sufferings, we can imagine the "hardships" in the Roman prison were indeed severe. Paul was held in chains as a common criminal. But God brings victory out of defeat: the very thing for which I am imprisoned is not in prison. I am here for preaching The Word, but it is not bound! The Word of God is with Timothy and with all others; it is spread over the wide Roman Empire! Wherever Paul or other inspired men had spoken or written, the Word of God was living and working.

Vs. 10. Because the Word of God is not bound and will accomplish its glorious purpose in the elect, Paul was ready to bear up under whatever hardships came his way.

Paul felt his remaining steadfast even in prison, was necessary for "the elect's sake"; i.e., he wanted to present the best possible example so as not to discourage a single one. If he could, in any way, help the least or the last of "the elect" to obtain what he was confident awaited him, he would suffer anything Nero wanted to bring upon him.

On the other hand, this sentence, "Therefore I endure all things for the elect's sake, that they also may obtain the salvation which is in Christ Jesus with eternal glory," could look backward instead of forward. Paul could have reference to what he had suffered, as well as what he is suffering. He could mean that he stood up under the sufferings described in II Cor. 11:16-33 and Rom. 8:35-39 because he knew his labor was not vain in the Lord.

The use of the word, "elect," reminds us of the need to understand the teaching of the New Testament on election. It is not our purpose to develop it here, but suffice it to say, no Bible student worthy of the name will fail to search the Scriptures diligently on this important subject.

It should be pointed out that salvation is "in Christ Jesus," and that there is no salvation outside of Christ. How does one come "into Christ Jesus"? Read Gal. 3:27 for an inspired answer from Paul.

The "eternal glory" of our salvation is here anticipated, and is certain of the fulfillment. Something of the power of the age to come should be reflected in the lives of those who will share it.

Vss. 11-13. Here is the fifth and last "faithful saying." We like the thought of Hendriksen that this is probably a part of an "early Christian hymn, a cross-bearer's or martyr's hymn." He says, with good effect: "Now the word 'for' indicates that in the hymn, something preceded." The probability is that the unquoted line which preceded, was something like, "We shall remain faithful to our Lord even to death," or "We have resigned ourselves to reproach and suffering and even to death for Christ's sake." (Ibid pp. 254,255)

The quoted lines are:

"For if we died with Him, we shall also live with Him:
if we endure, we shall also reign with Him:
if we shall deny Him, He also will deny us:
if we are faithless, He abideth faithful;
for He cannot deny Himself."

Please do not miss the point of quoting this hymn (if indeed it is). This is a conclusion to the thought that without a cross there is no crown; without a thorn there is no throne. We shall take up a discussion of each phrase as it appears:

If we died with Him When did this take place? We died when Christ died. Please read Rom. 6:8 and II Cor. 5:14 for a confirmation of this. Remember that this is applicable to all Christians. It was written to Timothy and the saints in Ephesus to offer them strength and challenge, but it is just as applicable to us. Paul said of himself, "I have been crucified with Christ, and it is no longer I that live, but Christ liveth in me." (Gal. 2:20)

(We have read the discussions which link this phrase, "If we died with Him" with a martyr's death, but we much prefer the above interpretation and can see no conflict with the context.)

When Christ died, we died. This identification of ourselves with Christ is a powerful motive for holy living. Such a motive was needed in this day of intense persecution.

We shall also live with Him This is the joyous advantage in dying with Him. We are as truly identified with His Resurrection as we are with His death. We have been raised together with Christ in this life, and it is but a foretaste of the life to come. If we do not live like Christ here, how can we hope to live with Him for eternity? If we do not live *like* Him, we cannot live *with* Him. The blessed thought is, He deigns to live with us and in us through the Holy Spirit (Rom. 8:9).

if we endure, we shall also reign with Him "Endurance" is more than begrudgingly bearing difficulties. "Endurance" is remaining steadfast amid all manner of trials. "Endurance" is a positive quality, not a negative one. Please associate this endurance with Christ; we are to endure or suffer *with* Him. "They who suffered with David in his humiliation were preferred with him in his exaltation; so it will be with the Son of David" (Henry).

Reigning with Christ is more than an offer of the hope of heaven. It is true right here and right now: "if we endure, we shall reign with Him." If we are willing to bear the reproaches and accusations found in fellowship with Jesus, we can also share in the triumph of overcoming evil with good. One day, all the daily trials and difficulties will be past, and we shall reign with Him forever in the new heaven and new earth.

if we shall deny Him, He also will deny us These words seem almost a quotation of Matt. 10:33 or Mark 8:38. Indeed, some commentators feel they are.

What is meant by denying Christ, and how could it be done? Commentators have read "final denial," "fatal denial," "hypocritical faith," etc., into these simple words, "deny Him." Did Peter deny Him? Did Jesus deny Peter? When we reject Him, we are rejected by Him. We are well aware that the final judgment day is inferred by the text, but please remember, that judgment day arrives every day for thousands of persons in the form of a visit from Death.

Every time we please ourselves instead of Jesus, we have denied Him. To remain in this state and die in such a state is to be forever denied by Him. When we are ashamed of Him or His Word in this wicked and adulterous generation, we have denied Him. Who is to say that such a person never owned Him in the first place?

if we are faithless, He abideth faithful, for He cannot deny Himself. This is a conclusion to all that has been said in vss. 11-13. This is not intended to be a discouragement, but an encouragement. If we fail, God remains faithful. We can always return to the solid rock; we have forever a norm of truth that does not change. If we turn aside, it is only because we choose to do so; it is not that God wants us to, or that there is some advantage in it.

Like the disillusioned prodigal, we can be sure there is a warm house, a loving father, and a cleansing bath awaiting our return from the pig-pen of the world.

God's faithfulness is a part of His very being: a part of His essence. He is essentially and eternally consistent. It is His nature to be so. Therefore, He cannot deny Himself. To deny His faithfulness is to deny His existence.

Fact Questions 2:6-13

60. Which is to be emphasized in vs. 6: the work of the farmer or the reward of the farmer?
61. What are the "fruits" of which the minister is the first to partake?
62. Give your own exegesis of vs. 7.
63. Verses 8 through 13 are a unit; explain of what and why.
64. Why "remember Jesus Christ"? Please answer in the context.
65. Why mention that Jesus was of the seed of David?
66. Why mention "according to my Gospel"?
67. We know Paul was very reluctant to say anything about his suffering. How does this thought relate to vs. 9a?
68. In what sense was the Word of God not bound? Show how God brought victory out of defeat.
69. Paul endured all things "for the elect's sake"; explain how his sufferings related to "the elect."
70. Show how vs. 10 could look either backward or forward in thought.
71. Who are the elect? Who does the electing? How?
72. Do we presently have salvation in Christ Jesus?
73. Which verses contain "the faithful saying"?
74. If the faithful saying was part of an early hymn, what was the thought of the part not quoted?
75. What is the purpose in giving this faithful saying?
76. When and where and how did we die with Christ? Are we presently dead?
77. In what sense are we to live with Christ?
78. Please define "endurance."
79. Show how we are presently reigning with Christ and how we will do so in the future.
80. What type of a denial is to be understood from vs. 12b? Is this a final, fatal denial?
81. If we deny Him, is it proof positive that we never knew Him at all? Do you agree? Explain.
82. Show how vs. 13 is a conclusion to vss. 6-12.
83. God's eternal faithfulness is a great source of encouragement. Discuss.

e. As a workman 14-19

Text 2:14-19

14 Of these things put them in remembrance, charging them in the sight of the Lord, that they strive not about words, to no profit, to the subverting of them that hear. 15 Give diligence to present thyself approved unto God, a workman that needeth not to be ashamed, handling aright the word of truth. 16 But shun profane babblings: for they will proceed further in ungodliness, 17 and their word will eat as doth a gangrene: of whom is Hymenaeus and Philetus; 18 men who concerning the truth have erred, saying that the resurrection is past already, and overthrow the faith of some. 19 Howbeit the firm foundation of God standeth, having this seal, the Lord knoweth them that are His: and, let every one that nameth the name of the Lord depart from unrighteousness.

Thought Questions 2:14-19

105. Of what "things" is Timothy to put them in remembrance? Did they already know? When and how did they learn?
106. What is meant by the word, "charging," as in vs. 14?
107. Please try to imagine the circumstances in which Timothy would carry out the instructions of vs. 14. Who is to receive this charge? Are those involved in the word-battles to be aware of "the sight of God"?
108. Who would be subverted? Why?
109. Does vs. 15 have anything to do with Bible Study?
110. How would Timothy know when he was "approved unto God"?
111. Timothy was to consider himself "a workman"; what were his tools? What was his job?
112. What could cause embarrassment to God's workman?
113. There are three possible readings for vs. 15b: (1) handling aright the Word of Truth; (2) a straight course in the Word of Truth; (3) rightly dividing the Word of Truth. Which do you prefer? Please, please make an effort to choose—it is important.
114. What is the meaning of the word, "profane," as used in 16a?
115. How could Timothy shun "profane babblings" without shunning the teachers of it? Explain.
116. Why could Paul be so sure that such vain talk would progress if not ignored?

117. In what way is false teaching like a cancer?
118. Why mention Hymenaeus and Philetus? Read I Timothy 1:20. Had Paul failed in his efforts to help Hymenaeus?
119. Is there anyone today who follows the teachings of the two mentioned in vs. 17? Be specific.
120. What resurrection is meant in vs. 18? Is not our baptism a resurrection? Cf. Rom. 6:1-4 and Col. 3:1-3. Explain.
121. Show how vs. 19 offers an answer to the false teachers, and a hope for the ultimate victory of truth.
122. What is the "firm foundation"?
123. Explain the use of "the seal" as here used.

Paraphrase 2:14-19

14 Put the Ephesians in mind of these great motives, earnestly testifying to them in the presence of Christ, and as they shall answer to him, not to fight about words (see I Tim. 6:4), as the Judaizers do, to no manner of use, but to the subverting of the faith and morals of the hearers.

15 Strive to behave so as at last thou mayest present thyself to God an approved unashamed workman, who hath rightly distributed the doctrine of the Gospel to all, according to their need.

16 But irreligious empty declamations resist, for they who use such discourses will increase to more ungodliness; they will proceed to deny the most essential articles of the Christian faith;

17 And their doctrine will eat, will destroy the souls of men, as a gangrene destroys the body. Of this sort of ungodly talkers are Hymenaeus and Philetus.

18 Who from the true Christian doctrine have wandered, affirming that the resurrection hath already happened; and by this impious babbling have overturned the faith of some concerning the resurrection of the body, and a future life in the body.

19 These false teachers, by denying the doctrine of the apostles, make themselves greater than the apostles. Nevertheless, the apostles being the foundation of God's Church (Eph. 2:20), stand firm in that honourable place, having this inscription as a confirmation of their authority, The Lord will make known them who are his: And, Let every one who nameth the name of Christ as his Lord, depart from wicked teachers, lest with them he be destroyed.

Comment 2:14-19

Vs. 14. Paul turns from a discussion of Timothy, to discuss those with whom Timothy is working. The great eternal truths of the Gospel, stated in verses 8-13, are to be implanted in the minds and hearts of the saints at Ephesus and surrounding area. Particularly should such truths be appreciated by the elders of the several churches.

Such persons had heard from Paul the same truths he has written to Timothy; therefore, he is but to "put them in remembrance." It is so easy to forget. How involved some people become in discussions about some fine point of the law. The "word battles" here being held were not about the law of God, but related to the "endless genealogies, the myths and fables of the traditions of the Jewish fathers."

When Timothy came upon a group of Christians gathered around two or three or more of the church leaders, listening to a heated discussion about some point of Jewish tradition, he was to stop such a meeting. He was to rebuke the leaders for starting such an argument. He was to remind them that such arguments carried no profit even if they came to a perfect agreement, and as it stood it was upsetting the faith of some of the newer converts. Some of the new converts would say, "If the church leaders cannot come to an agreement, who are we to hope to attain a knowledge of God's will?"

We have imagined a situation which we feel is close to the reality of Paul's day.

The word, "subverting," comes from the word from which we have "catastrophe." Such a situation as just described is indeed a catastrophe.

Vs. 15. "Timothy must be a workman, not a quibbler." The word, "study," in the King James version, has been very misleading to a number of people. To use this as a proof text for Bible Study is to miss the point of Paul's words. The expression, "give diligence," is much better; the thought relates to Timothy's attitude, not his practice. We hasten to add that if Timothy was to present himself approved unto God, a workman who needed not to be ashamed, handling aright the Word of truth; he doubtless meditated upon the word in order to so present himself, but the opening expression, "give diligence," relates to his attitude in approaching the Word of truth.

We shall all one day be arraigned before the judgment seat of Christ to give an account. It will be then that we shall want the approval of the one before whom we stand. The thought of such an examination is back of the phrase, "approved of God." Timothy was to conduct himself in his teaching and preaching in such a manner that on the great day of evaluation he would have nothing for which he should be ashamed. What a goal for every man of God!

In order to do this he must make a straight-forward use of the Word of Truth. We take this to be the meaning of the expression, "handle aright the word of truth." In contrast to the empty chatter of the word, "battles," Timothy is to offer a solid discussion of the revealed facts of the Gospel.

A good deal of controversy has arisen over the meaning of "handle aright"; some feel it retains the root meaning of "cutting straight." The meaning and application are the same if the root meaning is retained, or is not retained. Timothy will be approved of God when he makes the right use of the Word of truth.

Vs. 16. What shall be done with those teachers who persist in discussing the profitless points of Jewish tradition? Shun them; ignore them; when they approach you with a question, or attempt an audience with you, turn away from them. Be gentle and kind about it, but be positive and firm. It is not that Timothy or Paul were not interested in the concerns of others, for they were, but when divine truth was the issue, everyone except such persons as here described, knew God had revealed His Word through His inspired apostles and prophets, and anything else was "profane," or empty. Such action is an imperative, for such teachings have within them the germ of Satan.

Do not allow their presence. To do so is to ask for an overthrow of the cause of Christ. Error has a terrifying potency for progress. Stop it before it starts!

The basic error of such teachers as here mentioned, is that they felt the traditions of men were of equal value with the Word of God. Our Lord has something to say about such persons; read Matt. 15:7-9.

Vs. 17. Somehow, in their study and argument concerning profane questions, these false teachers came to believe that the resurrection was already past. If this word was allowed to be taught, it would grow like gangrene. This term is medical in background; it means, literally, "to find pasture." The spread of false teaching in the body of Christ is like the spread of gangrene in the physical body, and just as destructive.

Two examples of such false teachers are Hymenaeus and Philetus. We have heard of Hymenaeus before, in I Timothy 1:20; we cannot be positive that this is the same man, but it does appear more than likely. Of Philetus we know nothing.

Vs. 18. Evidently such men were equating the final resurrection with our new birth. A misapplication of Romans 6:1-4, or Colossians 3:13, would produce such a thought. Think of what implications are contained in this false word: (1) It would deny Christ's physical resurrection; (2) It would deny the possibility of the second coming; (3) The hope of the resurrection for believers would be gone; (4) All hope of meeting our dead loved ones is taken away; (5) We could not share in the Father's house of many mansions. No wonder such a teaching would overthrow the faith of the new ones in Christ in the city of Ephesus!

Vs. 19. What is "the firm foundation of God"? Is it the Gospel or the Church? If we are going to carry the figure of a workman in the house of God (the church), we would refer it to the church. Timothy is not to become discouraged in the face of apostacy, for the Lord's Church will stand though all Hell oppose it! Why refer to the Church as a foundation? In a basic sense, all members of Christ's Church are built upon the apostles and prophets (i.e., their teaching and preaching), Christ Jesus Himself being the chief cornerstone.

In another figure we can say we are builded in and upon one another. We believe Paul is saying here that a remnant or foundation will always be in the world. A solid core will always remain. There shall be two distinguishing marks of this foundation. One mark relating to God, "the Lord knoweth them that are His," i.e., God does have His people in every age. When there are apostates and when there are not. The second mark relates to man, "Let every one that nameth the name of the Lord depart from unrighteousness." In every age there have been those who loved the beauty of holiness and departed from the "spirit of the present age." Timothy could look about him in Ephesus and read this inscription in the conduct of a good number. When the fruit of the Spirit is present in the conduct of men, it is reasonable evidence that they belong to Christ (Cf. Rom. 8:9). To see the one, is to believe the other.

Fact Questions 2:14-19

84. What change is noted in these verses as compared with vss. 8-13?
85. What was the subject matter of the word-battles?
86. What was to be done when Timothy knew of such word-battles? Why was he to do this?
87. What is the meaning and import of the word, "subverting"?
88. Why not use vs. 15a as a proof text for Bible study? What does it mean?
89. How does the thought of the day of judgment relate to vs. 15b?
90. Give your explanation of the expression, "handle aright the word of truth."
91. What shall be done with those teachers who persist in discussing the profitless points of Jewish traditions?
92. Was it not very narrow and unkind to "shun" certain persons? Explain.
93. Explain the meaning and application of the word, "gangrene."
94. Who were Hymenaeus and Philetus?
95. What argument was probably used to show that the resurrection was already past?
96. How would such teaching spread? Didn't the saints at Ephesus have a knowledge of the truth?
97. What is the firm foundation of God?
98. Explain how the Church could be a foundation.
99. Discuss the twofold seal upon the foundation.
100. How did such information, as in vs. 19, encourage Timothy?

f. As a utensil 20-23

Text 2:20-23

20 Now in a great house there are not only vessels of gold and of silver, but also of wood and of earth; and some unto honor, and some unto dishonor. 21 If a man, therefore, purge himself from these, he shall be a vessel unto honor, sanctified, meet for the master's use, prepared unto every good work. 22 But flee youthful lusts, and follow after righteousness, faith, love, peace, with

them that call on the Lord out of a pure heart. 23 But foolish and ignorant questionings refuse, knowing that they gender strifes.

Thought Questions 2:20-23

124. To what does the expression, "great house," refer?
125. Who or what are the "vessels"?
126. The composition of the vessels is determined by someone other than the vessel. Are we to understand that we are predestinated to be either gold, silver, wood, or earth?
127. If the great house is the Church, how could there be dishonorable vessels in it?
128. From what should a man purge himself?
129. Is Paul saying in vs. 21 that a silver and gold vessel should clean itself up for better use? Or is he saying a wooden or clap vessel can change its nature and become gold or silver? Or is there yet another possibility? Please think carefully on this.
130. Discuss the meaning and use of the term, "sanctified," as in vs. 21. Do the same with the word, "meet."
131. Specify some of the "youthful lusts." Why are some desires particularly associated with youth? Is this a hard-and-fast rule?
132. Read I Timothy 6:11 and compare it with II Timothy 2:22. Show what II Timothy 2:22 adds to I Timothy 6:11.
133. How does the possession of a "pure heart" relate to the context?
134. Are the "foolish and ignorant questionings" of vs. 23 the same as those mentioned in 2:16? If so, why mention them again?

Paraphrase 2:20-23

20 Think it not strange that God permits wicked teachers to be in His Church. In a great house there are not only vessels of gold and of silver, but also of wood and of earthenware, and some of these vessels are destined to an honourable, and some to a dishonourable use.

21 If then, a teacher will cleanse himself well from these things, namely, from false doctrine, corrupt affections, and sinful actions, he will be a vessel appointed to an honourable use in the Church, consecrated, and very profitable for God's use, Who is the master of the house or church, being prepared for every good work.

22 Flee, therefore, those youthful lusts which young men placed over others are prone to indulge, and which render them unfit for the master's use: But pursue righteousness, fidelity, love, and peace, especially with them who worship the Lord from a pure heart.

23 Moreover, foolish and untaught questions (Titus 3:9) reject, knowing that they beget fightings.

Comment 2:20-23

Vs. 20. We take the reference to vessels in "the great house" to be church members, in the same sense that the wheat and tares of Jesus' parable were in the Church; and in the same sense that the good and bad fish of the parable of the net were in the church.

This is particularly a discussion of conditions existing in the churches in Ephesus and the province of Asia; however, what was true then is true now. In the great present day House of God there are indeed a variety of vessels. Some are valuable and profitable in the Lord's service (perhaps we should say, a few are), but many are as wood and earth in their value and service to our Lord.

Vs. 21. From what is a man to purge himself? Before we answer this question, please attempt to understand the figure here used. There are two types of vessels: one honorable—represented by those of silver and gold; the other dishonorable—represented by those of wood and earth. All Christians are in one class or the other. We are either honorable or dishonorable; we are either silver and gold or wood and earth. In the church at Ephesus were Hymenaeus and Philetus and their followers, as well as Timothy and certain faithful men. Timothy and those who were faithful to Christ were not to be contaminated by certain filthy members; they must purge themselves, or wash themselves, of them. In so doing they will become vessels unto honor: set apart for the Master's use. On the other hand, if any one of the dishonorable vessels chose to follow in the way of truth instead of error, they could, and would become vessels of honor. By their own choice they set themselves aside as useable in the Lord's House. We realize how abrupt is the change in the figure and also how the analogy is pressed beyond logic, but we honestly feel this is the meaning of the inspired writer.

Vs. 22. In order to be of honorable use in the great House of God, Paul admonishes Timothy to run away from youthful desires. Just what are those desires and why are they called "youthful"? We must not confine them to the lust of the flesh or sins of sex, although we should not exclude such. Mark once again that Paul does not say to fight and oppose such desires; to do such is not to win by overcoming them, but to lose by being overcome by them. The victor's crown belongs to the one who runs away. This is psychologically sound, for when we turn to run away, we transfer our attention and interest and thus break the hold of our previous interest. However, mark well that we are to have something from which to run. Pride, anger and prejudice are as much a part of youthful lusts as passion.

Paul has given almost the same advice to Timothy in his first letter. Read I Timothy 6:11. We discussed those virtues at length in the first letter. "Peace" is the only additional virtue here specified. Perhaps it is included because of the need for this quality in face of the strife certain persons were attempting to bring into the church.

There are others in this pursuit after holiness of character. They are those who call upon the Lord out of a pure heart. What a beautifully descriptive phrase. This is that profitable, valuable, pure company: those in whose hearts insincerity has no place.

Vs. 23. Such advice as given in vs. 23 must have been very much needed, for it was given twice before. Cf. I Tim. 1:4 and 4:7; also II Tim. 2:16. Do not dignify such foolish and ignorant questions with your attention. Avoid them in any way you can that will not bring reproach upon the cause of Christ. Titus was given the same admonition. Cf. Titus 3:9. "Such questionings, while having no useful end, tend to mere empty controversy, arousing the worst passions and breeding bitter enmities." (Harvey)

Fact Questions 2:20-23

101. In what sense are the vessels in the great house church members?
102. There are only two kinds of vessels in God's House. What are they?
103. Vs. 20 has a real application to the present church; show how.
104. From what is a man to purge himself? When he does, what will this do for him?

105. Is it possible for a wood or clay vessel to become one of silver or gold? How?
106. Why flee youthful lusts? Why not stand up and fight them like a man?
107. What is meant by "calling on the Lord out of a pure heart"?
108. Why refuse to answer some questions?
    g. As a bondservant 24-26

Text 2:24-26

24 And the Lord's servant must not strive, but be gentle toward all, apt to teach, forbearing, 25 in meekness correcting them that oppose themselves; if per-adventure God may give them repentance unto the knowledge of the truth, 26 and they may recover themselves out of the snare of the devil, having been taken captive by him unto his will.

Thought Questions 2:24-26

135. Define in your own words the word, "strive," in vs. 24. Didn't Jude say we should "contend"? See Jude 3.
136. How could the Lord's servant be gentle and, at the same time, shun, turn away, reprove, rebuke, and gag the mouths of some?
137. How is the word, "apt," used in vs. 24?
138. Give a hypothetical situation where the Lord's servant could be "forbearing."
139. Please notice that the forbearing is to be "in meekness." Define this word in this context; or is this the use and meaning of the phrase?
140. In what sense do certain persons oppose themselves?
141. What part does God have in producing repentance?
142. How does the knowledge of the truth relate to repentance? What is repentance?
143. Paul says some people are live captives of Satan, but they can escape. How?
144. What is "the snare of the devil"?
145. Whose "will" is concerned in vs. 26b?

Paraphrase 2:24-26

24 And the servant of the Lord must not fight, but be gentle toward all men, fit to teach (see I Tim. 3:2), patiently bearing evil:

25 In meekness instructing those who set themselves in opposition; if, by any means, God will give them repentance to the acknowledgment of truth.

26 And being caught alive by him out of the snare of the devil, they may awake to do the will of God.

Comment 2:24-26

Vs. 24. Christ's bondservant must not become embroiled in strife over words. In contrast, he should have the following four qualities: (1) Gentle toward all. He must be possessed of that heavenly judgment or wisdom, which is "first pure, then gentle, easy to be entreated" (Jas. 3:17). This does not mean weak or flabby. He is approachable and reasonable with *all* who come to him. (2) Apt to teach, i.e., having the ability and desire to do so. Instruction is a great part of his work for Christ. If he does not have a sincere, eager desire to communicate the message, he will not do much for Christ. (3) Forbearing. "Let your forbearance be known unto all men, the Lord is at hand" (Phil. 4:5). Unless we are aware of the presence of the Lord, we will not be very forbearing, especially to those who oppose us. This is such a needed quality; it indicates unselfishness and understanding. The forbearance of God is intended to lead man to repentance (Rom. 2:3,4), ans so should this quality enable us to assist God in this accomplishment.

Vs. 25. (4) "in meekness correcting them that oppose themselves." A man in sin is actually fighting himself. He is opposing all that is for his own best interests. But to cause him to see this is no easy task. It requires that quality of strength under control, defined as "meekness." It is such a comfort and strength to know that the man in sin or error is not himself; he is not living and enjoying life like God wants him to, and like he wants to himself. The man of God must be able to approach such a one with the truth that will give the errorist a vision of reality; this requires meekness.

The hesitancy in the expression, "if *peradventure* God may give them repentance unto the knowledge of the truth," reminds us immediately of Simon, the sorcerer, who was also taken captive by Satan (Acts 8:18-24). There is never any hesitancy on the part of God, for He is always ready to forgive us. But we are not always willing to admit our captivity. The truth comes from

God through His servant. If we want to change our minds about our belief and conduct, then we shall have been given from God the gracious gift of repentance. Somehow, error and sin becomes a part of man, and to change requires the power of God.

Vs. 26. God has provided the prescription, but you must fill it and take the medicine. It is possible (and surely desirable) to recover ourselves from the captivity of Satan. Timothy was going to have a joyful experience of helping some to do this very thing. The recovery is effected by a "return to soberness," or by "coming to your senses." When we can convince ourselves and others that sin and error do not make sense; that they do *not* match reality, we are on the road out. It is sad to be in bondage to Satan, but it is worse not to know it. Paul was discussing certain church members who had been "captured alive" by the Enemy. Satan does not want, nor does he have, any dead captives. We follow Satan to become his slaves. The deep sense of tragedy and futility, which has characterized man for ages, is but an indication that he has been working a long time in the slave camp of the devil. Man's freedom to choose is in choosing who will be his master.

We understand the little phrase, "having been taken captive by him unto *his* will," poses a problem as to whom the last pronoun, "he," refers. Is this the devil or God? We believe the easiest solution is to refer it to Satan; the context seems to support this understanding.

Fact Questions 2:24-26

109. Name, and explain briefly, the four qualities to be found in the Lord's servant.
110. Explain how a man in sin is actually fighting himself.
111. Why use the word, "peradventure," in vs. 25?
112. What is the "snare of the devil"?
113. In a sense, the errorists here described were drunk. Explain.
114. What does the sense of tragedy in life indicate?
115. Whose will is indicated in vs. 26b?

EXEGETICAL EXAMINATION OVER CHAPTER TWO OF II TIMOTHY

1. Discuss two characteristics of a child to be found in the minister and in the Christian. Discuss two qualities of a "good soldier of Christ Jesus."
2 Is there, in 2:2, the basis for "preacher training"? Discuss.

3. Point out the meaning of contending lawfully.
4. Give your interpretation of the "priority of reward" given to the farmer.
5. What is the point of Paul's summary as in vss. 9-13?
6. Discuss when, where, how, and why "we died with Him."
7. God's workman has responsibilities—name and explain two of them.
8. Why did Paul discuss the different kinds of utensils? i.e., gold, silver, wood, earthenware.
9. Discuss briefly two things we must "flee."
10. What is the responsibility of the minister as a bond servant? Please be specific.

PART TWO

Warnings 3:1-4:5

1. RECOGNIZE THE COMING APOSTASY 3:1-9

Text 3:1-9

**1 But know this, that in the last days grievous times shall come,
2 For men shall be lovers of self, lovers of money, boastful, haughty, railers, disobedient to parents, unthankful, unholy,
3 without natural affection, implacable, slanderers, without self-control, fierce, no lovers of good, 4 traitors, headstrong, puffed up,
lovers of pleasure rather than lovers of God; 5 holding a form of godliness, but having denied the power thereof: from these also turn away. 6 For of these are they that creep into houses, and take captive silly women laden with sins, led away by divers lusts,
7 ever learning, and never able to come to the knowledge of the
truth. 8 And even as Jannes and Jambres withstood Moses, so do these also withstand the truth; men corrupted in mind, reprobate
concerning the faith. 9 But they shall proceed no further: for their folly shall be evident unto all men, as theirs also came to be.**

Thought Questions 3:1-9

146. Why did Paul want Timothy to know about the grievous times?
147. To what period of time does the expression, "last days," refer?
148. What is meant by grievous times?
149. Have such times already occurred, or are we to look for them in the future?
150 Give two or three specific instances of self-love.
151. How could one identify a money-lover?

152. What is the difference in being boastful and in being haughty?
153. What is a "railer"? Against whom?
154. Has there ever been a time when children were not disobedient to their parents? Why associate this with a particular time?
155. Is there any connection in this list of sins? Such as a connection between unthankful and unholy, etc.
156. How could anyone become "without natural affections"?
157. Define "implacable."
158. Is the description here related to church members? If so, in what manner?
159. What is meant by the word, "good," in the expression, "no lovers of good"?
160. How would you define "headstrong"?
161. How would the expression, "puffed up," differ from boastful or haughty?
162. In this catalog of sins, which would you feel is the most serious in our present-day society?
163. Why hold any form of godliness if such sins are to be indulged?
164. From vs. 5b we learn there was another group besides this one from which Timothy was to turn away; name them.
165. Who are the "silly women" of vs. 6? How or why described as "silly"?
166. Are these apostates entering households, or physical buildings?
167. Of what sin do you surmise these women were guilty?
168. Why would such women be interested in learning? What were they being taught?
169. Who were Jannes and Jambres? Is the emphasis upon who they were or what they did? What did they do?
170. Some men have a cancer of the mind. How did such develop? What is the meaning of the term, "reprobate"?
171. These men will not get far in their evil efforts. Why not?
172. To whom does this phrase refer, "as *theirs* also came to be"?

Paraphrase 3:1-9

1 Besides what I formerly told thee concerning the apostasy (Eph. 4:1), this also know, that in the latter days, through the extreme wickedness both of the teachers and of the people, times

dangerous to live in will come:
2 For men will be selfish, covetous of money, boasters of their being in favour with God, and proud on that account, blasphemers of God, by the injurious representation which they give of him, disobedient to parents, ungrateful to benefactors, unholy,
3 Without natural affection, avowed covenant-breakers, slanderers of those who oppose their corruptions, immoderately addicted to veneral pleasures, fierce against their opposers, without any love to good men who maintain the truth,
4 Betrayers of trust, headstrong in whatever they undertake, swollen with pride, so that they will hearken to no advice, lovers of sensual pleasures more than lovers of God.
5 These wicked teachers, in order to deceive their disciples the more effectually, will have an appearance of godliness, by their care in performing the external duties of religion, but they will be utterly void of real piety. Now, from these turn away.
6 Of these teachers indeed they are, who go into houses, and, having the appearance of godliness, take the direction of the consciences and purses of ignorant women, who, being laden with sins, and led away by divers lusts, gladly embrace doctrine which reconcile the practice of sin with the hope of salvation.
7 These are devoted to the false teachers, on pretence of always learning; but they are never able to come to the knowledge of truth, because their teachers industriously hide it from them.
8 Now, in the manner that Jannes and Jambres resisted Moses, so by false miracles these teachers also, contrary to their conscience, will resist the truth; being men wholly corrupted in mind, and utterly incapable of discerning the true faith of the Gospel.
9 However, after deluding mankind for a while, they shall not proceed further: For their imposture shall be made very plain to all; as the imposture of Pharaoh's magicians also was to the Israelites, and even to the Egyptians themselves.

Comment 3:1-9

Vs. 1. Paul was a true prophet. His predictions began to be fulfilled in the day of Timothy. Indeed, such conditions as described by Paul have been fulfilled a great number of times in these last days. The last days refers to the entire time from the giving of the New Covenant to the Second Coming of Christ. We shall be content to define, in order, the men here described:

Vs. 2. (1) *lovers of self*—This is the parent stem to the tree of evil. How many foul sins are an outgrowth of this attitude? This is the man with ego at the center of his life. (2) *Lovers of money*—This is a natural outgrowth of self-love. We cannot pamper self without money. The sin and the sadness of money-love has been pointed out before in I Timothy 6:10. (3) *Boastful*—A loud-mouth braggard. About what does such a one boast? This is but a cover-up for the emptiness of his life. (4) *Haughty*—One who looks down on another. When one cannot obtain recognition by good work, his vain fancy will cause him to assume it: the lack of the genuine position and power will make him angry and frustrated. This is expressed in haughtiness. (5) *Railers*—We could call such persons blasphemers: those who speak against God and man. The ones who need the censure of both man and God are the first to offer censure to others. (6) *Disobedient to parents*—This is no light matter, for it indicates a deeper lack; a lack of respect or reverence for the person of God as well as the Law of the Lord. (7) *Unthankful*—When man feels he is sufficient unto himself, he sees no need to thank anyone but himself. How very nearsighted is such a view. (8) *Unholy*—When a man has no norm or standard from God as to conduct, nothing is sacred.

Vs. 3. (9) *Without natural affection*—This refers to the love parents have for their children, and children for their parents. It is called "natural" in the sense that even animals possess such an affection. Such wicked perverts are worse than brutes in their disobedience. Romans 1:23-31 is a commentary on this condition. (10) *Implacable*—Or a truce breaker. Such persons will not keep their word or be responsible for any agreement with others. (11) *Slanderers*—This usually refers to the destruction of the reputation of another by circulating lies. It is always done to the advantage of the one who slanders. (12) *Without self-control*—How ironical that the ones who want freedom and self-expression are unable to control themselves. Hiebert has so wisely said, "Man's freedom is his freedom to chose his master." (13) *Fierce*—This is the savage attitude toward all who oppose the selfish; animals hold this same attitude toward all who oppose them. (14) *No lovers of good*—Some translations indicate this means "no lovers of goodness," but we choose the thought of a generic application to all virtue. Such men as here described have no time or place in their life for virtue.

Vs. 4. (15) *Traitors*—If betrayal of others is to their advantage, they do not hesitate to betray them. (16) *Headstrong*—Such persons plunge ahead regardless of the advice of others, or the apparent consequences. They are like a bull in the arena who rushes to his death. (17) *Puffed up*—King James version translates this "highminded," because it has reference to an exalted opinion of self. Such persons are blinded by the smoke or fog conceit produces. (18) *Lovers of pleasure rather than lovers of God*—This phrase could summarize the basic attitude of those who serve themselves instead of God; who worship themselves instead of God. Those who love themselves worship at the shrine of sensuality. Whatever can tantalize one of the senses is held up as the object of love. The presence of an all-wise and powerful God is an embarrassment to them.

Vs. 5. (19) *Holding a form of godliness, but having denied the power thereof*:—After the record of the wicked life of such persons, it comes as somewhat of a shock that they would profess any religion at all. However, from what is here stated, we could even imagine some of these men as members of the churches to which Timothy ministered. All that is left of the Christianity of such men is the outward form; they are dead while they live. There is no power to overcome for they are servants of sin. The form of godliness is only maintained because of its advantage to them. What a tragic picture: the walking dead! It is no wonder Paul instructs Timothy to withdraw fellowship from such persons. This presupposes every effort has been made to restore such ones. It is to no avail; they are reprobate in heart and mind.

Vs. 6. Here is the reason for withdrawal of fellowship. Such persons are not content to corrupt themselves alone. They ingratiate themselves into the families of some of the church members. In such families they can find certain females who are open prey to their wiles. Such women are called "silly women"; the expression means "little or diminutive women." This has reference to their character or spiritual standing. Such evil men offer lessons in religion; silly women are their students. Such women were themselves "laden with sins" before these teachers appeared. Their conscience tormented them with guilt; thus were they heaped upon, or burdened down, with sin. Will they turn to the one who said, "Come unto me all ye that labor and are heavy laden"? No, no, they enjoy their sin; hence they continue to follow after the desires of the mind and body; such desires are aroused by Satan's offers through his servants.

Vs. 7. Such a tragic battle is the one waged in the heart of these women. On the one hand is some desire to know the truth, and on the other, the stronger desire to follow after the flesh. Such persons do not want a norm of truth, and for this reason they are ready to listen to false teachers. Their desire to know keeps them ever learning from the wrong source; hence they never come to a knowledge of truth.

Vs. 8. Now a consideration of the teachers themselves. Paul compares them with the two magicians of Pharaoh who opposed Moses when he came to Egypt to deliver Israel. The names of these men are not given in Exodus. They were mentioned often in Jewish traditions and were well-known by Paul and Timothy, as well as the rest of the Jewish nation. Paul makes use of the common traditional knowledge of their names for his own good purpose. Exodus tells of their efforts to oppose the truth of God through Moses. The incident in the court of Pharaoh is doubtless before the mind of Paul when he wrote. Such men were not interested in whether Moses was from God or not; they were there to defend their master. Such dupes are described as "corrupt in mind." The very means by which truth is perceived as distinct from error, has been corrupted or infected with disease. They are also described as "reprobate" or "counterfeit" concerning the Faith. Their teaching and work, when compared with the truth, are found wanting. Since they are compared with the court magicians, it could have been they were using magical powers in the false teaching. No wonder they had such an interested audience.

Vs. 9. These false teachers of the latter times will get no further than Jannes and Jambres did in the long ago. The miracles and teaching of Moses proved so far superior to these teachers that they soon began to look foolish to all. This is a most encouraging word: error and evil will be stopped. Even though Simon the sorcerer of the city of Samaria (Acts 8:9-13) practiced his evil art for a long time, there came a day when his folly was made known even to himself. When was that day? In the day when the truth of God, as preached by Philip, was placed squarely along side false practice and preaching. Timothy can be encouraged that error will be rejected as he preaches the truth, but he must preach the truth or there never will be such a victory.

Fact Questions 3:1-9

116. Why can we say Paul was a true prophet?
117. To what period of time does the phrase, "the last days," refer?
118. Define and apply in your own words ten of the nineteen characteristics of the evil men of the last days.
119. Verse six presents the reason for turning away from these men. What is it?
120. In what sense are we to understand the phrase, "silly women"?
121. Why would there be in such women an interest in learning?
122. Who were Jannes and Jambres?
123. In what way do these false teachers compare with Jannes and Jambres?
124. Timothy is assured of victory in spite of opposition. How?

2. WITHSTAND THE APOSTASY 3:10-17

Text 3:10-17

**10 But thou didst follow my teaching, conduct, purpose, faith, long-
suffering, love, patience, 11 persecutions, sufferings; what things
befell me at Antioch, at Iconium, at Lystra; what persecutions I
endured: and out of them all, the Lord delivered me. 12 Yea, and
all that would live godly in Christ Jesus shall suffer persecution.
13 But evil men and imposters shall wax worse and worse, deceiving and being deceived. 14 But abide thou in the things which thou
hast learned and hast been assured of, knowing of whom thou
hast learned them; 15 and that from a babe thou hast known the
sacred writings which are able to make thee wise unto salvation
through faith which is in Christ Jesus. 16 Every Scripture inspired
of God is also profitable for teaching, for reproof, for correction,
for instruction, which is in righteousness: 17 that the man of God
may be complete, furnished completely unto every good work.**

Thought Questions 3:10-17

173. Verses 10 and 11 are given as a contrast to something. What is it?
174. In what sense had Timothy followed Paul?
175. What is the difference between "conduct" and "purpose"?
176. Show the distinction between "longsuffering" and "patience."
177. Give two examples from the life of Paul to illustrate two of the qualities here mentioned.

178. Why does Paul refer to the persecutions and trials at Antioch, Iconium, and Lystra?
179. What general principle is shown from those specific examples?
180. If we are not suffering persecutions, is it an indication that we are not living a godly life?
181. Specify just how the Lord delivered Paul from some of his persecutions. Sometimes he was not delivered. Why?
182. Why give the promise of vs. 13?
183. What is meant by the use of the term, "abide," as in vs. 14?
184. Timothy was to trust what he had learned because of those from whom he had been taught. Explain.
185. In what way could the Old Testament Scriptures make Timothy "wise unto salvation"?
186. Is Paul saying that every Scripture is inspired of God; or that only those which are inspired are profitable?
187. Define in your own words: "reproof," "correction," "instruction," and show how the Scriptures fulfill these purposes.
188. If the Scriptures will furnish us unto every good work, why use uninspired literature?

Paraphrase 3:10-17

10 But what I have done for detecting and opposing deceivers thou knowest, who hast fully known my doctrine, manner of life, purpose in preaching, fortitude in danger, meekness under provocation, love to mankind, patience under sufferings.

11 Persecutions and sufferings, such as befell me in Antioch (Acts 14:50), in Iconium, (Acts 14:2,5,6), in Lystra, where I was stoned and left as dead (Acts 14:19,20): Such persecutions I endured; but out of them all the Lord Jesus delivered me.

12 I do not complain of my sufferings, as if I was the only persecuted servant of Christ. All, indeed, who wish to live godly in the Christian Church, shall be persecuted in this age.

13 Now the wicked teachers and sorcerers, of whom I speak, who by false miracles seduce the people, will for a while wax worse and worse, deceiving others, and being deceived themselves, till they are stopped.

14 But, instead of acting like these wicked teachers, continue thou in the belief of the things which thou hast learned, and with which thou has been instructed, knowing from whom thou hast learned them—even from me, an inspired apostle;

15 And that from thy childhood thou hast known the sacred Scriptures, which having foretold the doctrine, miracles, death, resurrection, and ascension of the Christ, exactly as they have come to pass, are able to make thee wise to salvation, by confirming thee in the faith which hath Christ Jesus for its object.

16 I am calumniated as contradicting Moses and the prophets, but I believe, that the whole sacred Scripture is divinely inspired, and is profitable for teaching the doctrines of the Gospel, for confuting those who err therefrom, for correcting those who sin, for instructing all in righteousness;

17 That the Christian minister, by the light derived from the Jewish revelation, may be perfect in the knowledge of the things he is appointed to teach, and thoroughly fitted for discharging every part of the good work he is engaged in.

Comment 3:10-17

Vs. 10. In contrast to the evil workers, is God's faithful servant Timothy. Paul, in this section, wishes to offer encouragement in the face of very difficult times; this is accomplished for Timothy by a reference to Timothy's conversion. Paul says, in effect: "You are not like these false teachers, for you have followed not in error, but in truth. Such truth was heard and observed through my teaching, conduct, purpose, faith, longsuffering, love, patience." We shall discuss each of the qualities in order, as they relate to Paul in his association with Timothy: (1) *teaching*—The message of Paul was accepted by Timothy for what it was in truth—the Word of God. Timothy followed it in the sense that he made it a part of his life. The teachings of Paul, like those of the Old Testament Scriptures, were to Timothy God's light on his pathway of life. They not only gave him direction in life, but illumination on the way. (2) *conduct*—This refers to manner of life, or general demeanor. What was Paul's manner of life? He said, "For me, to live is Christ" (Phil. 1:21). The same dedication to the will of God, the same surrender of all the powers of body and mind as found in our Lord, were also found in Paul. Timothy was attracted by, and to, such a conduct. Paul is now saying, "Stay with it!" (3) *purpose*—Paul's Master's passion was to preach the Gospel. To this purpose, Christ had called and commissioned him, and to this vision he was never disobedient. What greater purpose could Timothy have? (4) *faith*—The faith here mentioned could be equated with "faithfulness," but it probably refers to Paul's belief or trust in God's revelation. This confidence, if held by Timothy, would fortify him against error and sin. (5) *longsuffering*—Paul indeed suffered long at the hands of Gentiles, as well as his own nation. If Timothy is so to suffer, he will know how to conduct himself. (6) *love*—Paul's love was the kind he described in I Corinthians, the 13th chapter. The selfless devotion of the apostle stands out on every page of the record of his life. (7) *patience*—This word could also be translated, "steadfastness." Without the power to endure, other qualities lose their fruit before it is ripe. "In due season we shall reap, if we faint not," seemed to be the hallmark of Paul's work.

Vs. 11. (8) *persecutions*—The particular opposition was that which was endured on the first missionary journey in the home town of Timothy. Timothy knew of the efforts of the evil one to defeat Paul's work. The details of such efforts are not known to us, but they were to Timothy. A reading of Acts, chapters 13 and 14, will help in our understanding. (9) *sufferings*—Was Timothy present at any of the five beatings of the Jews? Did Timothy hear from the lips of the apostle the particular details of the perils in rivers, or perils among robbers? What were the perils in the city, as contrasted with the perils in the wilderness?

The things which befell Paul in Lystra and Iconium, as well as in Antioch, were of particular knowledge to Timothy. What tender scenes of Paul's devotion were in the memory of this beloved child in the faith? Was Timothy one of those who stood around to see Paul stoned? "The fearful scene in Lystra, when Paul was stoned and left for dead, the young disciple had probably himself witnessed" (Harvey).

This recital of suffering is all given for a purpose: Timothy was about to face similar difficulty. When he called to heart and mind the sufferings of his beloved father in the faith, most especially his suffering in the early days of Timothy's Christian life, he would be strengthened to also "rejoice in tribulation, knowing that tribulation worketh steadfastness" (Rom. 5:3).

In what sense could Paul say, "and out of them all, the Lord delivered me"? He was not delivered from beatings, for he was beaten; he was not delivered from jail, for he was thrown into jail. Paul is not saying, "God will deliver us from suffering," but he is saying, He will give us the strength to endure it. We are not delivered *from* such suffering, but *out* of them. He has never forsaken His own.

Vs. 12. Out of Paul's personal experience comes this general principle. The Christian is at war with the spirit of this present age. We can expect opposition if we are aggressively living for Christ. We cannot hope to live a holy life, except by vital union with Christ Jesus. But as we can be certain of the strength received by fellowship with Christ, so we can expect the hatred, misunderstanding, and persecution of the world. If we continue in a comfortable life with little or no opposition, we should re-evaluate our efforts to live for Him. If we have so adapted ourselves to the spirit of this present age of materialism and sensuality that we suffer no opposition, then we are no better than Lot in Sodom; indeed, we are worse!

Vs. 13. As the godly increase in their efforts to live for Christ, so do evil men increase in their efforts to live for Satan. The "evil men and imposters" could quite as literally be called "evil men and sorcerers, or magicians." Sin is never static. This verse describes the effects of sin and error in the heart of the sinner or errorist. Such men make great and rapid progress in the direction of evil; they "advance in the direction of the worse." This is the natural tendency of evil. It has within it the power of Satanic life. It will grow from bad to worse if given any encouragement. But sinners have within themselves their own punishment. "Living in an element of deceit, they come to be themselves deceived. Deception always involves self-deception" (DeWette). "This is the inexorable law of our moral being: he who perverts the truth, in the very act destroys his own power to see the truth, and opens his soul to the influx of error" (Harvey).

Vs. 14. The only safeguard against error is to be actively engaged in the promotion of the truth. Timothy need have no fear of being deceived while he "abides" in the teaching of the revealed truth. Timothy did more than to mentally assent to the truthfulness of Paul's message; he learned in such a manner as to be able to teach others; but not only so, he was fully persuaded within. Timothy obtained conviction from his learning. Until one is ready to commit his life to the teachings, he does not have the conviction necessary to labor as he should. Such conviction possessed Timothy; he was "fully assured."

The source of such conviction is ultimately the Sacred Oracles, but they are communicated through persons. There is disagreement as to what person, or persons, are meant in vs. 14b. Some would relate the expression "of whom thou hast learned them" to Paul, but others refer it to Timothy's mother and grandmother. It does seem like the latter opinion fits the context better.

Vs. 15. Here is the true source of Timothy's steadfastness. How young was Timothy when he began his study of the "Sacred Writings"? The Word, "a babe" refers to the earliest years of childhood. "The Jewish children were taught the Scriptures by memorizing them as soon as they could speak. Rabbi Judah says: 'The boy of five years of age ought to apply to the study of the Sacred Scriptures' " (Harvey). Timothy learned his ABC's from the Old Testament. This was not without instruction as to their meaning and application to life. Reasons for accepting the Sacred Writings for what they claim to be, are abundant within the writings themselves. Timothy first believed the writings were from God, and then he found within them the blessed boon of salvation through the promised Messiah. When Paul came to Lystra to point out the fulfillment of all promises in Jesus of Nazareth, Timothy found salvation—the end of the law.

Vs. 16. Here is the objective fact drawn from Timothy's experience. Here is a principle for all men of all time and circumstance.

Which translation shall we accept? Should this verse read: (1) "Every Scripture inspired of God is also profitable," or (2) "Every Scripture is inspired of God and profitable." We like the expression of Lenski on this question: "The one is just as correct as the other, as far as the Greek is concerned; and the meaning is exactly the same save for the insignificant shifting of the capula." (*Ibid.* p. 810.)

What does Paul say of the Scripture? (The Old Testament Scriptures, in particular.) He says five specific things: (1) It is inspired, or "God breathed." (2) It is profitable for teaching. (3) It is profitable for reproof or rebuke of sin. (4) It is profitable for correction of sin and error. (5) It is profitable for instruction or discipline in righteousness. We shall give, in order, a brief discussion of each of these five points.

(1) *Every Scripture is "God breathed."* The expression, "Scripture," is used more than fifty times in the New Testament, in either the singular or plural form, to refer to the Old Testament

as received and used by the Jews in the days of the Apostles. How shall we understand the use of the word, every"? We refer it to every portion of the Scripture as being inspired.

(2) *It is profitable for teaching.* The important element in teaching, is content. The Scriptures provide "God breathed" information to the teacher. He has the joy and awesome privilege of enlightening the mind and heart concerning what God has spoken.

(3) *It is profitable for reproof.* Once the Scriptures are accepted as God's Word, then we can be corrected thereby. All that is wrong can be removed. A conscience is developed and conviction stirred.

(4) *It is profitable for correction.* This is not repetitious of the preceding. *Reproof* refers to conscience and conviction; *correction* refers to information and alteration. The Scriptures furnish the divine norm, or standard, whereby we can measure our lives and teaching.

(5) *It is profitable for instruction.* The word, "instruction," is also translated "discipline." "For 'training,' Scripture trains, or educates, by guiding and inspiring the soul in holiness and right living. It is the manual of spiritual education" (Harvey).

Vs. 17. After considering the accomplishments of the inspired Scriptures, this verse seems a rather inevitable conclusion.

The Scriptures accomplish two glorious ends: (1) They equip the Christian in every area of life. What are the words of men when compared to the heaven-sent Word of God? When the teacher has taught himself in all the four areas specified in vs. 16, he is indeed *complete.* The Scriptures provide the means for creating "the whole man." Psychologically and philosophically, the Scriptures give a coherence to life nothing else can provide.

(2) Once the man of God is *one*, or is a *whole man*, then he can use what has made him whole to accomplish this same wholeness in others.

Fact Questions 3:10-17

125. When, where, and how did Timothy follow Paul, as indicated in vs. 10?
126. Of the nine particulars in vss. 9 and 10, define four of them.
127. What was the purpose in the record of Paul's suffering, as given here?

128. In what sense had God delivered Paul from his persecutions?
129. Some people in our day are worse off than Lot in Sodom. Who are they?
130. Explain the expression that "sinners have within themselves their own punishment."
131. What is the only safeguard against error?
132. Timothy did something more than to merely assent to the truth. What was it?
133. What were the immediate and ultimate sources of Timothy's conviction?
134. How young was Timothy when he began to learn of the Old Testament? Wasn't this too young? Many say the Old Testament is too difficult to understand.
135. In what sense did the Old Testament make Timothy wise unto salvation?
136. Explain in your own words the fourfold profitableness of the inspired Word.
137. Do you believe a secular education equips one for living, in a way the Scriptures do not? Explain and discuss.

EXEGETICAL EXAMINATION OVER CHAPTER THREE of II TIMOTHY

1. Give your own outline of this chapter.
2. Define and apply ten of the nineteen characteristics of the evil men.
3. Why did Paul describe in such elaborate detail, the sins of the last days?
4. What was the purpose of mentioning Jannes and Jambres?
5. In what manner had Timothy followed Paul? (Cf. vs. 10a.)
6. In what sense had God delivered Paul?
7. Give your own exegesis of vs. 12.
8. In what sense had the Old Testament made Timothy "wise unto salvation"?
9. Define "inspiration," as it relates to the Scriptures.
10. Are we to believe the Scriptures furnish us completely only as they relate to our religious life? Discuss.

3. PREACH THE WORD 4:1-5

Text 4:1-5

1 I charge thee in the sight of God, and of Christ Jesus, who shall judge the living and the dead, and by His appearing and His kingdom: 2 preach the Word; be urgent in season, out of season;

reprove, rebuke, exhort, with all longsuffering and teaching. 3 For the time will come when they will not endure the sound doctrine; but, having itching ears, will heap to themselves teachers after their own lusts; 4 and will turn away their ears from the truth, and turn aside unto fables. 5 But be thou sober in all things, suffer hardship, do the work of an evangelist, fulfill thy ministry.

Thought Questions 4:1-5

189. Is Paul delivering a charge or giving a testimony?
190. Is Paul calling God and Christ Jesus to witness for his charge? Explain.
191. What is the purpose of vss.1-5?
192. When and where will Christ judge the living and the dead?
193. Why testify in the presence of the Second Coming of Christ? Please show the purpose as it relates to the context.
194. What "kingdom" is meant in vs. 1?
195. The word, "preach," is also translated "herald." Explain the implication of this for the preacher.
196. What is meant by the term, "word," in vs. 2a?
197. Define in your own words the term, "urgent."
198. When is it "in season" for preaching, and when is it "out of season" for preaching?
199. Define the three words, "reprove, rebuke, and exhort."
200. Does Paul give here a divine formula for the development of a sermon? Please look carefully.
201. Two attitudes of the preacher are described. What are they?
202. I thought listeners were to do something more than "endure" the sound doctrine. How is the word, "endure," here used?
203. Who has the "itching ears"? Discuss.
204. What is meant by saying, "heap to themselves," teachers?
205. Why do some turn their ears away from the truth? What particular "fables" would be of interest to these persons?
206. Discuss the meaning of the word, "sober," as in vs. 5a. What "things" are included?
207. Specify three things you believe would be included in the work of the evangelist.
208. How would Timothy know he had fulfilled his ministry?

Paraphrase 4:1-5

1 I have fully instructed thee in thy duty, and thou art well acquainted with the Jewish Scriptures, in which the Gospel is both explained and confirmed; I charge thee, therefore, in the

presence of God, and of the Lord Jesus Christ, who will judge the living and the dead at His second appearing, when His kingdom shall be displayed in all its glory.

2 Preach the Gospel doctrine in purity; be constant and earnest in preaching it, whether it be seasonable or unseasonable to thyself; confute false teachers, rebuke sinners, exhort all under thy care, with the greatest patience when teaching them.

3 Thou oughtest to be very faithful and diligent in these duties now; for there will be a time when the people will not endure wholesome teaching, but having itching ears, which must be tickled, they will, by the motions of their own peculiar lusts, multiply to themselves teachers, who, to gain their favour, will sooth them in their vices.

4 And thus indeed they will turn away their ears from the true doctrine of the Gospel, and, by their teachers, they will be turned aside to believe fables, concerning miracles wrought in support of the greatest errors.

5 But watch thou at all times, and withstand the beginnings of these corruptions; patiently bear the ill treatment which the enemies of the Gospel will give thee; do the work of an evangelist diligently; fully perform the duties of thy ministry:

Comment 4:1-5

Vs. 1. This is Paul's final farewell word to his beloved child, Timothy. This whole section (vss. 1-5) is surcharged with emotion. Here is Paul's personal testimony, as well as a charge to Timothy. What he said of himself, he says to his son.

Paul practiced living constantly in the presence of God and Christ Jesus, but never was he more aware of his divine observers and participators than when preaching the Word. This is an awesome responsibility. This same Jesus will be our judge on that day when we shall all be manifested before Him. Those who are living when He comes will be judged; those who have died, will be called forth from the world of the unseen to also appear before Him.

The "kingdom," here mentioned, probably is best identified with the eternal kingdom where all Christians will reign with Him.

Vs. 2. "Herald forth the whole council of God." The preacher, or herald, has a message from the King of kings. He dare not change it or withhold it. He must tell it if all men refuse it.

Timothy, and all who follow after, are to be keenly conscious that they have a message bigger and more important than themselves, that must be heard. The attitude of the preacher toward his message and work is described in the words, "be urgent"; it means, "to be on hand." We might say, "Be right on the spot" (Lenski). This absorbing interest in what is being said and done, will give the preacher the enthusiasm necessary to communicate the feeling of the truth, instead of just words.

There is no season when the Word is not to be preached. There are times when it does not seem at all convenient; there are times when men will mock it, ignore it, oppose it. There are other times when men will welcome the herald and his good news. Above and beyond all outward circumstances, the preacher has a message that *must* be told.

Please mark carefully the divine elements in preaching. They are: (1) *Reprove* or *bring to the proof*—we might say, *convince*. Offer evidence and reason for your subject. (2) *Rebuke* or *chide —convict*. This is the application of the truth to life. (3) *Exhort* or *call to action*. Stir the motives of the listeners to act upon, or decide upon, what has been spoken.

The overmastering attitude in all preaching is to be one of long-suffering and instruction.

Vs. 3. There is a very good reason for this steadfast attitude in preaching. A time is coming when such a message and preacher will be needed. This is another prophecy of apostasy very much like I Tim. 4:1 and II Tim. 3:1. Timothy is to prepare himself and the leaders of the churches against such a day. The world has not changed, but some persons in the church will. There will come a time when healthy teaching will be shunned in preference to the diseased doctrine of false prophets. Such false teachers will be invited by the elders of certain churches (even in Ephesus), to spread their doctrine among them. Such false elders, with their false preachers, have "itching ears"; i.e., they are eagerly restless to hear something that will satisfy their fancy. This itch is hard to scratch, for even those who have it know not for sure what they want. As a result, they must try one preacher after another. If gathered together they would make quite a "heap." Thus does Paul Prophetically as well as sarcastically, describe the coming apostasy.

Vs. 4. Such persons will aggressively oppose the truth. Because of their own lusts and refusal to obey the truth, they have chosen to obey falsehood. For whatever reason, they have made their choice; they will not hear the truth; they want to hear fables. We have read much in these three letters concerning fables; it is probably with such fables that he is also concerned here. It is difficult to say why some prefer fables to truth, but we can know the reason relates to one of the following three: (1) lust of the eye, (2) lust of the flesh, (3) pride of life. (I John 2:15.)

Vs. 5. In contrast to those who have been intoxicated with false doctrine—"be thou sober in all things." The reference is to the alert attitude Timothy was to sustain. By being vigilant, he could detect such error before it influenced too many. In all his work, Timothy was to be alert. If, in the discharge of his duties of preaching and teaching, Timothy was faced with perils of various sorts, he was not to be surprised, but rather expect them and overcome them, through his faith.

Paul wishes Timothy to carry out every phase of the office of evangelist. It would indeed be difficult to do the work of an evangelist if one was not an evangelist himself. Timothy was neither a pastor nor a bishop; he was an evangelist. We refer you to our text on *THE CHURCH IN THE BIBLE* for a rather thorough study of the office and of the work of an evangelist.

"Fulfill thy ministry" has been translated, "make full proof of thy ministry." It means to fill up every part of it: to leave no area undeveloped. This would be no easy task in the face of the conditions described.

Fact Questions 4:1-5

138. What indications of the emotion Paul felt when he wrote 4:1-5 are noticed in the text?
139. What is meant by saying that Paul lived constantly in the presence of God?
140. Show how the preacher is like a herald.
141. When is it "out of season" for preaching? Explain the meaning of the word, "urgent."
142. Discuss the meaning and application of "reprove, rebuke, and exhort" in preaching.
143. Who has "itching ears"? Why? What is to be done about it?
144. Explain: "heap to themselves teachers."
145. Why do some persons prefer fables to the truth?
146. Give your own exegesis of vs. 5.

PART THREE

Testimony 4:6-18

1. ASSURANCE IN THE FACE OF DEATH 4:6-8

Text 4:6-8

6 For I am already being offered, and the time of my departure is come. 7 I have fought the good fight, I have finished the course, I have kept the faith: 8 henceforth there is laid up for me the crown of righteousness, which the Lord, the righteous judge, shall give to me at that day; and not to me only, but also to all them that have loved His appearing.

Thought Questions 4:6-8

209. What figure of speech is Paul using in vs. 6a? Does Paul say that he is a sacrifice for Christ?
210. How could Paul be so certain of a soon departure from this life?
211. Who was Paul fighting in the "good fight"?
212. Are we all running in a race? Who will win?
213. Why didn't Paul say he had kept *his* faith, instead of *the* faith?
214. If Paul had not kept the faith or finished the race, would he have received the "crown of righteousness"?
215. Are there various crowns for Christians? i.e., "crown of life," "crown of righteousness," etc.? Explain.
216. Why use the expression, "the righteous judge"?
217. Give the meaning of the phrase, "His appearing." Is this His first or second appearing?

Paraphrase 4:6-8

6 For the church is soon to lose the benefit of my ministry: I am already poured out on the sacrifice of the faith of the Gentiles, and the time of my departure hath come.

7 I have combated the good combat of faith (I Tim. 6:12), I have finished the race of an apostle, I have preserved the faith uncorrupted, for which I have combated.

8 All fears of death vanish when I think of the glorious reward which awaits me. Henceforth there is laid aside for me a crown, not of olive leaves, but of righteousness, which, with all its honours and privileges, the Lord Jesus, the righteous judge, will de-

liver to me at the last day; and not to me only, but to all them also, who, like me, conscious that they have served Him faithfully, long for His appearing to judge the world.

Comment 4:6-8

Vs. 6. Paul now turns to say a word for himself. He had previously directed his words to Timothy and his responsibilities. The apostle does *not* say he is the sacrifice given on behalf of Christ—as well he might have said it. He rather prefers to be considered only as the drink offering to be poured out in connection with the sacrifice (Num. 15:5; 28:7). Paul's blood was about to be poured out in his martyr's death. What Paul here says of his death, he could say of his whole life; it was poured out in the service and worship to Christ. Paul views death as a voyage: the ship is about to be loosed from its moorings; the grand trip into the presence of God and of Christ Jesus is about to be made; farewells are in order; the time of sailing is just at hand. This is not a voyage into oblivion, but an adventure into a very far better world. What an example to Timothy and all who follow.

Vs. 7. The apostle is glad to rest on his record. Paul does *not* say he has won every battle, but that he has remained in the fight until the end. Paul does *not* say he has taken first place in the race, but that he has finished the course; nor does he say that he was the champion of the faith, but rather, that he kept it. In all of this, he presents an example all can follow. We know this is the grand old veteran's record. We know of his trials and triumphs, but it is his steadfastness that is rewarded. All of us cannot do what Paul did, but all of us are expected to *fight*, *finish* and *keep*. Paul offered his example to Timothy and to all men of all time.

Vs. 8. Perhaps, to some, it is a moot question, but we wonder what happens to those soldiers who do not stay in the battle: those runners who drop out of the race, and to those believers who fall away from the faith. If the figure is to hold, we have no crown to offer for those who fail to finish. We prefer to fear, along with the apostle, lest having preached unto others, we should be a castaway. On the merit of Christ, and our sincerity in service, let us claim, with Paul, the crown of righteousness. The righteous judge has it for all who have loved His appearing more than the appearance of this world. We have it on the word of Paul that it is so.

Fact Questions 4:6-8

147. What is the general content of vss. 6-8?
148. Paul does *not* say he offers himself as the sacrifice in the service of Christ. What does he say of his offering?
149. How does Paul view death? Is this your concept?
150. How does Paul's record become a grand example for all Christians?
151. Are we given heaven because we are faithful? Discuss.

2. REQUEST FOR TIMOTHY TO COME BACK TO PAUL 4:9-15

Text 4:9-15

**9 Give diligence to come shortly unto me: 10 for Demas forsook
me, having loved this present world, and went to Thessalonica;
Crescens to Galatia, Titus to Dalmatia. 11 Only Luke is with me.
Take Mark, and bring him with thee; for he is useful to me for
ministering. 12 But Tychicus I sent to Ephesus. 13 The cloak that I
left at Troas with Carpus, bring when thou comest, and the books,
especially the parchments. 14 Alexander the coppersmith did me
much evil: the Lord will render to him according to his works: 15
of whom do thou also beware; for he greatly withstood our words.**

Thought Questions 4:9-15

218. Why the urgency in the request to come to Paul?
219. Where was Paul when Demas forsook him? Demas loved "this present world." What was the basic fault?
220. Is there any significance in the place where Demas went upon forsaking Paul? If so, what?
221. Was there any blame in Crescens going to Galatia, or Titus to Dalmatia?
222. Paul's attitude toward Mark has changed since we last heard of him. Explain.
223. Why send Tychicus to Ephesus?
224. If Paul was so near death, why request the cloak, books and parchments?
225. Do we know anything of the Alexander mentioned in 4:14? What is meant by saying, "The Lord will render to him according to his works"? Is this vindictive? Explain.
226. Why would Alexander the coppersmith be a problem to Timothy?

Paraphrase 4:9-15

9 As I have a great desire to see thee, make haste to come to me soon.

10 For Demas, in particular, having loved the present world more than was fit, hath forsaken me, and is gone to Thessalonica, expecting to be in more safety there than at Rome; Crescens is gone into Galatia, and Titus into Dalmatia.

11 Only Luke is with me. His attachment to me, and his zeal for the cause of Christ, are the more remarkable, that all my other assistants have left me. In thy way call on Mark, and bring him with thee, for he will be very useful to me in the ministry of the Gospel.

12 But when Tychicus comes to thee, do not think he hath behaved like Demas: I have sent him to Ephesus to supply thy place.

13 The bag which I left at Troas with Carpus, in my way from Ephesus after parting with thee, bring when thou comest, and the books contained in that bag, but especially the parchments.

14 Alexander the coppersmith hath done me many ill offices here. In particular, he hath stirred up both the unbelieving Jews and Gentiles in Rome against me. The Lord reward him according to his works.

15 Of that wicked person be thou also aware, wherever thou happenest to meet with him, for he hath greatly contradicted the things which I advanced in my first answer.

Comment 4:9-15

Vs. 9. It would appear that Paul is lonely. He longs for the companionship of one who knew him better than any other; one who shared with him the same concern for the advance of the kingdom. If Timothy did not hurry, it would be too late. There were yet many little matters of personal interest to discuss in the midst of disappointments and desertions and even death; he longed to see one whom he could trust.

Vs. 10. Col. 4:14; Phil. 1:24 indicates Demas was once a trusted co-laborer. Paul might well have said, "Demas has left me in the lurch." Some love "His appearing"; others love "this present world." The love for this present age is not centered on any one thing. It is the desire for the world's false security and pleasure that produces men like Demas. Why did Demas go to Thessalonica? Did he go there because he wished to carry on a trade? Because it was his home? It is useless to ask. The point is, that he went to the world to satisfy the desires of his heart; this was the wrong direction, regardless of where he went geographically.

We know nothing of the man here called Crescens or what he did in Galatia. Why Paul sent Titus to Dalmatia we do not know

Vs. 11. By saying, "only Luke is with me," we are not to understand that Paul is all alone, for vs. 21 indicates there were a number of other friends with him. Luke was the only fellow-worker of those several who labored with Paul, who yet remained in Rome. We need not remind the reader that this is the Luke who wrote the Third Gospel and also the Book of Acts.

John Mark has redeemed himself in the eyes of Paul. In an earlier reference, he was with Paul in Rome (Cf. Col. 4:10). There was a time when Paul would have said the exact opposite of what he said here of John Mark (Cf. Acts 15:38,39).

The faith of Barnabas in John Mark paid off. Whether Paul wanted Mark as a personal helper, or as one to minister the Word, is not at all clear from the context; either one could be true.

Vs. 12. Perhaps this is a reference to the coming of the replacement for Timothy. Tychicus was a busy man. He was sent to Ephesus and Colossia to bear the three letters of Ephesians, Colossians, and Philemon (Cf. Eph. 6:21; Col. 4:7). He could have been sent to Crete to replace Titus (Titus 3:12). He was with Paul on his third missionary journey (Acts 20:5).

Vs. 13. Paul is intent on a visit from Timothy. The detailed instructions in these verses (9-15), all relate to Timothy's preparation for the visit. Mark is to accompany Timothy; he is also to bring something besides John Mark. There is some disagreement among commentators as to whether Paul is requesting a cloak, or a portfolio for holding books. We prefer the thought of a cloak. Vs. 21 speaks of the winter when a warm cloak would be most welcome. Are we to believe that even in his last hours Paul wanted to read, and hence, the reference to bringing the books and parchments? We like Lenski's suggestion that these were copies of the Old Testament books which Paul wanted to use in his defense. These were personal copies which he had used over the years. He wanted to prove that his religion was but a fulfillment of the Jewish religion and offered no threat to the Roman government. This is only a matter of opinion, but it seems to be a good one.

Vs. 14. Why mention Alexander the coppersmith at this particular time? It was either because Alexander was on his way to Ephesus and would give Timothy trouble when he arrived, or that Timothy would meet him in Rome and would need preparation and warning. It is useless speculation to try to relate this Alexander with any other mentioned in the New Testament who wore the same name. A coppersmith is one who works in metals. not necessarily only in copper or brass, but in all metals. Just where and when or how Alexander did Paul much evil, is not known; it is usually made to relate to Paul's defense before the court. Paul is prophetic, instead of vindictive, when he says, "the Lord will render to him according to his works."

Vs. 15. It is a problem as to when or where Timothy would meet Alexander. It is also a problem as to what "words" are meant. Did Alexander oppose the words of the Gospel, or did he oppose Paul's testimony at the Roman Court?

Fact Questions 4:9-15

152. Why did Paul want Timothy to visit him in Rome?
153. What is wrong with love for this present world?
154. Why did Demas go to Thessalonica?
155. How are we to understand the expression, "only Luke is with me"?
156. Paul changed his mind about John Mark. Explain.
157. Why mention Tychicus (vs. 12)?
158. Why request the books and parchments?
159. Alexander the coppersmith showed Paul much evil. When and where?
160. Why warn Timothy concerning Alexander?

3. PRAISE FOR HIS LORD 4:16-18

Text 4:16-18

16 At my first defence no one took my part, but all forsook me: may it not be laid to their account. 17 But the Lord stood by me, and strengthened me; that through me the message might be fully proclaimed, and that all the Gentiles might hear: and I was delivered out of the mouth of the lion. 18 The Lord will deliver me from

every evil work, and will save me unto His heavenly kingdom: to whom be the glory for ever and ever. Amen.

Thought Questions 5:16-18

227. What is meant by the phrase, "my first defense"?
228. Is Paul saying that his Christian friends would not testify on his behalf before the Roman Court? If not, what is meant?
229. If certain persons forsook Paul in his hour of need, it would be laid to their account. Why then the expression in vs. 16b?
230. What proclamation of the Gospel is meant in vs. 17? What Gentiles?
231. Who is "lion" in vs. 17b? Is this literal or figurative?
232. Paul had certain expectations of deliverance from "every evil work," and yet he was beheaded. How can we reconcile the two thoughts?
233. What is the "heavenly kingdom" of vs. 18b?

Paraphrase 4:16-18

16 At my first answer, my fellow-laborers were so terrified that no one of them appeared with me in the court, but all forsook me. I pray God not to lay it to their charge!
17 However, though men forsook me when brought to my trials, the Lord Jesus, according to His promise, Luke 21:15, stood by me and strengthened me, that on such an occasion, and before such personages, through me the preaching concerning Christ might be fully declared, and that all the Gentiles might hear that it was so declared; and I escaped with such difficulty, that I cannot describe it better than by saying, I was delivered out of the mouth of the lion.
18 And the Lord Jesus will deliver me from every evil work, so that I shall do nothing for the preservation of my life inconsistent with my former preaching; and He will preserve me to His Heavenly Kingdom. To whom I gratefully ascribe the glory of faithfulness, goodness, and power, for ever and ever. Amen.

Comment 4:16-18

Vs. 16. The "first defense" doubtless refers to the trial of Paul before the Roman Court.

Vss. 16 and 17. Because of its descriptive qualities we quote from THE LIFE AND EPISTLES OF PAUL (pp. 832-834):

"We see from this statement, that it was dangerous even to appear in public as the friend or adviser of the Apostle. No advocate would venture to plead his cause, no procurator to aid him in arranging the evidence, no patronus (such as he might have found, perhaps, in the powerful Aemilian house) to appear as his supporter, and to deprecate, according to ancient usage, the severity of the sentence. But he had a more powerful intercessor, and a wiser advocate, who could never leave him nor forsake him. The Lord Jesus was always near him, but now was felt almost visibly present in the hour of his need.

"From the above description we can realize, in some measure, the external features of his last trial. He evidently intimates that he spoke before a crowded audience, so that 'all the Gentiles might hear'; and this corresponds with the supposition, which historically, we should be led to make, that he was tried in one of those great basilicas which stood in the Forum. Two of the most celebrated of these edifices were called the Pauline Basilicas, from the well-known Lucius Aemilius Paulus, who had built one of them, and restored the other. It is not improbable that the greatest man who ever bore the Pauline name was tried in one of these. From specimens which still exist, as well as from the descriptions of Vituvius, we have an accurate knowledge of the character of these halls of justice. They were rectangular buildings, consisting of a central nave and two aisles, separated from the nave by rows of columns. At one end of the nave was the tribune, in the center of which was placed the magistrate's curule chair of ivory, elevated on a platform called the tribunal. Here also, sat the Council of Assessors, who advised the Prefect upon the law, though they had no voice in the judgment. On the sides of the tribune were seats for distinguished persons, as well as for parties engaged in the proceedings. Fronting the presiding magistrate stood the prisoner, with his accusers and his advocates. The public was admitted into the remainder of the nave and aisles (which was railed off from the portion devoted to the judicial proceedings); and there were also galleries along the whole length of the aisles, one for men, the other for women. The aisles were roofed over; as was the tribune. The nave was originally left open to the sky. The basilicas were buildings of great size, so that a vast multitude of spectators was always present at any trial which excited public interest.

"Before such an audience it was, that Paul was now called to speak in his defense. His earthly friends had deserted him, but his Heavenly Friend stood by him. He was strengthened by the power of Christ's Spirit, and pleaded the cause not of himself only, but of the Gospel. He spoke of Jesus, of His death and His resurrection, so that all the Heathen multitude might hear."

Vs. 18. The Lord had delivered Paul at his first defense, and although he fully expected to be executed, he believed the Lord would give him the victory. "Not injury done to him by others, it is plain he did not expect deliverance from this, but sin done by himself, such as that of denying Christ" (Harvey). Such strengthening from the Lord will be extended all the way from earth to glory. God's grace will be sufficient until he reaches the Heavenly Kingdom. The hope of this deliverance produces a doxology. It might be well to note that this doxology is directed toward Christ, which is an indication of His divinity.

Fact Questions 4:16-18

161. What is meant by "no one took my part"?
162. Explain how Paul received strength from the Lord. Please do more than to repeat the words of the text.
163. In what sense was the message fully proclaimed by Paul?
164. What does Paul mean by saying he was delivered out of the mouth of the lion?
165. From what evil work did Paul expect to be delivered?
166. What is significant about the doxology?

CONCLUSION 4:19-22

1. PERSONAL REFERENCES 4:19-21

Text 4:19-21

19 Salute Prisca and Aquila, and the house of Onesiphorus. 20 Erastus remained at Corinth: but Trophimus I left at Miletus sick. 21 Give diligence to come before winter, Eubulus saluteth thee, and Pudens, and Linus, and Claudia, and all the brethren.

Thought Questions 4:19-21

234. Read Acts 18:2; Rom. 16:3; I Cor. 16-19 for further references to Prisca and Aquila. Where were they when they

received this greeting? Is there any significance in using the woman's name before the man's?

235. Why "the house of Onesiphorus"? Why not salute the man?
236. Is this the same Erastus as mentioned in Acts 19:22 and Rom. 16:23? Explain.
237. Acts 20:4 and 21:9 tells us more about Trophimus. Why not heal this good friend?
238. Why the urgency of reaching Paul before winter?

Paraphrase 4:19-21

19 In my name wish health to Prisca, and her husband, Aquila, and to the family of Onesiphorus.
20 Erastus, who accompanied me in my way to Crete, abode in Corinth. But Trophimus I left at Miletus sick, when I departed from Crete.
21 Make haste to come to me before winter; sailing being then dangerous. Eubulus wisheth thee health. So do Pudens, and Linus, and Claudia, and all the brethren with whom I have any intercourse.

Comment 4:19-21

Vs. 19. Prisca and Aquila have been in Ephesus before; indeed, they were among those who began the work there. This reference to them indicates, then, continuing loyalty and good work. We have already made reference to the house of Onesiphorus. We could conclude that Onesiphorus was with Paul, and this greeting was sent to his family in his absence.

Vs. 20. It is hardly possible that the Erastus here mentioned is the same as the man who was the treasurer of the city of Corinth, i.e., unless he resigned his job, for the Erastus here mentioned seems to have been a traveling companion to Paul. Lenski does not feel that the two references (Acts 19:22 and Rom. 16:23) are concerning the same man, and therefore identifies this one with the one in Acts 19:22.

Why leave a faithful worker for Christ sick, if it were possible to heal him? Evidently, healing was for a purpose other than the physical comfort of the afflicted. Even an apostle could not exercise this power at his own will. Miracles were for a sign (John 20:30,31) and where such a purpose was not present, neither was the healing. Shall we ask for a further confirmation of His Word today?

Vs. 21. The seas were open to travel until September or October. If Timothy delayed his coming until winter, it would be too late. Did Paul's beloved disciple arrive in time? We do not know; we should like to believe that he did.

Of the persons mentioned in vs. 21b we know nothing. It is vain to speculate. It is enough to know they were faithful Christians who were not afraid of the terrors of the arena.

Fact Questions 4:22

167. What does the greeting sent to Prisca and Aquila indicate as to their loyalty and work? Why mention Prisca first?
168. Where was Onesiphorus when this greeting was sent to his house?
169. Who was the Erastus here mentioned?
170. Why leave a faithful worker sick?
171. If Timothy did not come before winter, he need not come at all. Give two reasons.

2. BENEDICTION 4:22

Text 4:22

22 The Lord be with thy spirit. Grace be with you.

Thought Questions 4:22

239. In what sense did Paul believe the Lord could be with the spirit of Timothy?
240. If the Lord was with the spirit of Timothy, what would be the result?
241. The word, "you," in vs. 22b is in the plural form. What significance is this?

Paraphrase 4:22

22 May the Lord Jesus Christ be with thy spirit, to strengthen thee in all difficulties and dangers, as He hath strengthened me, (vs. 17). Grace be with you in Ephesus who maintain the truth. Amen.

Comment 4:22

Vs. 22. Here are the last words of the great Apostle. If Timothy could be constantly aware of Christ's approval or disapproval of his words and works, then Paul's prayer for him would be answered. If Christ is with our inward man, all is well.

The desire for all of heaven's favor upon not only Timothy, but all the saints in the Ephesian church, is a fitting conclusion to an unselfish Christ-centered life.

Fact Questions 4:22

172. How could Paul's prayer for Timothy be answered?

EXEGETICAL EXAMINATION OVER CHAPTER FOUR OF II TIMOTHY

1. Give your own outline of this chapter.
2. What is the content of "the word" to be preached? What is the manner to use in preaching?
3. What causes some folk to have itching ears?
4. What is the "work of an evangelist"? Be specific.
5. What was the purpose of vss. 6-8?
6. What is the meaning of "his appearing"?
7. If Paul was about to die, why did he give instructions concerning his cloak, etc.?
8. What was the first defense of Paul?
9. Give your own exegesis of vs. 17.
10. Are we to have the same confidence in the delivering power of God as expressed by Paul in vs. 18? Specify.

EXAMINATION OVER PAUL'S SECOND EPISTLE TO TIMOTHY

1. Produce the outline of the letter.
2. Give the place, time, tone, and purpose of this letter.
3. Paul expressed his gratitude in vss. 1:3-5. Specify that for which he was thankful.
4. Discuss two things that would keep Timothy from being ashamed.
5. Write a short paragraph on the commendable attributes of Onesiphorus.
6. How shall we "grow strong in the grace which is in Christ Jesus"?
7. What is meant by entangling ourselves in the affairs of this life?
8. What is the priority of reward received by the farmer?
9. Explain this sentence: "On account of this I endure all things on account of the elect, in order that they may obtain salvation."
10. Identify Hymenaeus and Philetus.
11. We have said the "solid foundation of God" is the church. Explain.

12. How do we become and remain a utensil of honor?
13. Explain three characteristics of the apostates of the last days.
14. Who are the "silly women" of the second chapter?
15. Discuss three ways Paul became an example to Timothy.
16. In what way is the Scripture a safeguard against apostacy?
17. What was the content of the charge Paul gave to Timothy?
18. What did Paul mean when he said: "do an evangelist's work"?
19. Upon what basis did Paul look forward confidently to the crown of righteousness?
20. Identify the following: Lemas, Crescens, Tychicus, Carpus, Alexander, Erastus, Trophimus.

Special Studies

by

H. E. Phillips

From his book SCRIPTURAL ELDERS AND DEACONS

Used by permission.

NO ELDER THEORIES

PROOFS OFFERED FOR THE "NO ELDER" THEORY

A—*There Is No Such OFFICE In The Church As ELDERS.* It is argued that there is no such thing in the church as an "office." That the expression "office of a bishop" in I Timothy 3:1 is from "episcopee" which means twice "visitation" and twice "oversight," but not at any time as "official" authority. It is further argued that this is a WORK and not an authority: "If any man desire the office of a bishop, he desireth a good WORK."

It is further contended that the word "office" in respect to a deacon in I Timothy 3:10, 13, is from the Greek "diakoneo" and is found 36 times in the New Testament, 24 times translated "to minister," and 10 times "to serve." Only twice is the word translated "office" and that is in this chapter. The reason given for this translation here is that the translators of the King James Version were mostly from the Episcopal Church, and the idea of "office" was prominent in their minds.

The word "office" in I Timothy 3:1 is from "Episcopee" and is defined in *Abbott-Smith's Greek-Lexicon* as: "Office, charge, esp. office of an episcopos." *Thayer's Greek-English Lexicon* gives a similar meaning.

But some contend that we cannot take these lexicographers for they do not always give the true meaning. Webster gives the meaning of "baptism" as: "Sprinkling, pouring or immersion," therefore, if we take one we must take the other.

This is not true because it is the work of a lexicographer to define words in their current usage—as they are understood at the time of their use. Thayer defines words, not as what they now mean, but what they meant when spoken. Webster defines words as they are understood generally today, and that is what he did in the case of "baptism."

But it is admitted in the above that twice the word in I Timothy 3:1 means "oversight"; and that twice in I Timothy 3:10, 13 the word means "work." Is it to be understood that anything that is a work is not of authority? Christ was and is in authority—supreme authority in the church—but he also had work to do. All men in authority, whatever degree it may be, must work in executing that authority. It is true that the "office of a bishop" is a "good work." But it is also admitted in the above argument that the word means "oversight." What is oversight? It means to oversee, to look over, to superintend. Does one appointed to look over the affairs of another have any authority at all? Authority always carries the idea of responsibility, and responsibility carries the idea of authority. If one Christian is in any way responsible for another Christian, to that extent he has authority and must exercise it in order to fulfill his responsibility.

The word "office" in I Timothy 3:10, 13 means to serve. But since this is a special sense of service, and office is the word to designate that service, the office of a deacon is simply the work of a deacon. But the fact that it is a work does not imply that there is no office. All Christians have an "office" to perform, which means a "work." In Romans 12:4, 5: "For as we have many members in one body, and all members have not the same offfice: so we, being many, are one body in Christ, and every one members one of another." All members of the body of Christ have an "office"—WORK to perform. All these officers are not the same—some have authority over others—but each has authority to do the work assigned him.

It is contended from I Peter 5:2: "Feed the flock of God which is among you, taking the oversight thereof, not by constraint, but willingly; not for filthy lucre, but of a ready mind,"—that the older members are to take the oversight, not in an official capacity but just to do the work.

In the first place, if the older members were to take the "oversight" or superintendency of the other members, it implies that much authority. You just can't get around the idea of authority in the oversight. In the second place, Peter is not talking about the older members, but those who are the elders—Peter himself was such an elder—to take the oversight. It is a perversion of the passage to say "older members." This would include women as well as men, which would put them in the "oversight."

It is also argued that in Hebrews 13:17: "Obey them that have the rule over you, and submit yourselves,"—does not imply an office, and then they refer to the marginal note of the Revised Version which says: "Obey them that are your guides or leaders." But if one is a guide or leader, is he not performing an assigned work? If so, the work is the "office" and the one who does the work is an "officer." And since he is to rule or guide, he has authority to do that. He is an officer in the office that rules.

B.—*There Is No Authority Of One Man Over Another In The Church.* It is argued that one member of the church does not exercise any authority over another member, else some would be submitting to man rather than to Christ.

This cannot be true for wives are taught to submit to their husbands in everything (Eph. 5:23, 24). If both are Christians, we have one Christian submitting to another by the authority of Christ. Again, in Ephesians 6:1 children are to obey their parents in the Lord. If both child and parents are Christians, we have one Christian submitting—obeying—to others. These passages destroy the above argument of no man over another in the church.

If we submit to men called "elders," we will have to do away with the authority of Christ, it is said. But to reject the authority of the eldership as Christ has appointed would do away with the authority of Christ. Any man to whom Christ has delegated authority must be recognized as such or we reject the authority of Christ.

But some say, "Christ said no one would exercise authority over another—Matthew 20:25, 26. There will be none in the church to exercise authority over any other."

Let us examine this passage and the conclusion drawn in this argument. When James and John with their mother came to Jesus they came "worshipping him." They did not regard him as a mere man or as a servant on this occasion, even though Jesus is pictured in some places as a servant. They regarded him as a King; not only that, but as THE KING. To say that a King is not an official is to totally ignore the meaning of the word. Then the request made by this mother for her two sons was that they might "sit, one on thy right hand, and one on thy left hand, in thy kingdom." It is clearly evident that she was speaking of their authority IN HIS KINGDOM. The right hand and left hand indicates supreme authority next to Jesus. When Christ sat at the right hand of God, it meant that he was given authority next to God. These recognized the authority of Christ, thus his official capacity as King. The parallel passage is found in Mark 10:35-45, and in verse 40: "But to sit on my right hand and on my left hand is not mine to give; but it shall be given to them for whom it is prepared." The mother is simply asking Jesus to disregard the other apostles and place her sons above them in authority.

Jesus answered: "Ye know not what ye ask." They did not understand the nature of his kingdom. Certainly they knew what they were asking for, but they did not understand that the kingdom of Christ was to be a spiritual kingdom without earthly authority. They did not understand that the greatness in his kingdom depended upon service rather than ruling authority. He asked them if they were able to endure his suffering—"drink this cup," and they answered ignorantly that they were. Mark adds, "to be baptized with the baptism that I am baptized with," meaning his suffering.

Now when the other ten heard that James and John had made this request they were angry. Their anger did not stem from the fact that James and John had asked for a favor, but that they had asked for authority over them. It was a known fact that the apostles of Christ were continually arguing about who was to be the greater, which they conceived to be the one in authority over the rest. Jesus then proceeded to show them that his kingdom was not like that of the Gentiles, which denoted all other than the Jews. Greatness in his kingdom did not depend upon official rank, but upon service, and Jesus cites himself as an example of service. He did not imply that he was not a king, an official in the kingdom.

In verse 17 he was talking to the twelve and not to all men. What he said to them included them only. The passage does not teach that there are no authorities in the kingdom of Christ. That is to completely miss the point of Christ's statement. He did not teach, by referring to the kingdoms of the Gentiles, that there would be no authority of officials in his kingdom; he said: "and they that are GREAT exercise authority upon them. But it shall not be so among you: but whosoever will be great among you, let him be your minister" (verses 26, 27). "And it shall not be so among you" refers to "greatness" rather than authority. The great of the Gentiles were those in authority, while the great in the kingdom of Christ were the ministers.

Since he was talking to and about the twelve apostles, he did not intend that they should exercise authority over each other. He said, "It shall not be so AMONG YOU." It is true that the apostles themselves were officials in the kingdom as "witnesses," "judges," and "rulers." But the apostles had no authority, one over the other, but all had equal authority under Christ.

C—*There is no need for elders to rule over the church as we have the Bible today.* It is contended that all Christians have the Bible today as a perfect guide and do not have need for men called "elders" to rule over them. If all obey the Bible, they obey Christ. If elders must follow the Bible in their rule, why cannot all follow the Bible? If this is true, they say, we have no need for elders today.

One cannot possibly follow the Bible without obeying the commands of Christ, one of which is to submit to the elders in each congregation. Christ has commanded it. Hebrews 13:17: "Obey them that have the rule over you, and submit yourselves." And I Timothy 5:17: "Let the elders that rule well be counted worthy of double honor."

But if elders are not needed because we have the Bible today, neither do we need preachers and teachers today. Just let each one follow the Bible. But we know that to follow the Bible we must have preachers and teachers of truth because the Bible requires it. It is absurd to say we do not need a thing because we have the Bible when the Bible itself demands that thing. One is not following the Bible when he denies that the church today needs elders to oversee the local work.

D—*We cannot have elders today because we have no inspired men: spiritually gifted men.* It seems that because some were inspired or had spiritual gifts to some measure, that elders today must have the same gifts, else we cannot have elders in the church. We do not deny that some elders in New Testament days were spiritually gifted men, but it is equally certain that there were some who were not.

It is argued that Acts 8:14-18 is an example of Peter and John going to Samaria after the church had been established there to give spiritual gifts, including inspiration, to make elders. When this inspiration ceased the elders ceased.

This is not the case, as will be seen by carefully reading this entire chapter. Elders are not one time mentioned as being made in Samaria, especially at this time. How could one imagine that Peter and John made elders by giving them the power of inspiration, when neither "elder" nor "inspiration" is mentioned in the chapter? The spiritual abilities given at Samaria were to enable the church to continue in its growth and edification, because the New Testament had not then been completed and they had no guide as we have today. The New Testament now does exactly what those spiritual abilities did then.

It is also argued that we know all elders were inspired because God ordered the early church to hear and obey them and submit to them. The Holy Spirit would not have told those people to obey the elders and then leave them exposed to error. Hence, elders were inspired, and when inspiration ceased, the elders as such ceased.

In the first place, where did God ever say: "hear and obey inspired men"? He said to hear Christ (Matt. 17:5; Acts 3:22). Christ is the only one to be heard in religious matters, but he speaks to us through his apostles and prophets.

In the second place, inspiration did not do one thing more for the men in the early church than the written word of God will do now. The difference in the spiritual gift of inspiration to preach and teach then and now is in the method of receiving the message rather than in delivering the message. Preachers are the same, the message is the same, but the method of receiving it is different. Then it came by direct inspiration, but now it comes through the written word of God. Elders are the same today as then. The spiritual gifts gave them the ability to do the work assigned them just as the word of God gives them the knowledge now.

In the third place, some elders received instructions from Paul. Why would Paul teach them their duties and tell them their responsibilities if they were inspired to know those things? In Acts 20:27, 28 Paul said, "For I have not shunned to declare unto you all the counsel of God. Take heed therefore unto yourselves, and to all the flock, over the which the Holy Ghost hath made you overseers, to feed the church of God, which he hath purchased with his own blood." Paul had declared to them the counsel of God and then told them their duty. Why this if they were all inspired?

In the fourth place, inspiration provided that the one who possessed it could not err in teaching, but then some elders did err in teaching, for Paul said, "For I know this, that after my departing shall grevious wolves enter in among you, not sparing the flock. Also of your own selves (elders) shall men arise, speaking perverse things, to draw away disciples after them" (Acts 20:29, 30). This proves that all elders did not have the spiritual gift of inspiration. But if some were inspired, it does not prove that elders were done away when inspiration ceased any more than it proves that preachers were done away with inspiration, for some preachers had the gift of inspiration.

In the fifth place, Hebrews 13:7 says that some have the rule. From I Timothy 5:17 we learn that the elders are to rule. Those who had the rule were not all inspired so far as the record shows. The general date of the Hebrew letter is about 63 A.D. In chapter 5:12, we learn that some had been in the church long enough to be teachers. Does that mean that they had been in the church long enough to be inspired? Some were teachers by living in the church long enough to learn the truth so as to teach it. In Titus 1:9, speaking of the elders, Paul says "Holding fast the faithful word as he hath been taught." Does this sound like inspiration?

In the sixth place, Paul did not mention inspiration as a qualification for the eldership in I Timothy 3 or Titus 1. If it had been essential it would have been mentioned along with the other qualifications.

It is argued that I Cor. 12:1-13 and Eph. 4:11-13 show that spiritual gifts included elders or pastors and that they were done away with the spiritual gifts when the perfect way was revealed (I Cor. 13:8-10). It is further argued that I Cor. 12:28 proves that the elders were done away by the term "governments," which passed away with other spiritual gifts. The following syllogism is given to prove it:

1. Elders, by implication, are included with the spiritually gifted men of I Cor. 12 and Eph. 4.

2. The spiritually gifted men ceased with the close of spiritual gifts.

3. Therefore, there are no elders or church officers today.

First, I Cor. 12:1-13 and Eph. 4:11-13 do not show that spiritual gifts included elders or pastors. Gifts were not the men as such in Ephesians 4:11, for verse 8 says, "Wherefore he saith, When he ascended up on high, he led captivity captive, and gave gifts unto men." These men as spiritually endowed workers were given to the church. Many things are gifts, but the word itself does not tell what is given. Christ is a "gift" (John 3:16), but it does not mean a spiritual gift of the Holy Spirit. These men were "gifts" but they had "spiritual gifts," or abilities. Men as men were not given to the church as "gifts" but men with spiritual gifts (elders included) were given.

Second, the passage tells how long the "spiritually gifted" men were to be in the church: "till we all come in the unity of the faith, and of the knowledge of the Son of God, unto a perfect man, unto the measure of the stature of the fulness of Christ" (Eph. 4:13). Now that we have the unity of the faith and the full knowledge of the Son of God which is revealed in the New Testament, we do not need spiritual gifts in men. But the spiritual gifts have ceased, not the men. The unity of the faith and the full knowledge of the Son of God supply these men now with the same that spiritual gifts supplied then.

Third, if elders are done away with spiritual gifts in these passages, evangelists and teachers are also done away. Even some Christians had spiritual gifts, such as the four daughters of Philip (Acts 21:9), but Christians did not cease when the spiritually gifted Christians ceased. The spiritual gifts just gave away to the complete word of God when it was revealed. But if it be admitted that preachers, teachers and Christians remain today, though not spiritually gifted, it must be admitted by the same rule that elders remain today in the same way.

The syllogism in the argument is not true because the conclusion is not in agreement with the premises. It should be:

1. Elders, by implication, are included with the spiritually gifted men of I Corinthians 12 and Ephesians 4.

2. The spiritually gifted men ceased with the close of spiritual gifts.

3. Therefore, there are no spiritually gifted elders or church officers today. But it does not follow that there are no elders of any kind today.

E—*We cannot have elders today because no one can qualify.* It is argued that the qualifications listed for a bishop are too perfect for man to reach, and, therefore, we cannot have elders today.

If this reasoning be true, it follows that no man could have ever been an elder, even in the early church, because no man is perfect. But we know the early church did have elders. We further know that these elders were not perfect, for those in Ephesus to whom Paul talked in

Acts 20 needed building up (Acts 20:32), and Paul prophesied that some of them would lead disciples away after them (Acts 20:30).

The standard for a Christian is perfect. If we follow the same reasoning as above, we must conclude that no one can be a Christian today because no one can be perfect. Every standard of God is perfect. An elder must measure relatively high in every qualification given in the word of God, but he must continue to grow.

F—*We have no elders today because we do not know how to appoint them.* It is argued that since the Bible does not specify HOW to appoint the elders, we cannot have them in the church today.

But the Bible does not tell us HOW to serve the Lord's Supper, or how many songs to sing in worship, or the order in which we should worship on the Lord's Day. Are we to conclude that we are not to have the Lord's Supper, sing songs of praise to God or worship on the Lord's Day just because God did not tell us just the procedure of doing these things? These are left to human judgment in full harmony with all Bible principles governing such matters. The same is true of appointing elders.

G—*We can have no elders today because we have no one to appoint them.* Three reasons are given why we do not have men who can appoint elders today, and, consequently, can have no elders.

1. In the New Testament times inspired men did the appointing and now we do not have inspired men, and therefore, can have no appointing.

2. There are three qualifications of elders that no man can know unless he is guided by the Holy Spirit: (1) Blameless (2) Holy (3) Just. One must be able to read the heart to know this, and only the Holy Spirit could guide men to select elders. Timothy and Titus received this power of inspiration from Paul and could appoint elders; today we cannot.

3. No one can lay hands on men today and give them the spiritual gifts they need to be elders.

Let us now examine each of these in order.

1. There is no indication anywhere in the Bible that inspired men were to do the appointing. Just because Timothy and Titus did the appointing of some of the elders, and Paul and Barnabas also did some appointing, it does not follow that only inspired men must do the appointing. These men preached also, but it does not follow that only inspired men can preach. It can not be proved that either Timothy or Titus was inspired. Paul told Timothy to teach what he had learned from him (2 Tim. 2:2); and from the Holy Scriptures (2 Tim. 3:14, 15); and Paul told him to study to be approved (2 Tim. 2:15); and to read

(I Tim. 4:13). They may have had some spiritual gifts, but it had no bearing on the appointment of elders.

2. Blameless, holy and just are qualities that can be known in every man. Jesus said a good tree brings forth good fruit, and by that we may know the tree. "By their fruit ye shall know them" Matt. 7:20). How does one tell the difference between a child of God and a child of the devil? Paul knew Peter was wrong by his actions (Gal. 2:11).

But these are not the only qualities of man that come in the same class. Any condition of the heart cannot be known by another except by his actions or words. What about faith and repentance? How can a preacher know one has really believed and repented of his sins before he baptizes him? Must the preacher be inspired by the Holy Spirit to know this? No. He determines the condition of the heart by his words and actions. Just so one can tell when a man is blameless, holy and just.

3. It has already been shown that elders do not need spiritual gifts today to do their work. They can use the word of God now. But the Bible teaches that some besides the apostles "laid hands" on men to appoint them elders, and none but the apostles could transmit the spiritual gifts (Acts 8:18). Timothy and Titus were not apostles and could not give any measure of spiritual gifts by the "laying on of their hands."

But besides all this, the "laying on of hands" did not always signify the giving of spiritual gifts. This act was for a number of things. The expression in the Bible may refer to unpleasant things also. Notice:

(1) Acts 4:3—The Sadducees "laid hands on" the apostles to put them in prison.

(2) Acts 5:18—Again the Sadducees "laid hands on" the apostles and put them in prison.

(3) Acts 6:6—Apostles "laid hands" on those selected by the multitude and appointed them to the work. Stephen was "full of the Holy Ghost." The multitude selected and the apostles "appointed," verse 3.

(4) Acts 8:17, 18—The apostles, Peter and John, "laid their hands" on some in Samaria to "give the Holy Ghost"—spiritual gifts.

(5) Acts 13:3—The church at Antioch "appointed" two whom the Holy Spirit had selected, to do a certain work. No spiritual gifts are indicated.

(6) Acts 28:8—Paul "laid his hands" on the father of Publius to heal him. No spiritual gift given, but a means of miraculous healing.

(7) I Tim. 4:14—The presbytery "laid hands on Timothy" with respect to some gift of prophecy regarding his work.

(8) 2 Tim. 1:6—Paul "laid hands" on Timothy to convey a gift of God—probably some spiritual gift.

(9) I Tim. 5:22—Paul told Timothy not to "lay hands" suddenly on any man. This refers to appointing.

We glean from these few passages that the "laying on of hands" sometimes meant "to arrest or take hold of"; sometimes "to appoint or designate"; sometimes "to transmit a spiritual gift of one kind or another"; and sometimes "as a means of miraculous healing." Spiritual gifts are not essential today to elders in performing their duties, as the word of God is sufficient, hence we have no need for men who "give spiritual gifts by laying on of hands."

H—*We do not have elders today because there is some work that no elder can do today.* It is argued that since there is some work that no man can do today, that was done by the elders of the early church, there can be no elders today. Following is a list of some of those things they say no man can do today.

(1) James 5:14, 15 teaches us to call for the elders of the church when one is sick, and they will come and anoint with oil in the name of the Lord and pray for the sick and he will be healed. This was miraculous healing and cannot be done by so called elders today.

Let us notice this passage. The healing of James 5:14 was really by the power of God. The oil poured on by the elders does not necessarily mean a miracle. Oil was used for several things in the Bible:

a. Appointing one to a charge (I Sam. 16:12, 13).
b. For medicine (Luke 10:34).
c. For food (Ex. 29:2).
d. For a cosmetic (Ps. 104:15).
e. For a light (Ex. 27:20).

Not one time is oil used to perform a miracle. Miracles were used to confirm the word, but when the word was fully confirmed and completely revealed the miracles ceased, but the preaching of that word did not cease. Since this passage says the oil was poured on sick people, it is more reasonable to believe that it was used for medicine. The elders are called to administer whatever aid they can to the sick, while at the same time praying for them. The writer here says the "effectual fervent prayer of a righteous man availeth much," and then uses Elias praying for the rain as an example (verse 17, 18). We read that the reference of Elias was not a miracle but by natural process: a cloud coming from over the ocean (I Kings 18:44, 45). So neither the oil nor the prayer would suggest that they were to perform a miracle. But if those elders did perform a miracle, would it follow that all elders are to perform miracles? Some preachers performed miracles at that time, but preachers are not to pass away because no preacher can perform miracles today.

(2) It is argued that no elder today can "lay hands on" another to give him spiritual gifts, and that was one work of elders in New Testament times. The presbytery (eldership) gave such a gift to Timothy (I Tim. 4:14).

It has already been shown that "laying on of hands" did not always mean the conveying of spiritual gifts. In fact it never referred to that except in the case of an apostle, and then it may mean something else as determined by the context. The "laying on of hands" in I Tim. 4:14 means the same as in Acts 13:3—appointing to some work. No elder as such ever laid his hands on any man to transmit to him a spiritual gift.

(3) It is argued that an elder can not feed the flock of God. No man is qualified today to feed anyone that the word of God does not better feed. The church can feed itself by studying the word. What can an elder feed that any other member of the church can not feed?

To feed the flock is to put the word before them and see that they learn it. Things that elders can do that others can not do in this realm is a matter of authority. Many can do certain things but do not have the authority or right to do it. The Bible calls those who are Christians "children" (I John 2:1; Eph. 5:8; Rom. 8:17; Eph. 5:1). Elders are the older, stronger children who have been commissioned by the Saviour to feed the others the word of God. One might make arrests for violation of a law IF he had the authority of the higher powers. Christ, who is head of the church, gave authority for the local church to the eldership. They can exercise that authority when others in the church can not, because of the authority given them by Christ through his word.

(4) It is also argued that one thing an elder can not do today is to rule and take oversight. Only the apostles and inspired men could do that, and as we have no apostles or inspired men alive today we have no one to rule and take oversight.

Again this is a matter of authority. If the Bible teaches that the congregation is to submit to those who are in the oversight, can one be submissive to Christ and not be submissive to the elders? Can a wife obey Christ without obeying his authority to submit to her husband? We have the writings of the apostles and inspired men today as a guide, but someone must see that it is obeyed and followed exactly as it should be. Who is to do this? Even the church in Jerusalem, where the apostles were, had elders, If they needed elders there, do we not need them today with the writings of the apostles?

As to the matter of authority, I can not walk out on the street and arrest a man for a traffic violation, but a policeman can because he has the authority to do it. If I were to become a policeman I would have the authority to do some things in that line that I can not now do. Others may be physically able to do some things—even all things—an elder can do, but he does not have the authority from Christ to do them. That is the difference. It is not to be understood that in all points I am making the elders policemen in the church. I am simply comparing the right to do things by authority over others.

I—*The Holy Spirit made elders in Ephesus, and since the Holy Spirit does not make elders now, we do not have elders today.* The Holy Spirit did make elders then, and He makes them now. The Holy Spirit makes elders just as He makes Christians. He gives the standard of qualifications, and when one complies with them he becomes a Christian. The same is true of the elders. When one complies with all the requirements to become an elder that have been given by the Holy Spirit, he is an elder made by the Holy Spirit. That is the very reason the list of qualifications is recorded in I Timothy and Titus.

J—*Some Churches did not have elders, so we all need not have them today.* This is based upon the assumption that at least the Bible does not teach that all churches had elders. For instance, the church at Corinth, the elders are not mentioned. But after the days of the apostles, Clement of Rome wrote an epistle to the Corinthians and at the close he mentions the elders. Paul appointed elders in every city where he preached (Acts 14:23), and it follows that he practiced the same thing at Corinth.

There is not a single argument made against the appointment of qualified elders in every church that will stand the test of God's word. "Beloved, believe not every spirit . . ." (I John 4:1).

THE RELATIONSHIP—APOSTLES, ELDERS, PREACHERS

I. THE RELATIONSHIP

A relationship exists between the apostles and elders, and between elders and preachers. This relationship must be respected, yet not transgressed. "For as we have many members in one body, and all members have not the same office: so we, being many, are one body in Christ, and every one members one of another" (Rom. 12:4, 5).

Since all these members are in the one body, the church of our Lord, and all the members have not the same work to do, but all are under the same Head—Christ, there must be a close relationship between all three classes considered here as public workers in the church: the apostles, elders and preachers. This does not necessarily mean that their work overlaps; but there is a connection and relationship in their work that makes for the unity of the Faith.

It must be understood in the study of this relationship that the terms: *Apostle, Elder,* and *Preacher* do not mean the same thing and do not refer to the same work. They are very distinct, one from the other. However, the same man may be an apostle, elder and preacher all at the same time. Peter is an example. He was an apostle (Matt. 10:2); an elder (I Peter 1:1; 5-2); and a preacher (Acts 2—the first gospel sermon). This does not mean that because Peter did or said a certain thing that any preacher may do the same thing, for Peter may have been acting or speaking as an apostle or an elder rather than as a preacher. It must be determined in what capacity he was speaking or acting to know whether it applies to certain men today. There is quite a difference in the scope of authority and the nature of the work of these three classes of men in the church.

II. APOSTLES AND ELDERS

When Christ delegated authority to a certain one, that one may exercise that authority, but another cannot assume it without violating God's plan. The apostles were granted an authority in the church that no other can take. (Matt. 16:19; 18:18).

A. *The difference in authority of apostles and elders.*

The authority of the apostles was universal in scope. Their rule and authority extended over all congregations equally. Their writings today are the authority of Christ in all churches of Christ. Paul said that he had the care of all the churches. (2 Cor. 11:28). When he exercised such authority it was only as an apostle and never as an elder or a preacher.

The authority of the elders is local in scope, never extending beyond the bounds that define a local church. There is never an exception to this rule in the New Testament. The elders have no rule over any person beyond the scope of their local authority in the church where they serve. When Peter acted in authority over different congregations, he did so as an apostle and not as an elder.

B. *The difference in the qualifications of apostles and elders.*

The work of the apostles was REVEALING AND CREATIVE as well as SUPERVISORY. The very nature of their work in revealing and creating suggested that there could be no successor to the apostles. The church has been established and the full will of God has been revealed, so there is no need for a further work of apostles. While, on the other hand, the elder's work is only SUPERVISORY and by nature requires succession to the office as long as the church exists.

The qualifications for the work of an apostle make it impossible to have apostles in the church today in the sense that we have elders. Notice some of the qualifications for this work:

1. An apostle must have been with Christ from the beginning of his ministry. (John 15:26, 27). Paul was the exception to this, but spoke of himself as "one born out of due time" (I Cor. 15-8). Today no one lives who has been with Christ from the beginning of his ministry, nor has one witnessed his resurrection as "one born out of due time." Hence, no one can qualify to be an apostle today.

2. An apostle must have been a witness of the resurrection of Christ (Matt. 26:32; 28:7; Acts 1:8; 2:32). No one can be an eye witness to the resurrection of Christ today, therefore, there can be no living qualified apostles today in the church.

3. An apostle must have been chosen personally by Christ for this work (Acts 1:2; Matt. 10:1-5). Christ does not personally select such men today, so there are no living apostles in the church now. This was so even in the case of Matthias (Acts 1:24).

The qualifications for elders are found in I Timothy 3 and Titus 1. Any good, experienced Christian father and husband can develop these qualifications today. There is not a single one that any good Christian man should not have, with the exception of experience, age and family relations.

C. *The specific duties of an apostle are different from the duties of elders.*

The work of the apostles was:

1. To be ambassadors of Christ (2 Cor. 5:20). They were his

personal representatives here on earth after he ascended to the Father. The elders are not personal representatives of Chirst today any more than any other Christian. The work of an ambassador is to speak for and represent a king or ruler in a foreign country. This is exactly the work the apostles did, but neither the elders, nor anyone else, has such duties today. Neither did the elders in New Testament times have such work to do.

2. The apostles were to reveal the will of Christ to all men. This has been done and completed. (Jude 3, 17; Gal. 1:8, 9). They were guided without error by the Holy Spirit to speak the full truth of Christ on all matters. (John 14:26; 16:13; Luke 24:49; Acts 2:1-4). The will of Christ is now complete and needs no addition. (2 Pet. 1-3; 2 Tim. 3:16, 17). Therefore, the active work of the apostles is no more. However, their writings are the sole authority in all matters of faith in the church today. The elders are not empowered to reveal the will of Christ in addition to what has been revealed by the apostles. The work of the elders is to see that the revealed will of Christ is kept by the "flock which is among" them.

3. The apostles are to be judges of God's people. (Matt. 19:28). There is a sense in which the apostles will "judge" while Christ is on the throne of his glory. This "judging" is the "binding" and "loosing" of Matt. 16:19. Notice when this judging is to be: "In the regeneration"—when men are regenerated or born again. That certainly means now. Also it is to be when Christ sits on the throne of his glory. He is now sitting on that throne. (Acts 2:30, 31). The *Israel* refers to the people of God today in the church. We have no fleshly Israel now so far as Christianity is concerned (Gal. 3:28, 29), but all Christians are spiritual Israel (Rom. 2:28; 9:6; Gal. 6:15). The word *twelve* signifies all because the whole of fleshly Israel consisted of twelve tribes. The apostles are "judging" through their writings today while Christ rules with all authority upon his throne.

But the elders have no such authority. They have no authority to "bind" or "loose" in matters of faith. That has already been completed in the work of the apostles.

D. *The relationship between apostles and elders.*

It has been shown that their work and scope of authority are in separate fields, but there is a close connection between their duties and the fields of their work. In the New Testament times when matters of importance to the church arose, both the apostles and elders assembled and considered the matter. (Acts 15:1-6—the matter of circumcision and the law of Moses). This matter was settled by the Holy Spirit and not by the authority of the elders. But the elders as well as the apostles saw that the matter was kept in accord with revelation. Both are under the authority of Christ; and both are working for the salvation of the world and the glory of God.

III. ELDERS AND PREACHERS

As in the case of apostles and elders and their relationship, there is a relationship between elders and preachers that must be observed strictly if both are to do their work properly and scripturally. The work of elders and preachers is different; although one might be both an elder and a preacher at the same time. He can do things as a preacher that he cannot do as an elder, or do things as an elder that he cannot do as a preacher. For instance, he may preach for several congregations but he cannot exercise the authority of an overseer in any congregation. Or he may exercise the oversight as an elder in a certain congregation but he can not exercise the oversight of several congregations at the same time.

A. *Preachers sometimes try to dominate elders.*

Preachers often ignore the eldership. Young preachers sometimes try to do their work without elders, thinking that they can better carry out their ideas and plans without the restraint of the eldership to check them. Many think they know more than the elders, and the sad part is that they sometimes do, but this does not authorize preachers to usurp control of the oversight. No doubt one of the reasons for inefficient elders today is the zeal of young, ambitious preachers who have not learned the standard of God's organization for the church.

In the *Apostolic Times* of May, 1951, on page 123, brother Rue Porter made this observation: "Among the problems confronting the church today, none seems to be more constantly coming up than certain questions relating to the eldership. That is, no doubt, due to the fact that new congregations are constantly gathered together and we have a great number of young and enthusiastic preachers who seem not to have realized as yet that the eldership as pictured in the New Testament is the picture of a perfect standard toward which every man chosen for that work should aim and strive. . . .

"Most of the men who have been made elders get little encouragement for the efforts they make. They are looked upon by some preachers and many members as a sort of *necessary useless* sort of men. Some of us will accept the advice of a man who was never chosen by any one to oversee, rather than follow the counsel of a properly selected and appointed eldership."

To this I say, Amen. One might as well ignore some expression of worship that God has ordained in the church as to ignore this arrangement in the organization of the church.

B. *Many preachers act as sole judges of who is and who is not qualified to be elders in a certain place, disregarding the Bible qualifications.*

We can all go to the Bible and determine who is and who is not a qualified elder. But when preachers say, "That is not necessary to be an elder," when speaking of some qualification, "I'll just appoint him anyway," that is going too far. Sometimes a preacher refuses to appoint, or allow to be appointed (as if he were the only judge), a qualified man to the eldership by giving some point of qualification that the Bible does not give. For instance, to demand that "apt to teach" means that the elder must be a seasoned, polished, public teacher or preacher. That is giving a meaning to this qualification that the Bible does not give.

Again in the *Apostolic Times,* May, 1951, page 123, brother Rue Porter says: "One congregation chose and appointed a man with others to serve them as elder, and a young preacher came along and decided that the congregation—most of whose members had been Christians and students longer than he, just didn't know enough to select men for the eldership, and so proceeded to attempt the 'unseating' of the elder to whom he objected! Of course the eldership and congregation were pretty prompt in teaching him a lesson he needed very much to learn. . . .

"It seems easy for inexperienced preachers to decide that they *know* just exactly what elders must be in order to be elders, but for some unknown reason seem unable to catch a glimpse of what a perfect preacher should be!"

C. *Preachers claiming the position and authority of elders when they begin regular work at a place.*

A few preachers are so careless in the Scriptures as to claim to be an "Automatic Elder" when they move to a certain place to begin regular work there. They argue this way: The elders labor in word and doctrine (I Tim. 5:17); the preacher also labors in word and doctrine, and since the preacher always labors in this field, and it is the work of elders, it follows that the preacher is automatically an elder where ever he labors. That is the real argument. Just such reasoning! One might as well argue as follows: The elders are to "teach" (Titus 1:9), but women also are required to "teach" (Titus 2:4), therefore, women are automatically elders. Would not this argument be as strong as the one above?

There are some things wrong with this system. (1) This would completely disregard the qualifications for an elder as given by the Bible. Just any boy-preacher would be an elder where ever he preaches. The qualifications for an elder might as well be scratched from the Bible. (2) In a congregation where elders have never been appointed this young preacher would be THE ELDER—a one man rule. (3) This would put a fence around the preacher that would block any move regarding his discharge from the pulpit, and also many of his other obligations. He would be in position to "block" any move by "the other elders" to do anything opposed by him. This would actually reduce itself to a one-man-rule.

Some preachers have actually contended that since it is the duty of the elders to feed the flock (Acts 20:28), and since some preachers do more feeding than the elders, the preacher MUST be one of the elders to have a scriptural arrangement. But it is also the business of preachers to feed (I Cor. 3:2). Just because some of the responsibilities of elders and preachers are very much the same, if not the same, is no reason to conclude that the one is equal to the other in all things. It was a responsibility of an apostle to teach, and it is also the responsibility of any Christian to teach the truth. Are we to conclude that every Christian is an apostle?

D. *Preachers exercising oversight in the place of the eldership.*

Some preachers follow the practice of denominationalism to make themselves THE PASTOR of the congregation where they preach. Why do some evangelists take this oversight? We give here three reasons for this practice.

1. In some places the elders are irresponsible and do not perform their work. This necessarily leaves the duties upon the shoulders of someone else, usually the preacher. He begins little by little to assume their work until finally he is acting as the eldership, even though he did not seek it in the beginning, then he tries to justify his practice in some way.

2. In some places there are no men qualified to become elders and either the membership places all responsibility and authority upon the preacher, or the preacher thinks he must assume the oversight in order for the work to go forward.

3. In some places the elders insist that the preacher take the leading part and make most of the decisions for them. It often forces the preacher into a position that he is not really seeking. But in all cases the evangelist of a congregation has no scriptural authority to take the oversight under any condition.

E. *Preachers exercising oversight over the elders.*

This is the most extreme claim toward popery we have found to date in the church of Christ. It is contended that preachers are not only EQUAL to the elders in the oversight, but are ABOVE them! Imagine a gospel preacher claiming OVERSIGHT over the elders of the church! But that is not the end. Imagine a gospel preacher claiming OVERSIGHT over not just one group of elders, but over SEVERAL elderships at the same time! This makes the preacher a sort of ARCHBISHOP.

In an article entitled *Over and Under The Eldership,* by I. C. Nance in the *Gospel Broadcast* of February 24, 1949, page 141, we find the following: "Whereas it cannot be shown that either Titus or Timothy, evangelists, were *ever under* any eldership *after* they began their work of evangelism, it can be definitely shown that both of them were *over* the eldership of at least one (and that's enough). Timothy was placed over the eldership at Ephesus by apostolic authority. And, Ephesus was an old, large, and established church which had had elders for years *when* this happened. Read all of First Timothy, understandingly. Titus, on the other hand, just a plain evangelist, was placed by apostolic authority over all the churches in Crete. Among his duties was the appointment of elders. Since an evangelist is given power to exercise 'all authority' over a number of churches and, whereas, an elder has only partial authority in only *one* congregation, it follows that the authority of the evangelist supersedes that of the elder or the eldership. Hence, Titus was over any eldership you might name in Crete. If not, why not?"

The direction of thought in this article is wrong and scripturally untrue. The Bible teaches that the elders have the OVERSIGHT of the flock which is among them. If the evangelist is among the flock he is under the oversight of the elders. Titus and Timothy would be included. No passage in all the Bible teaches that any evangelist, as such, ever had the oversight of one person in the church, must less a congregation or several congregations, Timothy and Titus included. Titus was told to "rebuke with all authority" (Titus 2:15), but that is a far cry from "oversee with all authority." The authority of an evangelist is toward the preaching of the word. This, indeed, is a most dangerous doctrine and leads directly to the popery of Romanism. This dereliction of plain truth by those who wear the appellation *Gospel Preacher* is deplorable.

F. *Elders exercising too much authority over preachers.*

Many times elders will keep placing their own responsibilities upon the preacher until he is actually trying to do all the work of the eldership. This is taking too much authority on the part of the eldership. Christ did not give the elders authority to delegate their responsibilities to others. They may assign certain work to others to do, but the OVERSIGHT and responsibilities for such can never be assigned to another.

Then some elders try to control a preacher when he is beyond the bounds of their authority. Some have asked: "Do the elders of one congregation have the oversight of a preacher who regularly works with them but goes away for a meeting to another locality? Are the elders still over him while he works there?" The answer is, NO. And the simple reason is that the elders cannot oversee ANY WORK beyond the local church of which they are elders. The elders where he is in the meeting at the time he is there have the oversight over him and his work. A congregation may send a preacher into a new field of labor and support him, but they do not exercise the oversight over him or those converts where he is preaching in that work. They may discipline him for an unchristian conduct while away in a meeting after he returns, or they may withdraw their support from him and mark him as a false teacher if he does not continue true to the word while at some other place preaching, but that is the extent of their authority over an evangelist whom they may be supporting when he is not laboring among them. When we study the scope of authority of elders this truth will become more evident.

THE ELDERSHIP AND APOSTASY

I. THE MEANING OF APOSTASY

The word *apostasy* is not found in the Bible by that term, but the expression, "depart from the faith" is exactly what Webster says *apostasy* means. In I Timothy 4:1 we read: "Now the Spirit speaketh expressly, that in the latter times some shall depart from the faith, giving heed to seducing spirits, and doctrines of devils." This is a prediction of an apostasy to come during the latter times, but here it does not tell where and how it will come—only WHEN. But Paul tells us that this apostasy —"the mystery of iniquity"—was already at work as he wrote the second letter to the Thessalonians (2:7).

We ask, WHERE will the departing from the faith begin, and HOW will it develop? Does the Bible tell us? We read where Paul called the elders from Ephesus to meet him at Miletus and there he gave them the charge to watch themselves and all the flock among them (Acts 20:28). He then adds: "For I know this," (this was a prophecy which Paul knew by revelation,) "that after my departing" (after his death, for he spoke of his departure being near as death approached—2 Tim. 4:6) shall grievous wolves enter in among you, not sparing the flock. Also of your own selves shall men arise, speaking perverse things, to draw away disciples after them."

As to WHERE this apostasy would come, Paul said it would come from among the elders of the church. All real apostasy from truth begins there directly or indirectly. The eldership creates, or allows to be created, some innovation in the church. They become divided over matters and carry it to the whole church for settlement; or they become weak in the discipline and allow worldliness to corrupt the flock of God. As long as the eldership is pure and godly the church in that place will be strong.

As to the HOW, Paul said it would come by "grievous wolves" entering to devour the flock by false teaching; and some of the elders themselves will speak perverse things to lead away disciples after them. History gives us the full picture of this prophecy of Paul. The *apostasy* depicted in the New Testament was to come "in the latter times," through the eldership of the church, and by false teaching and deception, even within and from among the eldership.

There is a very close relationship between corruption in the eldership of the church and the apostasy. Great care should be taken in selecting and appointing men to be elders because the wrong men can lead to a complete departing of the whole congregation from the faith. That is one reason why this matter is of a most serious nature to the purity of the church of Christ.

II. HOW APOSTASY DEVELOPED AMONG THE ELDERS

Apostasy is a slow working of error. It is a slow departure from the truth. One does not realize that he is drifting, in most cases, until he has gone into apostasy or very near it. Its working is like the facial change of a man. We take a picture and in ten years take another and notice the radical change in the face and features of a man, yet we do not really see the change from day to day because it is so gradual. Apostasy may well be called the cancer of the soul. Like this horrible disease of the body, it begins small and unnoticed and gradually works its way through and around the vital parts of the body until, by its slow working and growth, the body succumbs to its deadly work. It is often too late when the disease is located. The best and only safe-guard against this evil power in the church is a periodical and complete check-up often. This slow persistent working of apostasy is what devoured the early church, and it is what hinders the church today.

Apostasy follows three well defined steps. (1) A change in the divine pattern for the oversight of the church. The governing power must be changed before anything else can be changed. As long as the proper authority remains in the proper place and proper way in the church, apostasy is impossible. (2) The second step is to go beyond the word of God. These corrupt practices religiously must come from some authority beyond the Bible. Something must be added. Once the governing part of the local church is set aside and another substituted, the next step may be taken, and this consists of adding some practice which is not authorized in the Bible, or changing some doctrine of the Bible to suit man's desires. (3) The third step is into complete departure from the truth of God. If one change in the divine order is allowed, who can stop further changes? Paul warned against any advance beyond what is written. (I Cor. 4:6). The first step beyond what is written opens the way for any number of steps one would desire to take, and the person who takes the first step can never criticise or censure the one who takes ten or twenty, or even goes completely away from the Bible. How can the man who takes the first step from God's authority by disregarding the divine organization of the church justly censure or correct the man who has gone further and denied the divinity of Jesus, or has denied the inspiration of the Bible? Is not one as much in disobedience as the other? Regarding this very principle James said to keep all the law, yet to disobey in one point is the same as disobeying in all points. (James 2:10). How many commandments of God must one disobey to be lost? It can be easily answered by the principle James gives.

Let us notice briefly just how this apostasy worked in the eldership of the early church. The following is a very brief summary of the working of many years. If the reader is interested in a more thorough study of the development of the various denominational systems in their departure from God's order, he is referred to any good, authoritative church historian or any contemporary writer with these events.

A. The first step was taken when the bishops of a congregation decided to elect a chairman or spokesman for them, and gradually allowed this chairman or spokesman to become their chief. After a few years of this arrangement it was easy to drift into the practice of all other elders of that congregation submitting in most matters to the judgment and demands of the chief elder. This became the general practice in the larger congregations and finally developed into the office of *archbishop.* No doubt this did not appear to those involved to be a serious thing. It was just an "expedient," a method to increase the efficiency of the eldership. But it was a step toward apostasy.

B. This move that created the office of ARCHBISHOP led to another departure. After a few years the *archbishop* in the larger cities began to reach out and take under control the smaller churches in surrounding towns. Two reasons may be given for this arrangement: (1) The educational and influential superiority of the city bishops over the country bishops. (2) The financial and numerical pre-eminence of the city churches over the country churches. This action came as a direct result of the archbishop idea. The same idea is in process of development within the churches today. The elderships of "big" churches are having the elderships of "little" churches channel their money and authority through the "big" churches to do "big" things. Anything larger than the local church is not the New Testament church. The second step was to have ONE elder over several churches.

C. The third step was to organize the archbishops. These chairman bishops of several towns were organized into a "diocese" or county. From the archbishops a chief was appointed. This developed into the office of *Cardinal* or chief archbishop. This act puts one elder over a section of the country.

D. Still later one of the cardinals was elected from the group to become the chief elder over the church universal, now called the *Pope.* When this step was taken, the next naturally led to claiming authority for this chief elder which has never been given to any man, not even the apostles. This is the system of departure that started among the elders in a small way. No doubt it seemed to them such a small thing that one would have been branded a "crank" or "hobby-rider" to voice an objection to it. The departure was so gradual that it was not noticed by the majority of people. The same can be true in the church today.

III. SCRIPTURAL ELDERS ARE THE SAFEGUARD AGAINST APOSTASY

There is a NEED for elders today in the church. Many things must be decided about the work and worship of the church. The time of assembling, the place of meeting, the order in the worship, the preparation for the worship, who shall preach and teach, and many other decisions are important. Somebody must do this directing. Is it to be decided by a majority vote, by the preacher or by the eldership? The latter is to make such decisions and is responsible to God for them being done scripturally. We need elders today in the church to do the work of overseeing the flock.

There is no greater work nor higher responsibility than that of the bishops of the church. When one reaches the good degree of Christianity that is required of the elders he has reached the very peak of usefulness in the church.

The elders need a pat on the back and a word of encouragement from the members of the church when they do a good work. We all need encouragement, but especially so when the heavy responsibility of the oversight is laid upon the shoulders of a man. The elders would work much harder and more earnestly if we would give them the encouragement they deserve when their work is well executed.

There must always be a plurality of elders in each congregation. This is one of the best safeguards against apostasy. The following passages of Scripture will show that there was a plurality of elders in each church: Acts 11:29, 30; 14:23; 15:4; 20:17; Phil. 1:1; I Tim. 4:14; 5:17 Titus 1:5; James 5:14; I Peter 5:1, 2.

There can never be less than two elders in each local church. Some ask, How many should there be in a congregation? The answer is, "If ANY man . . ." Any and all men in each congregation who can qualify should be appointed. The more qualified men appointed, the more work can be done and the more efficiently it can be done.

Another question of interest: If all the elders die except one, can he remain an elder in that congregation? He can if others are appointed to take the places of those who have died, but he cannot be scripturally THE ELDER. That is exactly what he would be if he remained the only elder. There is no place in all the New Testament that teaches a one man rule in the local church. This would not disqualify him as an elder but it would disqualify his rule as THE ELDER.

Each church must be autonomous (self-governed). If one congregation drifted from the truth, others would not be affected by governmental ties. With each church governed by its own elders it safeguards against apostasy of the whole church.

A plurality of elders in each church will provide a supply for the deficiency in any one man. The strong, spiritual characteristics of several men blended together is a safer oversight than just one man.

IV. WHY MORE MEN ARE NOT QUALIFIED TO BE ELDERS

No doubt the first reason to mention why many are not qualified elders is the lack of energy and will to develop the godly characteristics needed to be a scriptural elder. It is not easy to obtain a good knowledge of the Bible, to live a life above reproach, and to govern and guide a family so as to keep them in the way of the Lord. That is what one must do to become an elder.

A second reason is that there has been such mass substitutions for the eldership today that many have grown to disregard Bible instructions for the elders. Many churches have substituted an office called *Leaders* to take the place of the eldership. These *leaders* do not have to be qualified according to the Bible, and since they hold the same office, the qualifications are considered unimportant.

A third reason is the abuse of the eldership in some quarters. This has caused men not to desire the work. When they do not desire the office of a bishop, they will make no effort to qualify. The reason many do not desire this work of oversight is because they have seen and heard the continual abuse and complaining of churches toward the elders. They have heard members speak of them in an unchristian way. They have seen them accused of many things of which they were not guilty. The lack of respect and honor for the bishops has caused many young men never to set their goal to be an elder.

The work of efficient elders is the highest, most noble and needed work among us today. The man who qualifies and does the work of an elder is as near God as he can get on this earth. They are deserving of the deepest and greatest of our love and respect, for "they watch for your souls, as they that must give account."

The fourth reason is that the lack of preaching and teaching on the subject has caused many to fail to qualify. Many preachers have purposely tried to keep men from reaching the point to be recognized as qualified men for the eldership. Others have been so unlearned on the subject that they could not preach the truth on the eldership. They do not want to lose any power or control over the church where they preach. In some places the membership of the churches have never heard a gospel sermon on the subject of the qualifications for the eldership. One might as well leave out any other phase of scriptural teaching as this one.

Special Studies

by

W. Carl Ketcherside

Used by permission.

MUST ELDERS BE MARRIED?

"*Mias gunaikos andra.*" These are words of Paul. They were written to both Timothy and Titus. They constitute one qualification for an elder. What do they mean? The King James Version translates them "the husband of one wife." The Revised Standard Version says "married only once." Does the expression mean that marriage is essential to being a bishop? Almost before the last apostle died this was a matter of controversy. It has continued to be so in every generation since. This question bothered the reformers of the nineteenth century, both here and abroad.

On Wednesday, August 4, 1880, the annual conference of Churches of Christ in Great Britain met at Huddersfield. Brother G. Y. Tickle presented a paper on "The Eldership." Later, he published it in *The Christian Advocate,* of which he was editor. Here is an excerpt from the printed version:

"I respectfully submit that there is nothing in the directions given to either Timothy or Titus to make it imperative that they should be married men, and that they should have children. . . . The *one*, as opposed to plurality, is evidently the emphatic word. But it may be asked, Does it not even in that case include the injunction that he must be a married man? Most assuredly not. If the apostle has before him a man with a plurality of wives and intends to exclude *him* from the eldership on that ground, you have no right to say that is equal to having a single man before him who is to be excluded simply on the ground of his being unmarried or a widower—for to be consistent the language must exclude both."

At the same time, Bro. David King was editor of the *Ecclesiastical Observer.* He took exception to the speech made at the conference. This provoked Bro. Tickle to write in the next edition of his paper as follows:

"When we presented our paper on 'The Eldership' to the Annual Meeting we did not expect, and had no desire that it should escape the sifting of a full and fair criticism. We know that it is only by such means that the question can be lifted out of the ruts which a superficial exegesis has sunk for it, and be made to move forward on broad apostolic lines. That the Editor of the *Ecclesiastical Observer* should allow the whole of our positions, some of them so widely divergent from those he has accepted so many years as unassailable, to pass unchallenged, was not at all to be expected. We have felt, therefore, no surprise either as to the points of his attack, or to the manner in which the attack has been made, but we are bound to say we have never known the Editor so rash and heedless as he has shown himself in this critique on our paper."

After another rebuttal by Bro. King, the controversy was suspended by Bro. Tickle in these words:

"We do not think it would be profitable to enter into further controversy on this subject. D. K. intimates that he is not satisfied with the reply in our last issue. We were not *altogether* satisfied with his attack and are not *at all* satisfied with his rejoinder. If we answered in the same vein, we are sure dissatisfaction would be increased on both sides. So we prefer to let the matter rest where it is, in the hope that the brethren may be enabled to look away from the men and their little contention to the question in its different phases and on its merits, carefully weighing all that has been advanced in the way of argument in the balances of truth and right reason."

Interest in the issue has been heightened in some sections of the disçiple brotherhood in this country in the last two years. A Pennsylvania reader posed the following question to a fellow editor:

"If a man has all the qualifications to be an elder except that he has no children, his wife being childless and thus he has no children through no fault of his own, would that in itself bar him forever to serve as elder?"

The reply as published went far beyond the original question, for it would appear that the querist assumed that an elder must be married. But the editor responded in these words:

"If brethren generally will be gracious enough not to hang me on Haman's gallows, I would like to say that I think we have stretched the domestic qualifications for bishops out of proportions. Paul's stipulations to Timothy and Titus deal with a 'normal' situation, and *normally* men old enough to be bishops are married and have children. But does Paul draw the line on bachelors or childless married men? I think not. Our straight-laced interpretations would bar even Paul himself from being an elder. The 'husband of one wife' qualification literally means 'a one-woman man,' which is likely a moral restriction against polygamy. Most all scholars take this view, if that means anything. The 'Church of Christ' stands almost alone in its idea that bishops must be married men, an interpretation that is linguistically weak. With such a liberal view I would, of course, say *No* to the above question. I am always amazed at brethren who think a man must be a husband and father in order to oversee a church, and yet believe that an evangelist who sets the church in order and trains men to be bishops can be either single or childless."

I was not disturbed by this reply. But I must admit that I was amazed at the reaction of many. They actually became emotionally upset and agitated. Instead of bringing forward proof to sustain their position and to show any fallacy in the reasoning of the editor, they began to whisper that he was unsound and unsafe. Some quit taking his paper on the ground that they did not want to read anything which disagreed with their position. My attitude is just the opposite of that. I have long ago determined that I do not learn by reading after those in perfect agreement with me. Those who are not, present things to challenge my thinking. They force me to re-evaluate my convictions. I am thus made to test all things so that I may retain what is good. Accordingly, when I read such an article I invariably follow a three-point program. First, I read it over very carefully to ascertain just what the author intends to convey; secondly, I examine such proofs as he presents by the proper criterion; thirdly, I formulate my own convictions in the light of my personal investigation.

For several months in MISSION MESSENGER I have been conducting a survey of the eldership. Having considered the moral qualifications of the presbyters, I have arrived at the place where I must deal with the domestic requirements. The first question is whether or not a man must be married to qualify. Strictly speaking, the question is what Paul intended to convey in the expression "*mias gunaikos andra.*" That is what should concern us. We ought not to be interested primarily, in whether these words confirm a qualification we have set up. We must seek to find what qualification they set up. Since I am dealing at such length with an issue which may appear to my readers to be of minor importance, I offer as justification the fact that I am of the sober opinion that we can never restore the church of God to its ancient order without restoring the polity ordained by the holy apostles. Any matter related to the government of the congregation of saints is important. This particular one has taken on added importance at this time.

I am deeply indebted to, and appreciative of, the great scholars who have done so much in clearing the ground for those of us possessed of humbler intellects. I doubt that any person now living has a more profound respect for scholarship than the writer. Yet, I recognize that the mere fact that the "Church of Christ" stands almost alone in its idea that bishops must be married men, is not in itself, proof of either correctness or error in thinking. I shall seek to be objective and not concerned with the idea of any "church." What did the inspired envoy of the Lord say, and what did he mean?

"Mias gunaikos andra." In generations past men of great learning have held conflicting views. These words have been said to have the following connotations:

1. To forbid concubinage.
2. To forbid polygamy.
3. To forbid remarriage after divorce.
4. To forbid digamy, or deuterogamy (a second marriage after the death of the mate).
5. To demand that elders be married men.

At the outset, it must be admitted that most all scholars positively reject the last as being a proper interpretation. There are some notable exceptions to which we will later call attention. But it is likewise true that a careful poll of the same scholars may prove that a majority of them reject the idea that Paul was opposing polygamy by his statement. They believe rather that he was opposing deuterogamy, that is, a second marriage after death of a companion.

Goodspeed translates: "Only once married." James Moffatt: "He must be married only once." The Berkeley Version: "One wife's husband," with an added footnote: "If married at all." The New Testament in Plain English has "Married only once." The Revised Standard Version reads: "Married only once," with the footnote: "Greek *the husband of one wife.*"

On the original language itself, Kenneth S. Wuest, in his book on *The Pastoral Epistles* has this to say:

"The two nouns are without the definite article, which construction indicates character or nature. The entire context is one in which the character of the bishop is being discussed. Thus one can translate 'a one-wife sort of husband' or 'a one-woman sort of man.' We speak of the Airedale as a one-man dog. We mean, by that, that it is his nature to become attached to only one man, his master. Since character is emphasized by the Greek construction, the bishop should be a man who loves only one woman as his wife. It should be his nature to thus isolate and centralize his love."

Edmund J. Wolff, D.D., Professor of Church History and New Testament Exegesis in the Theological Seminary, Gettysburg, Pennsylvania, says:

"Public sentiment at the time looked with disfavor upon the contraction of marriage after the death of one's consort. It was held to be unseemly, if not immoral. To forego a second wedlock was regarded as a mark of high moral strictness. Even the heathen deemed it unbecoming for a widow. It, therefore, behooved one about to step on the high pedestal of pastoral oversight to conform to public sentiment—as long as it was not sinful, and to set an example of self-restraint."

Henry Alford, D.D., one time Dean of Canterbury, concurs in this view as shown by his statement:

"The view then which must I think be adopted is that . . . St. Paul forbids second marriage. He requires of them pre-eminent chastity, and abstinence from licence which is allowed to other Christians. How far such a prohibition is to be considered binding on us, now that the Christian life has entered into another and totally different phase, is of course an open question for the present Christian church at any time to deal with. It must be as a matter of course understood that regulations, in all lawful things, depend, even when made by an Apostle, on circumstances: and the superstitious observance of the letter in such cases is often pregnant with mischief to the people and the cause of Christ."

The reader is no doubt familiar with Vincent's Word Studies in the New Testament. In espousing the above position, the author says:

"The opposition to second marriage became very strong in the latter part of the second century. It was elevated into an article of faith by the Montanists, and was emphasized by Tertullian, and by Athenagoras, who called second marriage 'a spurious adultery.'"

Among the commentators who believe that the apostle was forbidding second marriages are Bloomfield, Wiesinger, Van Oosterzee, Huther, Ellicott, Wordsworth, and Faussett. There are a number of others who dissent from this view, among them H. H. Harvey, D.D., of Hamilton Theological Seminary, who declares:

"It seems clear, therefore, that the disqualification here intended is not remarriage after the death of a wife, but polygamy, or the having at the same time more than one living wife."

To complicate this explanation, Alfred Plummer, M.A., D.D., affirms that:

"Polygamy in the Roman Empire must have been very rare. It was forbidden by Roman law, which did not allow a man to have more than one lawful wife at a time, and treated every simultaneous marriage, not only as null and void, but infamous. When it was practiced, it must have been practiced secretly. It is possible that when St. Paul wrote to Timothy and Titus, not a single polygamist had been converted to the Christian faith. Polygamists were exceedingly rare inside the Empire, and the Church had not yet spread beyond it."

As to the rarity of polygamy in the days of the apostles we have the testimony of E. F. Scott, Professor of Biblical Theology, Union Theological Seminary, New York.

"This has sometimes been taken to imply that only married men were eligible, but a rule of this kind would be contrary to the whole passage, which deals with character rather than status. Neither can it be polygamy which is forbidden, for this was never practiced in the civilized regions of Asia Minor. Perhaps Moffatt is right in translating *he must be married only once*. . . . But perhaps the meaning is simply that a bishop must show an example of strict morality. As a man of mature years he would presumably be married, and in the married relation, above all others, he must be above reproach."

Edward Hayes Plumptree, D.D., Professor in King's College, London, suggests another alternative:

"A third explanation is, perhaps, more satisfactory. The most prominent fact in the social life of both Jews and Greeks at this period was the frequency of divorce. This, as we know, Jewish teachers, for the most part, sanctioned on even trifling grounds (Matt. 5: 31, 32; 19: 3-9). The apostle, taking up the law which Christ had laid down, infers that any breach of that law (even in the case which made marriage after divorce just permissible) would at least so far diminish a man's claim to respect as to disqualify him for office."

Walter Lock, D.D., in The International Critical Commentary, reaches about the same conclusion:

"To be unmarried would incur no reproach: such a requirement (marriage) would be scarcely consistent with the teaching of our Lord (Matt. 19: 12) and of St. Paul (1 Cor. 7: 7, 8); so the writer is only thinking of the character of a bishop, *if* married; as in verse 4 he deals only with his children, if he has children. . . . It also implies, and was probably meant to imply, not divorcing one wife and marrying another."

Paul E. Kretzmann, Ph.D., D.D., in Popular Commentary of the Bible, offers the following:

"That a pastor lead a chaste and decent life, confining his attentions to his wife, if he have one, as he normally will, not living in concubinage or bigamy, or rejecting a woman to whom he is lawfully betrothed for another."

N. J. D. White, D.D., in The Expositor's Greek Testament sets forth the view:

"It does not mean that the episcopus must be, or have been married. What is here forbidden is digamy under any circumstances."

Nothing is more apparent to the researchist than the wide area of disagreement among the scholars. They are not agreed upon what the apostle meant. They are not even agreed upon what he did not mean. It is true that a majority take the position that Paul did not intend to set up the married state as requisite to office. On this point, we quote from R. C. H. Lenski, who says:

"The emphasis is on *one* wife's husband, and the sense is that he have nothing to do with any other woman. He must be a man who cannot be taken hold of on the score of sexual promiscuity or laxity. It is plain that Paul does not say here that none but married men may enter the ministry, that every pastor must be married."

John Peter Lange, in his comments upon the passages under consideration, says:

"The view that Paul speaks here only of the married state, as a *conditio sine qua non* for the episcopoi, or that he merely discourages anything unusual, immoral, or illegal in the married life of such officers, does not fully explain his language."

Scott's Bible agree with the thought expressed by Lange and others, with the words:

"Some have inferred from this text, that stated pastors ought to be married, as a prerequisite to their office; but this seems to be a mistake of a *general permission*, connected with a restriction, for *an express command*."

A. S. Peake, M.A., D.D., lends the weight of his opinion to the same view, saying of the passages:

"Sometimes wrongly interpreted as alluding to polygamy or adultery, or of forbidding celibacy."

Professor T. Croskery, D.D., in The Pulpit Commentary, also declares:

"It does not necessarily compel pastors to marry, like the Greek church. . . . It seems to mean that the pastor was to be 'the husband of one wife,' avoiding the polygamy that was then common among the Jews, and the system of divorce still so common in that age, and remaining faithful to the wife of his choice."

We need to be careful, lest we leave the impression that all of the commentators and historians are united in the view that Paul did not set up marriage as a qualification. Carlstadt, the illustrious contemporary of Luther, and the fiery reformer, who advocated that a destructive process was the only method of reform, was a notable exception. This man, who was anxious to introduce into ecclesiastical and civil affairs an unconditional adherence to the obvious and literal construction of the Scriptures, steadfastly contended that the bishops should be married men.

Thomas M. Lindsay, D.D., Principal of Glasgow College, in his book, "The Church and The Ministry in the Early Centuries," says:

> "Titus is told that a presbyter or elder must be a man who is above suspicion, who is a faithful husband, and whose children are Christians of well-regulated lives."

In a footnote on the same page is contained the following explanation:

> "'A faithful husband' appears to be the best translation of *mias gunaikos andra,* one who acts on the principles of Christian morality and is not led astray by the licentious usages of the surrounding heathenism."

But Macknight in his work on "The Epistles" dissents from this view, in this language:

> "The direction I have been considering does not make it necessary, to one's being a bishop, that he be a married person. . . . But the apostle's meaning is, that if such a person be married, he must, as was observed above, have only one wife at a time."

Albert Barnes concludes that the apostle intended to prohibit polygamy, but writes:

> "This need not be understood as requiring that a bishop should be a married man."

In the face of all of this contradictory material what is the honest student to do? What did the apostle actually mean by the terms he used? It is possible we may not be able, at this late date, to definitely determine, in the absence of more complete testimony. Certainly we should not be arbitrary or dogmatic in our personal views. We need to proceed with caution and becoming humility, lest we advance an interpretation, then make of it a creed, and proceed to disfellowship others because they will not bow to our will. There is a difference between what the apostle said and what men think that he meant.

It is an easy matter for us to ignore the results of research and investigation and cling to a traditional view without regard to its validity. But this is not an honest approach to the revealed word of heaven. One of our greatest difficulties is that, having taught a thing for so long, we become lifted up with pride. We feel that we cannot change for this would be an admission of error! Or, perhaps, we learn better, but conclude that silence is the better part of valor. If we remain still and say nothing on the issues that are raised, we can retain the plaudits of the masses; whereas, if we speak out boldly we may be hated and hounded as troublers of Israel.

The writer does not feel that he should suppress his honest views in order to please men. In the next issue those views will be clearly set forth and the reasons given for them. Those reasons may not satisfy all of our readers. They may be deemed as insufficient to justify the conclusion reached, but they will be presented in kindness and love, and those who differ will not be castigated nor driven out by the editor. It is our very fervent prayer that you shall read this review again very carefully and save this issue until the next appears. In the meantime, we believe that there is one thing of which all may be certain, and that is that the enforced celibacy of the Roman Church is contrary to the word of God.

In our first article on this subject, published in MISSION MESSENGER last month, we reviewed the positions taken by various scholars. We urge you to read it as a preparation for this second article. It will demonstrate the great differences that exist as to the meaning of the language used by the apostle. It will also show that only a small minority of scholars entertain the view that marriage is a requisite for the eldership.

Those of us who have always contended that a bishop must be married should face up courageously to the difficulties which must be met in the defence of that position. Let me cite but a few. Jesus speaks with commendation of those who "have made themselves eunuchs for the sake of the kingdom of heaven" (Matt. 19: 12). I understand this to refer to those who desist from marriage to advance the kingdom. Is it logical that one who deprives himself of marriage for the sake of the kingdom, should be deprived of an office or function in that kingdom, on the basis that he is not married? Again, we learn from the scriptures that continency is a gift (Matt. 19: 11) and that it is a special gift from God (1 Cor. 7: 7). Shall a man be barred from the eldership becauses he exercises this gift, or, if he desires the office of bishop, must he deny the gift of God?

The expression "husband of one wife" as relates to the bishop, is on par with the expression "wife of one husband" as pertains to the widow in 1 Timothy 5: 9. It is generally conceded, we believe, that the latter expression means that a widow is not to have married again after the death of her husband. In view of this, is it not implied that Paul, instead of setting up marriage as a qualification, was simply stating that no twice married man could qualify? If it be agreed that "husband of one wife" is a correct rendering, is the emphasis to be placed upon "husband" or "one." If we were laying down a qualification of marriage for a position, would we say that a man had to be the husband of *one wife?* If Paul intended to establish marriage as a requisite to office, why did he not use the word for "married" since he was familiar with it and employed it frequently?

On the other hand, we should not feel that this is the only position beset with problems. Those who settle upon other meanings also have difficulties which they must meet. Certainly the language employed by the apostle meant *something,* and it meant just *one thing* when written. It is not a fair or wise approach to say that it could have included a number of various things, for this spirit would do despite to all interpretation, and it is the resort of shallow thinkers and surface reasoners who do not handle the word skilfully.

In presenting my own view as to the question in our heading, I must admit that I do so with some reluctance which I did not feel five years ago. Always before, when writing upon this topic, I have been bold, forward and positive. I merely stated my position derived from years of traditional teaching. It never occurred to me that any person would be so rash as to question it. I admit that I did not strive to find out what the apostle meant, for I thought I already knew. Now that I am again faced with the necessity of declaring my thoughts I find myself both humbled and hesitant. Yet I cannot be true to my readers without expressing my feelings.

My conclusion is that a bishop should be a married man. This is in opposition to the world's scholarship. It may seem presumptuous to array myself against the battery of great reasoners whose opinions I have cited. Surely I must present the bases for arriving at such a conclusion. I know these will be attacked and sifted, and they should be. It may be proven that they are inadequate and insufficient to justify my position. I submit them in all honesty and sincerity. They are my own. I have not consulted with others on the matter. No one else need be charged with them. My only justification in disagreeing with the scholars is that "God hath chosen the foolish to confound the wise." Here are the reasons which lead me to believe that bishops should be married.

1. The primitive community of saints, being Jewish, was patterned after the synagogue in government. It is my personal feeling that the synagogue, which was a spontaneous production of the Babylonian exile, was used of God to

cushion the shock of transition from Judaism to Christianity. This theme I hope to develop in a future book if God spares my life. At the present, it is sufficient to say that all scholars of note agree that the congregation in Jerusalem was a Messianic synagogue, with its permanent form of government developing along the lines with which the people were familiar. Out of the great bulk of material before me, I present statements from two writers of note.

The first quotation is from Arthur Penrhyn Stanley, D.D., Dean of Westminster, in his "Lectures on the History of the Jewish Church," Vol. 3, Page 409:

"And thus, inasmuch as the synagogue existed where the Temple was unknown, and remained when the Temple fell, it followed that from its order and worship, and not from that of the Temple, were copied, if not in all their details, yet in the general features, the government, the institutions, and the devotions of those Christian communities, which springing directly from the Jewish, were in the first instance known as 'synagogues' . . . and afterward by the adoption of an almost identical word 'Ecclesia,' assembly house."

The second quotation will be found in "The Temple Dictionary of the Bible" by W. Ewing, M.A., and J. E. H. Thomson, D.D., under the article "Synagogue."

"It is not difficult to trace the foundation and practice of the Apostolic Church to the Synagogue system, and to see that we have nothing to do with the Temple worship, which was meant to be unique and to be devoted to the sacrificial ritual. . . . Every detail of the Primitive Church organization is synagogal—the equality of elders and rulers (Acts 20: 17, 28), the episcopal power vested in the presbyters, the daily ministration (Acts 6: 1), the matter of collections, the use of the word angel (Rev. 2: 1) for the presiding elder, and the general order of Christian worship: all are synagogal and presbyterian."

It should not be necessary to tell the serious student that the last word in the quotation has no reference to a denomination in the Protestant world, but to a form of government.

The Jewish disciples were familiar with the rule of elders in the synagogue. (See MISSION MESSENGER, June 1957, page 8). It is conceivable that when the apostles visited a synagogue and reasoned from the Jewish Scriptures, proving that Jesus of Nazareth was the Messiah, the entire synagogue might be converted, in which case there would be no necessity of a change of government, worship or procedure, except the addition of the Lord's Supper. But the Jews had a high regard for the married state and the home. For that reason they taught that a priest should be neither unmarried or childless, lest he be unmerciful.

Dr. Alfred Edersheim, D.D., Ph.D., in an article on "Marriage Among the Hebrews," says:

"Thus viewed, marriage was considered almost a religious duty, that is, not from lust, nor for beauty, nor yet merely for wealth. For whatever woman was, either for good or bad, she was always superlatively. Stringing together several portions of Scripture, it was argued that an unmarried man was without any *good* (Gen. 2: 18), without *joy* (Deut. 14: 26), without *blessing* (Ezek. 44: 30); without *protection* (Jer. 31: 22), without *peace* (Job 5: 24); indeed, could not properly be called a man (Gen. 5: 22)."

The same writer in his "Jewish Social Life in the Days of Christ" has this to say:

"We can understand how, before the coming of the Messiah, marriage should have been looked upon as of religious obligation. Many passages of Scripture were at least *quoted* in support of this idea. Ordinarily, a young man was expected to enter the wedded state (according to Maimonides) at the age of sixteen or seventeen, while the age of twenty may be regarded as the utmost limit conceded, unless study so absorbed time and attention as to leave no leisure for the duties of married life. Still it was thought better even to neglect study than to remain single."

In the same book, the author, himself a Jew who came to believe in the Messiah, has this to say about those who had charge of the conduct of public worship, as well as of the government and discipline of the synagogues:

"They were men learned in the law and of good repute, whom the popular voice designated, but who were regularly set apart by 'the laying on of hands,' or the 'Semichah,' which was done by at least three, who had themselves received ordination. . . . The special qualifications for the office of Sanhedrist, mentioned in the Rabbinical writings, are such as to remind us of the directions of St. Paul to Timothy (1 Tim. 3: 1-10)."

Our next authority is C. D. Ginsburg,

LL.D., who writes in "Early Attendance at the Sanctuary" as follows:

"It was deemed most desirable that he who acts as the mouthpiece of the people should be able to sympathize with the wants of the people, and should possess those moral and mental qualifications which became so holy a mission. The canon law, therefore, laid it down that 'even if an elder or sage is present in the congregation, he is not to be asked to officiate before the ark; but that man is to be delegated to officiate who has children, whose family are free from vice, who has a proper beard, whose garments are decent, who is acceptable to the people, and who has a good and amiable voice, who understands to read properly the Law, the Prophets, and the Hagiographa, and who knows all the benedictions of the service' (*Mishna Taanith,* 2:2). How strikingly this illustrates the apostolic injunction, 'A bishop must be blameless, the husband of one wife, vigilant, sober, of good behavior, and modest . . . one that ruleth well his own house, having his children in subjection with all gravity, . . . not a novice, . . . he must have a good report of them that are without' (1 Tim. 3:1-7, with Titus 1:1-9)."

It would not have been necessary to set forth marriage as one of the qualifications for the presbyters who were selected by the congregation at Jerusalem and appointed to administer the affairs of the community of saints. The brethren who constituted that community were all Jews. They regarded themselves as a synagogue of disciples of the Nazarene. Their superintendents and administrators selected by popular voice would be married men. And we believe that this pattern would be followed in other congregations, even those remote from Palestine. "For ye, brethren, became followers of the churches of God which in Judea are in Christ Jesus" (1 Thess. 2:14).

2. The whole tenor of the teaching seems to indicate that a presbyter will be a married man. It may be argued that a *definite rule* of marriage based upon the mere statement "*mias gunaikos andros*" is linguistically weak, but we do not think it will be seriously disputed that the context relates to one who is domestically situated as the head of a household. And just as a gem loses part of its luster out of the setting designed for it, so it is sometimes difficult to appreciate fully a passage isolated from the general frame in which it is placed.

Edward Hayes Plumptre, D.D., Professor in King's College, London, has this to say:

"Both this verse and verse 4 appear to take marriage for granted. It is obvious that in a community much exposed to the suspicions or the slanders of the heathen, this would be a safeguard against many of the perils to which a celibate clergy have always been exposed."

Much along the same vein is the statement of J. R. Dummelow, M.A., Queen's College, Oxford, who says the expression probably means that a presbyter must be faithful to his wife, "a man of one woman." He adds, "In any case the presbyter or bishop is contemplated as a married man."

3. The Holy Spirit presents an analogy in which the home, or household, sustains a relation to the congregation of God, and it is in ruling the first that one demonstrates his ability to govern the second. A presbyter must "rule well his own house." He must have "his children in subjection with all gravity." The purpose of this qualification is not to determine his ability to beget offspring but to afford a demonstration of his ability to govern them. The argument is that "If he know not how to rule his own house how shall he take care of the church of God?" The word for house is *oikos* "the inmates of a house, all the persons forming one family, a household." A part of this family are children. In ruling them, the candidate for the eldership shows his ability to govern. If he is not married and has no children how can he demonstrate this ability? How can the congregation know he will be able to take care of the church of God if they have never seen a demonstration of his ability in a household? Can a congregation select a man to govern the church of God who has not demonstrated ability to rule his own house, including his children?

But what about the argument that by setting up marriage as a qualification, Paul would render himself, Barnabas, and Timothy, disqualified for the office? We propose to allow David King to answer this.

"We consider that either polygamy or celibacy disqualifies for the eldership. It has been urged that celibacy cannot do so, as, in that case, Paul and Timothy would have been disqualified; certainly they would, and there is no evidence they were not. No one can produce proof that they were qualified for the elder's office, and nowhere are we taught that the qualifications for an apostle, an evangelist, and an elder are the same. On the point now immediately under notice, nothing could be more fitting than that apostles and evangelists, whose work largely required them to move from place to place, and generally rendered impossible a settled home, should be unmarried; while on the other hand, nothing is more seemly and desirable than that overseers in one church, whose duties require settled residence and involve frequent interposition between husband and wife, parents and children, should themselves be married men, who have given evidence that they understand and rightfully deport themselves in that relationship. No one can fail to see that such, other circumstances being equal, could not but present a fitness for the office which the unmarried are without. This is our conclusion after years of thoughtful investigation, and after reading, perhaps, all that can be said on either side."

What should be our attitude toward brethren who honestly differ from us and who think that we make a rigid interpretation without proper justification? Here is how Brother King resolved that issue.

"Still the fact remains, that thoughtful, learned, pious brethren conclude that it is not certain that the intention is wider than the exclusion of the polygamist, and, therefore, they decline to reject an unmarried man who is, in all other respects, qualified. Now, we are not prepared to say that these brethren must of *necessity* be wrong. That they are wrong we have little or no doubt, but the impossibility of their being right is not here affirmed. How then shall the difficulty be met? Each church must meet it for itself, and the understanding of the majority must prevail. Not that the church shall decree what the interpretation shall be; but that each member determine for himself, whether the person, or persons, named has, or have, the required qualifications; each to determine this according to his own understanding of the terms, and the declared will of the majority must be taken as the church-recognition or non-recognition of the fitness of the men submitted for their judgment. But just here comes in an important consideration, which to some extent should influence the decision. There *is* perfectly safe and certain ground. If only those are ordained who possess the other qualifications and who also are married, everyone will know that the requirements are fully met. Thus perfectly safe and reliable ground invites to occupation."

What course shall I pursue personally? Since starting this series I have learned of a group of brethren in another part of the world who do not consider marriage as a necessary qualification. They will not reject a man who is otherwise qualified but has never married. Suppose I should visit them and labor among them, as I have been invited to do. Would I seek to divide them over this issue? Indeed I would not! If asked to explain my position I would offer my interpretation in meekness and humility. I would avoid becoming dogmatic or arbitrary. I would not tell them that I could not worship with them, nor serve under an eldership, with one or more constituents unmarried. I could not conscientiously appoint such a brother to office with my present attitude, but I would not make an unwritten creed of my interpretation and divide brethren into "a married elder faction," and "an unmarried elder faction." If I have not grown much in knowledge in recent years I trust that I have at least grown in grace.

To any of my brethren, at home or abroad; to those who fellowship me and those who do not; I would like to say that I will be pleased to read anything you have to say on this issue which may help to throw additional light on the matter. I do not solicit your personal opinions, for I have more of my own than I know what to do with. But if there is some scripture I have overlooked, or some point of logic or reasoning I have failed to see, you will be my friend if you point out my shortcoming, and call my mistakes to my attention. I want to be right above all things else. I am willing to learn from any person who can teach me.

God willing, I shall deal with the questions concerning the children of bishops in my next issue. I trust that you will look forward to that, and that God may bless us all with a deeper insight into His revelation of truth.

ELDERS AND CHILDREN

The question of whether or not elders must have children in order to qualify has long been discussed. The editor humbly submits his views on this issue in the form of questions and answers.

1. Is it your position that a man must be married to qualify as an elder?

Yes, and I gave my reasons for so thinking in the November edition of this paper. I admit there are difficulties presented by this position, but it seems to fulfill the requirements better than any other. Those who desire to study the opposite view, and all should do so, may see it set forth by Bro. Ralph Graham, in *Bible Talk.*

2. Do you think that an elder must have children?

Yes, I do, because he is contemplated as the head of a family, or household, and he must demonstrate his ability to take care of the church of God by ruling his own family well (1 Tim. 3:5). In connection therewith, it is said he must have his children in subjection with all gravity.

3. Does the term children **imply a plurality, or could a man with one child serve, if he possesses the other qualifications?**

The word "children" does not necessitate a plurality. It is used in its common application, and neither legally, naturally, or in the Old and New Testaments does it convey the idea of a compulsory plurality.

4. Can you illustrate what you mean by "legally" and "naturally"?

Yes. In this state, there is a law which stipulates that "All parents having *children* under the age of sixteen years must enroll them in school." Could parents having only one child evade that law? Indeed not!

In normal conversation we use the term "children" in the same fashion. If the Parent-Teachers Association invites to a meeting all parents who have children enrolled in the school, it certainly would not be limited to those who had two or more in school.

5. Give us examples in the Old and New Testaments to illustrate your view.

A good case in point is that of Sarah, at the birth of Isaac. "And she said, Who would have said unto Abraham, that Sarah should have given children suck? for I have born him a son in his old age" (Gen. 21:7). Here the term "children" is certainly equivalent to "a son."

In 1 Timothy 5:4 "any widow who has children" is to be supported by them. This certainly would not eliminate one son or daughter from any obligation, for that would contradict verses 8 and 16 where the singular is employed. Such examples could be multiplied far beyond our space to accommodate them.

6. If a couple having no children of their own, adopt children, would this satisfy the requirements?

Certainly it would. The qualification is not based upon a man's physical ability to beget offspring, but upon his ability to rule or govern the family circle. A wife might be sterile even though her husband was not. If a couple adopts children and they demonstrate ability to rear them in subjection, the qualification is met.

7. Then why could not a man qualify by teaching public school and governing children?

Because the relationship sustained in a school is different than that in a home, and the government of a congregation is analogous to that of a home. There is more to "ruling a household" than maintaining youngsters in subjection. That is but one phase of it. An elder will be called upon to counsel and advise in domestic difficulties involving husbands and wives, parents and children, employers and employees, etc. It is to qualify him to deal objectively with all such cases that he must be the head of a household so he may know "how to care for the church of God."

8. Do the scriptures teach that an elder's children must be members of the church, in order for him to qualify?

I do not think so. I believe that the statement "having faithful children" in Titus 1:6, is misunderstood by a lot of people. Of course, I may be in error about it myself, but I merely give my view of it, after making very careful and earnest study, as objectively as I know how to do so.

9. Do not most of the modern translations imply that the expression means "children who are Christians"?

Yes. Some of them even use the expression. For instance, *The Twentieth Century New Testament* says, "Whose children are Christians." But this is not a translation. It is a commentary. It expresses what the translators thought the apostle meant, not what he said. There is no word for "Christian" in the text, and it is not a translation to use this word for the term that does appear.

10. Does not Thayer in his lexicon say the term means one who has become convinced that Jesus is the Messiah and the author of salvation?

Actually, Thayer does not say that. He merely translates the words of Prof. Grimm to that effect. Strictly speaking, belief *in Jesus* is not included in this word at all. It simply means "trustworthy, of good fidelity," and relates to one who can be relied upon. There is not one thing in the term itself to indicate belief in any specific person, proposition or thing.

11. Then why did the lexicographers assign it a specific application?

That is easily understood. The term *pistos* appears in a New Testament framework or background. In many cases, it has to do with a state of conviction relative to Jesus as the Messiah. The lexicographers of New Testament usage would obviously slant their thinking in that direction in any case of question. I think they have done so here. They thought the contextual usage justified it; I do not think so. The term is applied to God, Christ, servants, stewards, and the word, as well as to children.

12. Do you have some justifiable basis for disagreeing with these authorities?

That all depends upon who is to be the judge of what constitutes a justifiable basis. The Bible says "Every way of a man is right in his own eyes," but it also says, "The way of a fool is right in his own eyes." I think that I am correct in my conviction that a man may be appointed to the eldership before his children are old enough to accept the gospel and assume the responsibility of the Christian life.

13. On what ground do you reach that conclusion?

First, let it be remembered that the strict meaning of the term *pistos* is "trustworthy, reliable." Qualifications relating to the children were written by the apostle to Timothy at Ephesus, and Titus at Crete. I do not think they differ. Whatever was required of children in one place would be required in both. If an expression used in writing to Titus is obscure or ambiguous, it may be explained in the language to Timothy, or vice versa. The statement to Titus is "having faithful children," and to Timothy, it is, "having his children in subjection." I conclude, then, that faithful children are children in subjection to the will or rule of the father. Faithful children are those who are trustworthy and reliable because they are in subjection to paternal government. Paul defines what he means when he says "Faithful children *not accused of riot or unruly.*" This is the negative attribute, while trustworthy is the positive.

14. Is it not to be presumed that children who are reared by Christian parents will obey the Lord when they get old enough?

That does not necessarily follow. God said, "I have nourished and brought up children, and they have rebelled against me" (Isaiah 1: 2) and I do not think that earthly parents are any better than God. The fact that God's children rebelled against him is no reflection against the way in which he nourished and brought them up. We need to be careful in assuming that a profligate child is always a reflection against the parents, lest we reflect against the fatherhood of God.

15. If a man had one or more children, under subjection, yet none were old enough to become Christians, I take it you would ordain him as elder.

Of course, that is not the only qualification. But if a man was fully qualified otherwise, and his children were under subjection and obedient to his discipline, I would appoint him as elder, if the congregation selected him. The qualification is not the ability to get your children into the church, as desirable as that may be, but to govern and control the family circle. I know a man who reared his family in a denominational influence, and they were always very close as a family. All became members of the denomination. When the father was somewhat advanced in years, he and his wife became convinced that denominationalism was wrong, and obeyed the pure gosel. The children, all being married, would not leave the denomination in which they were reared. But this faithful, godly man could qualify as a bishop over the flock of God.

Extracts by FRANK HAMILTON *from*

The BIBLE *and* WINE

BY THE LATE

FERRAR FENTON, M.R.A.S., M.C.A.A., ETC., ETC.

(Translator of the Complete Bible into Modern English)

A. & C. Black, Ltd.

4, 5 & 6 Soho Square, London, W. 1.

13th July, 1938.

Frank Hamilton, Esq.,
6701 Atlantic Avenue,
Ventnor, N. J.

Dear Sir:—

We shall have no objection to your reprinting this as you suggest, provided that the reference to the Translator of the Complete Bible appears on the title-page as in proof which we are returning herewith.

Yours very truly,

A. & C. BLACK, Ltd.

(H. A. G.)

The Bible and Wine

"Thus saith Jehovah: As the new wine is found in the cluster, and one saith, Destroy it not, for a blessing is in it: so will I do for my servants' sake, that I may not destroy them all"—Isa. 65: 8.

(See also Deut. 32: 14 and Jer. 48: 33.)

Having now completed the examination of the Old Testament, and its teachings upon the uses of fruits as foods or drinks, I proceed to do the same by a careful survey of the Greek text of the New Testament, and the methods in which the old Greek and Mediterranean nations prepared the fruit of the vine-plant for use in their domestic life. This latter, of course, can only be learned as to technical details from writers outside the Gospels, who treated the subject as one of agriculture and manufactures, but who, by living at the same period as the Evangelists and Apostles, were personally acquainted with the matter to which both refer.

GREEK TEXTS OF THE NEW TESTAMENT

Oinos, Oinon, Texts in Greek.

Oinon, the Grape-tree or Vine-plant.

Oinion, the fruit of the Vine or Grape-plant. It is also used to denote various kinds of drinks or confections of other succulent fruits, such as the date and lotus fruit, according to Liddell and Scott's Lexicon. According to Professor Samuel Lee, of Cambridge University, the root of the Greek word is undoubtedly the Hebrew vocable, *Yain,* Wine; which, as I have before shown, under the sections of my essay devoted to the philology of that Hebrew noun, was not confined to an intoxicating liquor made from fruits by alcoholic fermentation of their expressed juices, but more frequently referred to a thick, non-intoxicating syrup, conserve, or jam, produced by boiling, to make them storable as articles of food, exactly as we do at the present day. The only difference being that we store them in jars, bottles, or metal cans, whilst the Ancients laid them up in skin bottles, as Aristotle and Pliny, and other classic writers upon agricultural and household affairs describe. Consequently the contention of some of my correspondents that the Greek *oinos, always* meant fermented and intoxicating liquor is totally inaccurate, and only arises from ignorance, or prejudice in favour of the delusion of the commentators of the Dark Ages, who fancied drunkenness was the highest delight, and intoxication an imperative Christian practice; because Mohammedan Arabians were a sober people.

Oine, and *Oinon,* the Grape, or Vine-plant. *Oinos,* wine, or drink made from any fruit or grain, such as dates, apples, pears, barley, the lotus seed. If specially indicated as made from Grapes it is called *Oinos 'ampelinos.*

As in the Hebrew "*Yain,*" the word does not in Greek always signify fermented intoxicating drink, but grapes as fresh fruit, dried as raisins, or prepared as jam, or preserved by boiling for storage, or as thick syrup for spreading upon bread as we do butter; and that syrup dissolved in water for a beverage at meals, as described in the Hebrew Bible by Solomon and others, and amongst Greek writers by Aristotle, and Pliny amongst the Roman ones. This mixing of the syrup with water ready for use at meals is alluded to in more than one of our Lord's parables. The liquid was absolutely non-alcoholic and not intoxicating. Grape-juice was also prepared by heating it, as soon as possible after it had been squeezed in the press, by boiling, so as to prevent fermentation, and yet preserve its thin liquid form as a drink. To ensure this certain resinous gums were dissolved in the juice, or sulphate of lime, or what is commonly called gypsum, was put into it, as is now done in Spain, to make the liquid clear and bright, and pervent subsequent fermentation arising from changes of atmosphere. All these plans for producing a non-intoxicating wine are still followed extensively in every grape-growing country of Southern Europe and Asia, as of old. Similar wines made in France can now be obtained in London from Ingersoll and Melluish, of 10 Eastcheap, E. C. This is not a paid advertisement, but noted because I believe it may benefit some readers to know the fact, and to support my statements in the text.

It should never be forgotten that when reading in the Bible and the classic pagan writers of "Wine," we are seldom dealing with the strongly intoxicating and loaded liquids to which that name is alone attached in the English language, but usually with beverages such as above described. They were as harmless and sober as our own teas, coffees, and cocoas. Had they not been so, the ancient populations would have been perpetually in a more or less pronounced state of drunkenness, for they had none of our above-noted herb-made drinks to use as a part of their dietary. These facts should never be forgotten when we read of "wine" there,—for it was simple fruit syrup, except where especially stated to be of the intoxicating kinds, which latter the Prophets and Legislators always condemn.

Leaving further exposition, I now turn to the New Testament.

REFERENCE IN ST. MATTHEW

St. Matthew 9: 17: "Neither do they pour new wine (fresh grape-juice) into old wine-skins; for if they did, the skins would burst, and the wine (grape-juice) be spilt, and the skins destroyed. On the contrary, they pour fresh juice into new skins, and both are safe together."

Only a determination to misread this metaphorical illustration of the subject which Jesus was discussing with the disciples of John, can pervert this passage into a recommendation or sanction for habitual use of intoxicating liquors. That the *oinon,* that is "fresh grape-juice" (if literally translated), referred to had not been fermented to the still liquid form is clear, for if it had been so it would not "burst the old wine skins" by beginning to ferment in them on account of the yeast or acid with which the old skins were saturated, setting up the alcoholic action. To keep the juice of the grapes sweet and wholesome it needed to be *specially* prepared before being poured into new sweet skins, when it would keep pure and benefit men as an article of diet, as His auditors knew well, as a syrup or jam, such as the ancient writers upon agriculture and domestic economy inform us were in common daily use.

Jesus wished to show John's disciples that before He could form an Organization or Church to be the instrument of continuing His doctrines, He had to prepare His disciples by a course of mental education to receive His spiritual teaching, freed from the "dead rituals" of the Sadducean priesthood of Jerusalem, and then inspire them with a newly-created Organization to preserve and serve out the Gospel doctrines to mankind.

The interpretation put upon His parable by the ignorant commentators of the Dark Ages, that He was insisting upon the drinking of intoxicants, is little short of blasphemy, and it is a disgrace to our better informed age that writers should say that "Christianity has given a sacred character to wine and its use," as some I have read declare, "in opposition to the Mohammedan condemnation of it." By "wine" this writer clearly says he meant alcoholic liquor.

REFERENCES IN ST. MARK

St. Mark 2:22: "Nobody pours new wine into old wine-skins; but if done, then the new wine (that is, the fresh unprepared grape-juice) would burst the skins, and both the wine and the skins would be wasted. On the contrary, new wine must be put into new skins."

To this passage my preceding comment will apply; but the following citation will demand a special consideration from both myself and readers, for it has been curiously distorted by commentators from its true bearing. It is—

St. Mark 15:20-24: "And when they had insulted Him they took off from Him the purple robe, and clad Him in His own attire, and led Him out for crucifixion. Then they seized a passer-by, who was coming up from the country—Simon the Cyrenian, the father of Alexander and Rufus—forcing him to accompany them, to carry the cross, and took Him to Golgotha (which means Skull-field), where they offered Him wine medicated with myrrh: *but He refused to drink it.* There they crucified Him, and divided His clothing among themselves, casting lots as to what part each should take."

The question suggested in the above, to which no one seems to have found an answer, is: Why did Jesus refuse to drink the wine, *medicated with a narcotic* by the Centurion, out of a feeling of mercy to the victim, whom he knew had been unjustly condemned to death upon a false accusation, and that Pilate had been driven to condemn him by terror for his own personal safety, after the Sadducean priests had threatened to accuse him to the Emperor at Rome as a confederate with Christ to incite a revolt of the Jews against the Empire, unless he did hand Jesus over to their will to be crucified? This narcotized liquor does not seem to have been offered to the two robbers who had been convicted of real crime, and therefore we must conclude, as I have done, that it was an act of mercy from the Centurion who commanded the detachment of soldiers, specially to Jesus. Then why should Christ not have drank it? He would know the kindness of heart of the soldier, and the nobility of soul that inspired the feeling of mercy. Then why did He not accept the act of mercy?

"Oh!" is the only answer I have ever read, or heard spoken, "Our Saviour refused the narcotic wine because He did not wish to diminish in the slightest degree the cruel tortures of the death He was about to suffer for mankind!"

As to the bodily torments, He was only to suffer the same as the two miserable robbers, His companions in the method of death. Consequently there must have been a far more powerful reason for His refusal than that commonly given. What was it?

Was it not the following?—Upon that day Jesus the Messiah had entered upon His office of the Eternal High Priest of Mankind, and was about to sacrifice the Paschal Lamb, His earthly body, upon the cross. St. Paul, commenting upon the fact, wrote: "Do you not know that a little ferment ferments the whole mass? Clean out the old ferment, so that you may be a sweet mass, *and thus you will be unfermented.* For Christ, our Passover, was sacrificed for us, so that we might keep a Festival, not with an old ferment, neither in a ferment of filth and wickedness, but, on the contrary, with unfermented purity and truth" (1 Cor. 5: 6-8). By this we can perceive that the Crucifixion not only occurred during the Passover week, but was done by Christ "offering Himself," that is, His body upon the cross at the Passover to free mankind from sin, but He was also spiritually the High Priest fulfilling the duties of His office of Sacrifice (Heb. 10: 22-28).

As the officiating High Priest was, by the Law given through Moses, prohibited from "drinking intoxicating wine" during the period of his ministration, before entering the Sanctuary, or whilst engaged in its duties, to refresh my reader's memory I give the whole passage from Leviticus, chap. 10, vers. 8-11.

"Then Moses spoke to Aaron and commanded: 'You or your sons with you shall not drink of wine or an intoxicant when you are going to the Sanctuary, so that you may not die. This is an everlasting institution for your posterity.

" 'For you shall distinguish between the sacred and the common, and between sin and purity, so that you may teach the sons of Israel'."

These Divine Laws, and the statements of the Apostles, show *why Jesus refused to drink of the drugged wine offered to Him by the pagan but merciful Centurion, or by his order;* the wine was the ration liquor served out to the Roman soldiery as part of their dietary, and was fermented as well as drugged, and so was an intoxicant, and forbidden to Christ as our High Priest, and also as an Israelite humanly; and the whole nation was also prohibited during the seven days' Preparation for the Passover from having any fermented thing in their dwellings or to drink fermented liquors,—*and Jesus came to "fulfil the whole law."* He obeyed it absolutely, and refused both as Priest and as an Israelite to drink the intoxicant offered to Him. He did not abstain with the object of securing to Himself the utmost of bodily agony; nor is any such motive suggested in the Gospels. As a further illustration of the continuous force of this command in regard to the ministering priesthood from the Hebrew Church of God to the Christian one, I now subjoin the striking passage from St. Luke's Gospel in chap. 1, vers. 11-16:—

REFERENCES IN ST. LUKE

"Then a messenger of the Lord appeared, standing at the right of the altar of incense. And on seeing him, Zacharias was struck with awe, and gave way to fear.

" 'Fear not, Zacharias, said the messenger, addressing him, 'for your supplications have been heard, and your wife Elizabeth will give birth to a son for you, and you shall give him the name of John. He will be a joy and delight to you, and many will exult at his birth, for he shall be distinguished in the presence of the Lord, and shall drink no wine or strong drink.[1] But he shall be full of the spirit of holiness, even from his birth, and shall turn many of the sons of Israel back to the Lord their God, and will advance in His presence in the spirit and power of Elijah'."

Upon the above no comment is needed.

Luke 5:37: "No one pours new (that is, fresh grape-juice) wine into old wine-skins; for if he did the new wine would burst the skins and the wine be spilt, and the skins destroyed. On the contrary, new juice must be stored in fresh wine-skins, and both will be preserved."

This may seem in contradiction of the foregoing, but that it is not the reader can ascertain if he turns to my exposition of the equivalent text of Matthew's Gospel, chap. 9, ver. 17, upon page 5 of this essay.

Luke 7:33: " 'To what, therefore,' He added, 'shall I liken the men of this generation? They are like children sitting in a market-place, and shouting out to one another,

> *"We piped to you, and you did not dance;—*
> *We wailed, and you did not weep!"*

For John the Baptizer came neither eating bread nor drinking wine; and you say, "A demon possesses him!" The Son of Man comes eating and drinking; and you say, "Look at Him! —an eater and drinker of wine,—a friend of taxgatherers and profligates!" Wisdom, however, will be justified by all her children'."

In this striking passage from the Gospel there is not the slightest encouragement for the habitual use of intoxicants of any kind, by whatever name they may be called. The whole force of the reproof of our Lord to the men of His day lay in the falsehood of the statements of His and John's critics.

[1] See Num. 4: 2-4.

That is, that the charge against John, the Nazarite, was a lie, and the libel against Jesus was also a lie, both invented by malicious adversaries, because the two inspired teachers denounced the hypocrisy and vices of that age, and of all succeeding ones. Only a perverse effort to justify themselves in drunkenness could ever have made commentators distort the narrative into a command to Christians to drink alcoholic liquors as a sacred duty, and to impose them upon all the converts they make from amongst hereditarily sober nations or tribes.

Luke 10:29-37: "A lawyer . . asked . . 'Who is my neighbor?'

"Jesus in reply to him said, 'There was a man who, on going down from Jerusalem to Jericho, fell among robbers, who both stripped and wounded him, and went away, leaving him half dead.

" 'It happened also that a priest was going down the same road, but seeing him, he passed on the other side. And in the same way a Levite also, when he got to the same place, looked at him and passed along. But a certain Samaritan on a journey came to where he was, and seeing him, took pity, and went to him and dressed his wounds, making use of oil and wine. Then, setting him upon his own beast, he conveyed him to an inn, and took care of him. And as he was leaving the following day, he threw down two denarii, and said to the host, "Attend to him; and whatever more you spend I will repay you upon my return." Which, therefore, of these three do you think proved a neighbor to him who fell amongst the thieves?'

" 'He who pitied him,' was the reply.

"Jesus then said, 'Go you and do the same'."

Wine is certainly mentioned in this beautiful illustration of what constitutes true humanity and neighborly kindness, but there is not in it any command to drink intoxicants, or statement that the 'wine' used with the oil to prevent inflammation of the wounds was a fermented alcoholic liquor. Therefore it cannot justify missionaries in teaching the converts they make from the habitually sober Mohammedan and Hindu peoples, or from barbarous tribes in Africa or elsewhere, that the Christian Faith demands they should, as one of the first acts to prove their adoption of it, drink intoxicating wine in its most sacred rite of the Holy Sacrament, and to habitually do so in domestic life to show they are not influenced by their former religions, with the result always following, according to very wide testimony, that those converts become, as did the converts of those ardent missionaries who of old "crossed sea and desert to make even *one* proselyte," and by the example of their personal vices made the convert a double "child of Hell" to what he had been as a heathen, instead of becoming a son of God. To justify my comment, the reader (and the missionary) have only to read the history of the extermination of the New Zealanders, the Sandwich Islanders, and the Fijians under the curse of intoxicants, and fornication, its attendant, within thirty to fifty years after their profession of the Christian religion. These are facts, not wild assertions, and it is shameful that our missionaries should shut their eyes to the terrible history, and refuse, when their attention is directed to it, to inquire into the cause.

REFERENCES IN ST. JOHN

St. John 2: 1-10: "There was a marriage at Cana in Galilee; and the mother of Jesus was present; and Jesus was invited to the marriage with His disciples. And when the wine ran short, Jesus was spoken to by His mother, who said to Him:—

" 'They have no more wine.'

"Jesus said to her in reply:—

" 'What is that to you and Me, mother? Has not My time yet come?'

"His mother then said to the attendants, 'Whatever He bids you, let it be done.'

"Now, there were standing there, for the Jewish purifications, six stone water-jars, holding from two to three firkins.

"Jesus said to them, 'Fill the jars with water.'

"They accordingly filled them to the brim. He then said to them,—

"Now draw out, and take to the master of the feast.

"They accordingly did so. And when the master of the festival had tasted the water which had become wine--(not knowing where it came from, although the servants who had drawn the water knew)—he called the bridegroom, and said to him:—'A man usually serves out the best wine at the beginning, reserving the inferior until the guests have tasted, but you have kept the best wine until now'."

Probably the above is one of the most misunderstood, and misrepresented passages in the whole of the Gospels.

The misunderstanding has arisen from imposing upon the ancient Greek text, and ancient Jewish habits of food and drink, entirely the modern and Northern European conception, that the word "wine" always means intoxicating liquor. Amongst the old Orientals and the Romans, such an idea was not attached to "wine" as a universal conception. On the contrary, their "best wines" were not fermented at all, as I have shown from the Old Testament above, and will now go on to do with Roman classical writers.

The ordinary drink of the Romans, learned writers tell us, was juice of the grape, *which they mixed with water, both hot and cold*—(the same as the "mingled" or "mixed" wine of Solomon, and the parable of Jesus about the royal feast at the King's son's marriage), and sometimes with spices. Fermented wine was rare in early Roman times; was only used as an act of worship in the temples, and men under thirty years of age, and women all their lives, were forbidden to use it, except at the sacrifices.[3]

Fresh grape-juice was called *mustum*, and to make it keep without fermentation *it was boiled until it became thick*, like our *treacle, or molasses*, and in that state was named *defrutum*, that is, "made from fruit," and stored away in large jars for future use, to be eaten spread upon bread, as we do butter or treacle, or mixed and stirred up in water, as we do sugar in tea, to make a drink, as stated above. The Greek scientist, Aristotle, says that by keeping for a time in the skins or jars,

[3] Valerius Maximus, Book ii. 1, 5; vi. 3; Aulus Gellius, Book x. 23; Pliny xiv. 13.

it became as thick as butter, and had to be cut out by spoons. The Roman writer, Pliny, records that when the grape-juice was boiled down to *one-third of its bulk,* to secure the finest flavor,—that is, to be made into the "best wine,"—it was called *sapa,* from which word comes our vocables, "sapid," well-flavored, and "savory," delicious in taste.[4]

To give variety of flavor, herbs and spices were often boiled in the juice during its preparation.

Such was the "best wine" of the Ancients, the sweetest and nicest flavored to the taste,—not as we imagine and mean, the most intoxicating, when we speak of "best wine."

It is practically certain that the "wine" created by Christ at Cana was of the non-intoxicating kind, which, as I have shown by the references to them, the ancient writers upon agriculture and domestic economy say was, "the ordinary drink of the people" in daily life. The knowledge of that fact disposes of the argument I have heard even good ministers of religion found upon the narrative, asserting that the guests were all drunk before the miraculous wine was produced, and therefore that Jesus decided to make them more so, to show His disciples and the people the sacred nature of intoxicants.

I am not exaggerating when I state this, for I have more than once had that very argument brought against me in private discussion over the subject. And indeed the old translations seem to justify their contention. I need not add that these old versions were made innocently by men ignorant both of the Greek and Hebrew domestic habits, and therefore of the idiomatic powers and import of their languages.

REFERENCES BY ST. PAUL

Rom. 14:21-23; chap. 15:1-3: "It is noble not to eat flesh, or to drink wine, or anything by which your brother is made to stumble, or is offended, or is weakened.

"You have faith? Have it by yourself before God—he is happy who does not convict himself by what he approves! and all not originating from faith is sin. And we, the strong, ought

[4] Pliny, Book.

to support the weakness of the feeble, and not to indulge ourselves. Let each make himself pleasant to his neighbor to promote loving-kindness. For Christ did not indulge Himself."

What a loving but forcible reproof the above is to our missionaries, whose mania for denouncing the Mohammedan and Hindu peoples for not habitually drinking intoxicating liquors is notable. Nay, I may add, forcing their converts to drink them as the first and most essential sign that they have become Christians, until, as a fact, the names "Christian" and "drunkard" are held in the popular mind of Asia and Africa to have the same meaning,—"All the Sahibs' servants in Calcutta are 'Christian' now," said Mr. Bayard Taylor's native attendants to him during his travels in India, "for they all drink brandy!" And that is the popular idea of the essence of Christianity. I know this from personal acquaintance with educated Asiatics, and it is painful to hear them speak on the subject—at least, to my feelings.

"I did not know our religion had spread so much in India," the American statesman says he answered.

"Oh, yes, it has," was his attendant's reply, "*for they all drink brandy!*"

I surely need not ask our missionaries to reflect on this record.

Ephesians 5: 18-21: "Be not drunk with wine, in which there is folly; but instead be full of the Spirit, speaking to yourselves in psalms and hymns and spiritual songs, singing and dancing in your hearts to the Lord; giving thanks at all times for everything, in the name of our Lord Jesus Christ, to the God and Father,—and supporting one another in a reverence of Christ."

The Apostle here refers to intoxicating drink, which he condemns, not to the simple unfermented grape-juice he did in Rom. 14: 21, which I quote immediately above. Surely I need not add a comment.

1 Tim. 3: 8: "Deacons should be grave; not deceitful, or addicted to much wine, nor greedy for money, but they should preserve the secret of the faith with a pure understanding."

In this rule for the ministers of the Church there is no indication whether the Apostle speaks of the ordinary domestic unfermented wine of his day commonly used then in domestic life, as I have shown, or of the same juices fermented so as to be intoxicating. Probably he meant the latter, ***which he clearly forbids.***

1 Tim. 5:23: "No longer drink water alone, but use with a little wine for the stomach, because of your frequent infirmities."

This advice of the Apostle to his friend is the favorite field of battle of those who claim the habit of using intoxicating drinks to be commanded to Christians. But St. Paul could hardly have so contradicted himself in his prohibition of the habitual use of intoxicating wine to the ministers of the Church as he had done (see 3:8 above), and a few lines afterwards have ordered Timothy, who held an Apostolic position in it, to regularly drink such liquor? It is only gross ignorance of the customs of olden times, and of the idiomatic use of the Greek language that originated the absurd import thus put upon St. Paul's words. "Stomach wine," or "*wine for the stomach,*" the old writers upon Greek medicine tell us, was grape-juice, prepared as a thick, unfermented syrup, for use as a medicament for dyspeptic and weak persons, and there cannot be a doubt but that was the "wine for the stomach," the Apostle told his friend to "use" a little of mixed with water, which it is evident that Timothy, like other pious Jews of that period, restricted himself to, and had drunk previously, so as to avoid breaking the Levitical command against priests drinking "wine or strong drink" during the course of their ministry. However, as the passage has been made, by mistranslation and perversion, a serious stumbling-block, I venture to give it as in the Greek:

"No longer drink water alone, but use with a little wine for the stomach, because of your frequent infirmities."

The Apostle's use of the dative case, which must be rendered in English by the adverb "with," indicates that "a little stomach wine" should, as a medicament, be mixed, or "mingled" as in other parts it is translated, ***with water,*** as the syrup anciently prepared from grapes and other fruits was done for use as a tonic to the stomach in cases of dyspepsia. When this fact is known, the absurdity of teaching that this bit of advice is a sacred sanction for always drinking intoxicant wine, in the place of water as a beverage, will be seen. Missionaries to pagan nations ought especially to avoid repeating the false rendering of the versions of this Epistle, which are unfortunately by irreflection put into their hands.

Among the recommendations of this book is the following from the Dean of Durham, D.D.: "The book is full of the most interesting matter, and I feel sure that you have rescued the Bible from the degrading imputations of taking sides with the disciples of drink. I wish the truths contained in it could be forced into people's heads. It ought to be spread broadcast."

PART TWO

INTOXICATING WINE AT THE HOLY COMMUNION

Extracts by Frank Hamilton *from*
THE BIBLE AND WINE by Ferrar Fenton.

The Anglican bishops at the Lambeth Conference also declared, "That the example of our Lord *necessitates* the use of fermented (and therefore alcoholic and intoxicating) wine in the administration of the Lord's Supper." This is indeed a strange statement for bishops of the Church of God to have made. I ask, What historical or other facts have the bishops in proof of this God-dishonouring statement? and I answer, None. They have simply made it because the Roman, Greek, and Anglican Churches have used intoxicating drink for commemorating Christ's great act of atonement for the sins of men for generations. But their using it is no proof that Jesus Christ used it at the first institution, or that it was used by the Apostles and the sub-Apostolic Churches. If Christ did use it, it never should have been used; and there is not a trace of evidence to show that His "fruit of the vine" was intoxicating. We know that at the end of the second century and onwards heathen customs were gradually introduced into the Christian system, and took the place of Apostolic usages.

There is no divine authority for the use of wine at all, fermented or unfermented, at the Passover; and at what period it was introduced by the Jewish priests no one appears to know. But all agree that Almighty God absolutely forbade even the presence of *bharm* (yeast, ferment, leaven) at the Passover, because it is the cause of putrefaction. It putrefies or rots fruit, corn, vegetables, etc., etc., and is the emblem of corruption, disease, and death, and not of life. Fermentation is putrefaction, and it would be almost, if not quite, impossible in our Lord's time to have found any fermented wine that did not contain *bharm* (leaven). And therefore, according to the teaching of the bishops, Jesus Christ, the divine Son of God, used and sanctioned the use of the very thing which had been strictly forbidden to be even present in the dwellings of the people at the Passover!

Now, Jesus Christ described the wine that was being used at His Passover as the "fruit of the vine," *e.g.*, the offspring of the vine, or that which is borne of the vine. Now, the vine does not bear intoxicating drink. The fruit of the vine is not intoxicating. There is no alcohol in the fruit of the vine. It is pure, good, wholesome, and health-giving, a beautiful emblem of the life and strength-giving grace of our Lord and Saviour Jesus Christ. Intoxicating wine is the emblem of disease, sin, and death. Moreover, just think of the condition the party keeping the Passover must have been in; for the Jewish *Mishna* (chap. 10) says: "A person shall not have less than four cups of wine, even if they be given to him from the fund devoted to the charitable support of the very poor. Each cup must contain the quarter of a quarter of a hin—that is three gills English measure—so that the four cups would contain twelve gills, or a bottle and a-half (three pints)." So Dr Lightfoot tells us (Vol. 9, p. 151). If the wine used was fermented grape-juice, the four cups would contain about six ounces of pure alcohol, equal to twelve ounces of proof spirit; and when we remember that each member of the family of twelve years of age and upwards had to drink four cups, twelve gills, it is certain that, if the wine was intoxicating, they must have been drunk at the end of the feast, especially the women and the boys and girls who were not accustomed to the use of intoxicating wine. How terrible to think of the mass of drunkenness in the Jewish families on the Passover night!

It is perfectly revolting to think that our Lord and Saviour could countenance or sanction such a man-injuring and God-dishonoring system.

Jesus Christ was God's High Priest. And Almighty God had strictly forbidden the priests to use intoxicating wine when ministering before Him. In Lev. 10: 8-10 it is written: "The Lord spake unto Aaron, saying, Drink no wine nor strong drink, thou nor thy sons with thee, when ye go into the tent of meeting, that ye die not: it shall be a statute for ever throughout your generations: and that ye may put difference between the holy and the common, and between the *unclean* and the *clean.*" God had also forbidden the presence of all fermented things at the Passover Service. It was therefore impossible for His Incarnate Son to act contrary to the Father's will, for He said, "I am come not to destroy the law, but to fulfil it" (Matt. 5: 17).

Although the customs of the Jews are no certain guide to Christians in this matter, yet it is an undeniable fact that vast numbers of pious Jewish families have used unfermented wine at the Passover all down the ages, and are using such wine now year by year. It is simply "the fruit of the vine." They cut up a quantity of raisins and place them in an earthen vessel, and add water to them, and allow them to simmer in the oven for a time, then separate the juice from the skins and pips, then put it in the Passover vessel, and they use the wine (juice) for the Passover Service.

In our Lord's time there was always an ample supply of the pure "fruit of the vine," which was preserved in an unfermented state.

The theologians have taught, and alas, still teach, that the contents of the cup which our Lord said was His blood was of the same nature as the thing which the Scriptures had said was as the poison of serpents—as the adder's poison. How can such a death-producing thing be a fit emblem of the life-giving power of the blood of Jesus Christ?

It is painful to realize how the Churches have erred, and misrepresented Christ, and misled the nations by forcing the use of intoxicating wine on the Lord's table and upon mankind.

The general word for wine, *oinos,* is never used in Holy Scripture to describe the wine used at the Lord's Supper.

Is this by chance, or is it of design? Surely it is of design, because *oinos* might be intoxicating, but the fruit of the vine never is.

According to God's command (Lev. 10:9) and the teaching of the Jewish *Mishna,* they were not allowed to drink intoxicating wine when serving before the Lord. How terrible it is to be taught by Christian theologians that Christ broke the divine law, and taught His infant Church to break the law He Himself had made, for He was the lawgiver with the Father and the Holy Ghost.

If the wine which was used at the first institution was intoxicating, then the great body of Nazarites, Rechabites, the followers of John the Baptist, and especially the Essenes (a vast multitude of the best of the people), would be prevented partaking, because they never used intoxicating wine of any kind. Jeremiah's description of the Nazarites might fairly be used to describe these holy people. They "were purer than snow, whiter than milk, more ruddy in body than rubies" (Lam. 4:7). These people were all abstainers from intoxicating drink, and were in much favor with the Lord. Surely it is not possible that the Lord of life would cause all these people, who were the cream of society in that day in Jerusalem, to violate their consciences by forcing upon them the intoxicating cup.

It is most trying to many communicants who are abstainers to be forced either to partake of the intoxicating wine or to pass the cup. It is especially trying for them to have to take their children to the holy table, where they will taste intoxicating drink for the first time. And some of it is most intoxicating, having not less than from 10 to 30 per cent alcohol in it.

The four passages in the New Testament (R.V.), in which is given the account of the Institution of the Lord's Supper.

ST. MATTHEW
26: 26 to 29.

26 And as they were
eating, Jesus took
bread, and blessed,
and brake it; and he
gave to the disciples,
and said, Take, eat;
this is my body. 27
And he took a cup,
and gave thanks,
and gave to them,
saying, 28 Drink ye
all of it; for this is
my blood of the
covenant, which is
shed for many unto
remission of sins.
29 But I say unto
you, I will not drink
henceforth OF THIS
FRUIT OF THE
VINE, until that day
when I drink it new
with you in my Fa-
ther's kingdom.

ST. MARK
14: 22 to 25.

22 And as they were
eating, he took
bread, and when he
had blessed, brake
it, and gave to them,
and said, Take ye:
this is my body. 23
And he took a cup,
and when he had
given thanks, he
gave to them: and
they all drank of it.
24 And he said unto
them, This is my
blood of the cove-
nant, which is shed
for many. 25 Verily,
I say unto you, I
will no more drink
OF THE FRUIT OF
THE VINE, until
that day when I
drink it new in the
kingdom of God.

ST. LUKE
22: 15 to 20.

15 And he said unto
them, With desire I
have desired to eat
this passover with
you before I suffer:
16 For I say unto
you, I will not eat
it, until it be ful-
filled in the kingdom
of God. 17 And he
received a cup, and
when he had given
thanks, he said,
Take this, and di-
vide it among your-
selves, 18 For I say
unto you, I will not
drink from hence-
forth OF THE
FRUIT OF THE
VINE, until the
kingdom of God
shall come. 19 And
he took bread, and
when he had given
thanks, he brake it,
and gave to them,
saying, This is my
body which is given
for you: this do in
remembrance of me.
20 And the cup in
like manner after
supper, saying, This
cup is the new cov-
enant in my blood,
even that which is
poured out for you.

I CORINTHIANS
11: 23 to 26.

23 For I received of
the Lord that which
also I delivered unto
you, how that the
Lord Jesus in the
night in which he
was betrayed took
bread; 24 and when
he had given thanks,
he brake it, and said,
This is my body,
which is for you;
this do in remem-
brance of me. 25 In
like manner also the
cup after supper,
saying, This cup is
the new covenant in
my blood: this do,
as oft as ye drink it,
in remembrance of
me. 26 For as often
as ye eat this bread,
and drink the cup,
ye proclaim the
Lord's death till he
come.

NOTE.—In no one of these four passages does the word oinos, "wine," occur.

The fruit of the Vine before and after it is fermented.

THE COMPONENT PARTS of THE FRUIT OF THE VINE, UNFERMENTED.	THE COMPONENT PARTS of THE ALCOHOLIC LIQUOR into which the Fruit of the Vine is CHANGED BY FERMENTATION.
Gluten.	*Alcohol.*
Gum.	*Acetic Acid.*
Aroma.	*OEnanthic Ether.*
	Extractive.
	Succinic Acid.
	Glycerine.
	Bouquet.
Albumen.	*Albumen.*
Sugar.	*Sugar.*
Tannin.	*Tannin.*
Tartaric Acid.	*Tartaric Acid.*
Malic Acid.	**Malic Acid.**
Potash.	*Potash.*
Lime.	*Lime.*
Sulphur.	*Sulphur.*
Phosphorus.	*Phosphorus.*

EXPLANATION.—The reader will observe at the top of the Left Table, in a bracket, the names of three constituents, *Gluten, Gum* and *Aroma,* which do not appear in the Right Table. These are the constitutents of the grape which are wholly destroyed by fermentation.

At the top of the Right Table will be seen in italics, seven constituents, *Alcohol, Acetic Acid, OEnanthic Ether, Extractive, Succinic Acid, Glycerine,* and *Bouquet,* which are not constituents of the grape, and do not appear in the Left Table. These are entirely new products, generated out of the three constituents of the Left Table, which have been destroyed by fermentation (putrefaction).

Other constituents appear in both Tables. The introduction of the italic letters in the Right Table is intended to indicate that the proportions of the constituents in which they occur have been materially diminished in the transformation of grape-juice into alcoholic liquor. The thick black letters represent what is left of the original grape after fermentation.

Thus it will be seen that by a triple process of destruction, addition, and abstraction—the result of fermentation—*grape-juice loses all the essential qualities of* "THE FRUIT OF THE VINE." It should be specially noted that, in parting with its gluten and gum, and with nearly the whole of its sugar and albumen, the nutritive and life-sustaining qualities of the fluid are destroyed, for it is to these constituents that grapes owe their value as human food.

Thus it is demonstrated that

ALCOHOLIC WINE is not the "FRUIT OF THE VINE."

There are *Thirteen* different words or vocables used (in the Bible); *Nine* in the Hebrew and Chaldee, and *Four* in the Greek, all of which are rendered by the European translators indiscriminately as "Wine or Strong Drink," although all intrinsically are solid substances, but which may be turned into intoxicants by human ingenuity. When, however, we examine the passages where these words are used, we find the sacred writers speak, in the most numerous cases, of them, not as intoxicants, but as foods, which was their ordinary form of consumption. *Where distinct reference is made to them as means after human manipulation of intoxication, drunkenness, and debauchery, their use in that form is invariably condemned and vehemently denounced by the Prophets and Moralists of the Bible as the causes of personal sin and national ruin.* Their use in these forms of alcoholic liquors, or fermented wine, was absolutely forbidden in the religious ordinances of the Temple or Altars, and especially from the sacred rites of the Passover, and to all priests during the period of their ministrations.

Grape Juice, unfermented, is "WINE," and a lawful emblem.

ST. CYPRIAN, A.D. 230.—"When the Lord gives the name of His body to bread, composed of the union of many particles, He indicates that our people, whose sins He bore, are united. And when He calls WINE SQUEEZED OUT FROM BUNCHES OF GRAPES His blood, He intimates that our flock are *similarly* joined by the varied *admixture of a united multitude*."—Epst. 75 ad Magnum.

THE FOURTH COUNCIL OF BRAGA, held A. D. 675.—Reference being made to some who used no other wine but what they pressed out of the cluster at the Lord's Table, and to others who communicated with the unpressed cluster, the Council condemned the use of uncrushed grapes with water—thus, by implication, allowing the use of expressed grape-juice. (Dupin *Eccl. His.* p. 20, 3rd. Edition, pub. 1724. Bingham, *Ant. of the Christ,* Ch. v. 410).

THOMAS AQUINAS, 13th Century.—"In unripe grapes the juice is still in process of being *developed*, and has not yet the form of wine: *therefore* this Sacrament cannot be fulfilled in the juice of *unripe grapes*."

"The juice of *ripe* grapes, on the other hand, has already the form of wine; for its sweet taste evidences a mellowing change, which is its completion by natural heat (as it is said in the Meteorologica, iv. 3, not far from the beginning); and for that reason this Sacrament can be fulfilled with the juice of *ripe grapes*."

ST. ANSELM, Archbishop of Canterbury, A. D. 1096.—"He behaved so that all men loved him as their father. He bore with even mind the ways and weaknesses of each. To each he supplied what he saw they wanted. Oh, how many, given over in sickness, has he brought back to health by his loving care! You found it so, Hereward, in your helpless old age, when disabled by years, as well as by heavy infirmity, you had lost all power in your body except in your tongue, and were fed by his hand, and *refreshed by wine squeezed from the grapes into his other hand*, from which you drank it, and were at last restored to health. For no other drink, as you used to say, could you relish, nor from any other hand." (Quoted from *Eadmer* by **DEAN CHURCH, in his life of St. Anselm, p. 81, new ed., Lond., 1882.)**

There is much danger to some Communicants in Communicating in Fermented Wine.

Dr. B. W. RICHARDSON, F.R.S.—"Dr. Kerr has drawn no imaginary picture of the danger menacing reformed drunkards in taking the Communion in Fermented Wine. I say the danger is very great indeed in regard to a considerable number of people. The physician's room is, in fact, a confessional. Very often statements are made to us physicians which are made to no others. In respect of this very question, hardly a month passes but some one speaks to me on this very point. I could at this moment, if it were right to do so, name at least ten persons who wish to accept the Communion, and who do not go to it from the fear lest they should fall back into those ways from which they have been rescued."—CHAIRMAN'S speech, Church Homiletical Society, Chapter House of St. Paul's, London, Nov. 1st, 1881.

The REV. NEWMAN HALL, LL.B.—"Unfermented Wine has been adopted at Christ Church, Lambeth, for the Holy Communion, by the unanimous opinion of the minister and elders. The Rev. N. Hall explained from the pulpit the reasons for this decision. There were many reclaimed drunkards in our churches, who feared that the taste of alcohol might act upon them like a spark to gunpowder. This was no idle fear. He had been told in Edinburgh, on good authority, of two elders of churches who had thus fallen. The previous week he had been told by a brother minister of a drunkard in the West of England who was frequently taken home in a wheelbarrow from the public-house. He became a teetotaller, and, as was hoped, a Christian. He joined a Congregational Church. The next Sunday again he tasted the intoxicating cup, and that very week was taken home intoxicated. Mr. N. Hall referred to his own father, who, as deacon of an Independent Church, and then as elder of Surrey Chapel, during 30 years, handed the cup to others, but never tasted it himself."

A young minister of the Orthodox Presbyterian Church changed from unfermented to fermented wine at his communion services, because he was taught that otherwise he would dishonor his Lord, who made, drank and used intoxicating wine.

DID THE LORD JESUS CHRIST DRINK INTOXICATING WINE?

The theologians have taught all down the ages that our blessed Lord and Saviour did drink intoxicating drink as His ordinary everyday drink, because they say there was no such thing as unintoxicating wine in His day. But the eyes of some of the most learned of *our* day appear to be opening wide enough to see that the theologians were wrong.

Dr. Kynaston, Professor of Greek at Durham University, says: "We cannot prove from the words in the Bible that our Lord did or did not drink intoxicating wine." This is a step in the right direction. The theologians have also taught equally definitely that *oinos* always meant intoxicating wine; but Sir Richard Jebb, Professor of Greek at Cambridge University said that "*oinos* is a general term, and might include all kinds of beverages."

Anacreon, who wrote some five hundred years, B.C., Ode lii, says:

> "Only males tread the grapes,
> Setting free the *oinos* (wine)."

Here, at this early period, we see that the juice in the grapes was called (wine) *oinos*. And all sane persons know that the juice in the grapes is not intoxicating. Nothing is clearer to those who have studied this question than that the Hebrew word *yain* and the Greek word *oinos* were, as Professor Sir R. Jebb says of *oinos*, general words in those early days, and were used to describe sometimes the fruit on the vines, the juice in the grapes, the juice when it was being pressed out, when it was preserved in an unfermented state and therefore unintoxicating, and when it was fermented and intoxicating

There is overwhelming proof that there has been in use all down the centuries, in all grape-growing countries, grape-juice fermented and intoxicating, and also an abundance of grape-juice preserved in an unfermented state, and therefore not intoxicating; and both have been called wine.

But the unintoxicating, in addition to being called wine, has been called by various other names, such as *glukus, vinum, mustum, sapa, careum, siraeum, hepsema, pekmez, new wine.* A great many more names might be added, but a full description may be seen in Dr. Norman Kerr's book on *Wines, Scriptural and Ecclesiastical,* also in the *Temperance Bible Commentary* by Dr. F. R. Lees and Dr. Dawson Burns. These words mainly describe a wine made from grape-juice by reducing the juice to a sweet liquid by boiling. It was too thick and too sweet to drink pure. And this is a main reason why the Greeks and Romans added so much water to it before drinking, and also why water was added to it before it was used at the Lord's Supper. Water was also added to the intoxicating wine to reduce its intoxicating power.

Varro speaks of "gathering wine."

Cato of "hanging wine" (grapes on the vine).

Columella of "unintoxicating wine."

Celsus says: "Gather the berries of the myrtle, and from them express wine."

Ovid says: "And scarce can the grapes contain the wine they have within."

Ibycus says:

> "And new born clusters teem with wine,
> Beneath the shadowy foliage of the vine."

Goethe beautifully says:

> "And bending down, the grapes o'erflow
> With wine into the vat below."

There is therefore clearly no justification whatever for the misleading statements of the theologians, viz., that there was no such thing as unintoxicating wine in the days of our Lord. And it is equally clear that there is no proof, either in holy Scripture or out of it, that our Lord ever drank intoxicating wine.

It is no more true to say that the word "wine" always meant intoxicating wine than it is to say that the word "bread" always meant fermented bread just as the word "bread" sometimes meant fermented bread and sometimes unfermented. So the word *oinos* (wine) sometimes was used to describe the grape-juice when it was fermented and sometimes when it was unfermented. St. Matthew 26: 26, "Jesus took bread and blessed it." Here it is not stated whether the bread was fermented or not, but we know it was unfermented (unleavened), because it was the Passover bread. Haggai 1: 11, "I called for drought upon the corn, and upon the new wine, and upon the oil." It is clear that the new wine in this verse means the growing grapes, for if the wine was in the casks or skin bottles the drought could have no effect upon it. The translation in this passage, like many others, is misleading; instead of "new wine" it should be "vine-fruit" (*Thirosh*). Thank God! there is therefore not even a trace of evidence to prove that our Saviour Jesus Christ ever drank or sanctioned the use of intoxicating drink.

HISTORY SHOWS THAT THERE HAS BEEN UNFERMENTED WINE ALL DOWN THE AGES

The theologians have denied the existence of unfermented wine and have asserted that all drinks described by the words *shekar, thirosh, yain,* or *oinos* were fermented and intoxicating. This theory I have already controverted, but it is most important in this discussion to show that unfermented wine has been well known, and has been drunk and used more or less for sacramental purposes all down the ages.

It has been known by many names, but the thing itself has existed, and does exist, in many countries at this day. In fact, all the grape-juice the earth produces could be preserved in an unfermented state.

I have shown that it was well known and much used by the Hebrews, Greeks, and Romans. Isaiah says: "Buy *yain* (wine) and milk." Aristotle says: "*Oinos glukus*" (thick sweet wine) is wine, though it is not so in reality, for its taste is not vinous, therefore it does not intoxicate."

Columella speaks of "unintoxicating good wine." He also gives the following recipe for preserving it unfermented, *i.e.*, "That your *must* may always be as sweet as when it is new, thus proceed. Before you apply the press to the grapes take the newest *must* from the lake, put it into a new amphora, bung it up and cover it up very carefully with pitch, lest any water should enter, then sink it in a cistern or pond of pure cold water, and allow no part of the amphora to remain above the surface. After forty days take it out; it will remain sweet for a year" (Book 12; ch. 29). And if for one year, it is equally true to say it will remain sweet for many years.

Rev. S. Robinson, Missionary at Damascus, when writing on the food of the country, says: "The fruit of the vine is a substantial part of the people's food from August to December. Bread and grapes are substantially the food of the people. The fruit of the vine is preserved in substance as thick as honey, and called *dibs*."

Pliny, who lived in the apostolic age, says: "The first of the artificial *wines* has *wine* for its basis; it is called *adynamon* (*i.e.*, without strength), and is made in the following manner: twenty sextarii of white *must* are boiled down with half that quantity of water until the amount of the water is lost by evaporation. This beverage is given to invalids (stomach wine that Timothy was advised to take a little of) to whom it is apprehended that *wine* (*i.e.*, fermented wine) *may prove injurious*" (Book 14: ch. 19).

Dr. H. Adler, Chief Rabbi of the British Empire, says: "I know of no authority for limiting the use of the word 'wine' to fermented wine" (Speech, Medical Society, London, Feb. 20th, 1883).

Sir James Miller, Professor at Edinburgh, Surgeon to Queen Victoria, said to an extensive wine-grower on the Moselle: "Have you any unfermented wine—juice of the grape?" And received for reply: "Tuns, ten years old" (*Nephalism*, pp. 147, 148).

The juice of the grape has been preserved in an unfermented state in all grape-growing countries, and in some for 3,000 years, and it has been called "wine." It is called "wine" by nearly all the great travellers and in ancient and modern dictionaries. It is sometimes called "new or sweet wine" in the Bible.

A short time ago I met a missionary who is laboring in Syria, and I said, "Do the natives preserve their grape-juice in an unfermented state and use it as drink and food?" And the answer was, "Yes, they do; it is thick and very sweet, and is in common use in the villages in Syria. They make us presents of it, and we eat it with porridge and drink it mixed with milk, also use it as you use golden syrup with bread." Here we have the very custom continued to our day, referred to by the prophet Isaiah (55: 1), where he says, "Come, buy wine and milk without money and without price." I have drunk some of this myself, and it is a delightful drink. It is simply the Greek *glukus,* or the Latin *mustum* or *defrutum,* mixed with milk.

PHILIP SIDERSKY, a Christian Jew, told Mrs. Hamilton that at the Passover Supper the Jews squeeze the juice from a bunch of grapes into the chalice.

FRANK HAMILTON.

227.
83077
D516/2
88-21638
DATE DUE
Faculty
May 25
RES Goldman
JUN 1 9
NOV 1 1
SEP 21 '94
AUG 11 '95
SEP 12 '96
Paul's letters to Timothy and Titus
14589
DeWelt, Don
227. 83077 D516
Rome
Three Taverns
Appii Forum
Puteoli
DALMATIA
Amphipolis
Appollonia
Athens
SICI
MELITA
(Malta
Phenice
Lasea
CLAUDA
THE MEDI
IN THE
Names of Ro
0
100
200
300
Modern place names are shown in italics, thus: Cairo
E31